The International Library of Sociology

ECONOMICS OF MIGRATION

Founded by KARL MANNHEIM

The International Library of Sociology

ECONOMICS AND SOCIETY
In 11 Volumes

ECONOMICS OF MIGRATION

by

JULIUS ISSAC

with an introduction by
SIR ALEXANDER CARR-SAUNDERS

ROUTLEDGE

ROUTLEDGE

Taylor & Francis Group

First published in 1947
by Routledge, Trench, Trubner & Co., Ltd.

Reprinted in 1998, 1999, 2000, 2002
by Routledge
2 Park Square, Milton Park, Abingdon, Oxon, OX14 4RN
or
270 Madison Avenue, New York, NY 10016

First issued in paperback 2010

Routledge is an imprint of the Taylor & Francis Group

The publishers have made every effort to contact authors/copyright holders
of the works reprinted in *The International Library of Sociology*.
This has not been possible in every case, however, and we would
welcome correspondence from those individuals/companies
we have been unable to trace.

British Library Cataloguing in Publication Data
A CIP catalogue record for this book
is available from the British Library

Economics of Migration
ISBN 978–0–415–17526–5 (hbk)
ISBN 978–0–415–60514–4 (pbk)
Economics and Society: 11 Volumes
ISBN 978–0–415–17819–8
The International Library of Sociology: 274 Volumes
ISBN 978–0–415–17838–9

Publisher's Note
The publisher has gone to great lengths to ensure the quality of this
reprint but points out that some imperfections in the original
may be apparent

CONTENTS

CHAPTER IV

MIGRATION AS A MEANS OF ADJUSTING A DISHARMONIOUS DISTRIBUTION OF POPULATION

CHAPTER V

THE CONTROL OF MIGRATION

CHAPTER VI

THE EFFECT OF MIGRATION

CONTENTS

AUTHOR'S NOTE

THE main object of this study is to examine the causes and effects of the great international migrations which have taken place during the last hundred years. I have not attempted to estimate from past migratory trends the volume and nature of the movements which might be expected in the future. Such an attempt seemed to be inappropriate at the present moment, immediately after the end of the second world war, when the whole pattern of international relationships is being remoulded. I thought, however, it might be useful to draw some conclusions from past experience as to the contribution which a resumption of international migration might be able to make towards world reconstruction, and to discuss various measures likely to serve this end.

I gratefully acknowledge the great help in the preparation of this book by all who have read and criticized the manuscript or parts of it and have provided most valuable suggestions. To Sir Alexander Carr-Saunders I am greatly indebted for his unfailing encouragement and guidance throughout the work. In its earlier stages I had the privilege of Professor L. Robbin's advice. I wish to express my thanks in particular to Mr. N. Kaldor and Mr. A. Radomysler for the stimulating discussion of various economic aspects of migration and to Mr. R. R. Kuczynski and Dr. L. I. Dublin for valuable suggestions on demographic questions. In dealing with conditions in the U.S.A. I greatly benefited from discussions with Professor E. F. Penrose of Stanford, and Professor J. Folsom of New York. A first version of this study has been approved by the University of London for the Award of the Ph.D.

J. I.

INTRODUCTION

IT is impossible not to be aware of the importance of the movement of peoples in human history, but it is only of those movements which have taken place since the sixteenth century that we have any accurate knowledge. During the last four centuries the peoples of Europe have overflowed and have established themselves as the masters of new continents, and indeed as the sole inhabitants of large parts of these regions. In view of the interest and importance of these events, especially to the inhabitants of these islands whence so large a proportion of the migrants came, it is surprising that they have not been more thoroughly investigated. There is room for further historical study and also for closer sociological and economic analysis. It is to the latter field that Dr. Isaac offers his book as a contribution.

It is an appropriate moment for such a work. A definite phase in the story of European migration closed in 1914. Up to that date for some hundred years or so freedom of exit and entry had generally prevailed. Before 1914, there were signs of a change, but after 1918 we enter upon a new epoch in the story of these movements. Entry was no longer free and unimpeded; quotas and other devices severely restricted the number of those permitted to enter most countries of immigration. Government action was not limited to such countries; certain countries of emigration, Italy for example, set themselves to keep their people at home. Our government, after several decades of neutrality in the matter of emigration, resumed the policy of encouraging and assisting those who wished to take up residence in the Dominions. Though other countries were also not unfavourable to the emigration of their subjects, the net result of the measures taken was greatly to reduce the volume of movement which would otherwise have occurred.

Whatever may be said against the particular policies pursued between the two wars, as regards both the motives which inspired them and the results achieved, it may be urged that some governmental action in this field was justified and, perhaps, overdue. The movement of masses of people, whether out of or into a country, is not a matter in which any government, given the widened conception of governmental responsiblity now generally accepted, ought to disinterest itself. There is no reason to suppose, however, that there will be any return to unrestricted movement; it may, indeed, be taken for granted that such migration as will take place will be regulated.

The first need felt by those who wish to consider how a policy of regulation should be designed is knowledge of the recent growth and present trends of the populations concerned. Information on this subject has been greatly expanded in recent years; in particular, indices have been devised and are regularly published which give a measurement of the vital forces at work in many countries. No less important is the analysis of the economic aspect of migration movements. Too little attention has been paid to this side of the matter hitherto, especially in this country; we have become aware of the purely demographic facts of the situation, the sparsity and slow rate of increase of the populations of the Dominions, for instance, but we have not infrequently been content with discussions of measures of which the economic implications were neglected. These problems are treated by Dr. Isaac in some detail, and this is one of the features of his work which makes his book of real value. Lastly there are the numerous sociological problems involved, using that term in a wide sense. Here we are in contact with somewhat intangible issues, such as assimilation. Though generalization may be difficult, much may be learnt from a study of what has happened in different circumstances; assimilation, we find, is largely a matter of the attitude of the immigrants and of those among whom they have come to live.

In the present state of world affairs it is, perhaps, too much to hope that the task of regulating migration will be approached with an unbiassed and objective outlook. Two things, however, may be said. Migration is a test case in international relations; those relations will never be satisfactory until, in the ordering of migration, the peoples concerned have not only risen above erroneous, partial and narrow views, but have also absorbed what can be learnt from dispassionate attention to the demographic, economic and sociological problems involved. Secondly, there must be adequate literature upon which their attention can be focussed. Such literature is not too abundant to-day; hence there should be a warm welcome for the present contribution by Dr. Isaac.

A. M. CARR-SAUNDERS.

CHAPTER I

THE SCOPE OF THE INQUIRY

1. MIGRATION AS DISTINCT FROM OTHER MASS MOVEMENTS

In the course of history mass movements of peoples have occurred in various forms. These are usually classified as:

Invasion,
Conquest,
Colonization,
Migration.

Invasion has been defined as the thrust of a primitive and virile people from its own territory into that of a more highly developed State. It involves the whole or a large proportion of the invading people, and is achieved by their physical superiority in numbers or in the use of force. The wandering of the peoples which led to the end of the Roman Empire and the beginning of the Middle Ages, fits well into this definition; so do other movements of peoples which took place during the Middle Ages, e.g. the invasion of the Huns and Magyars into Europe and of Tartar tribes into Asia Minor. Such movements continue for generations before the masses become definitely settled.

In the case of *conquest* a well-developed State attacks less advanced peoples and incorporates the conquered territory into its own political system. Conquest is not always accompanied by large-scale permanent transfer of nationals of the conquering country to the conquered territory. Under the Roman Empire, for example, conquests were followed by only a slight flow of Roman settlers and traders into the new provinces; Spain's conquest of Mexico and Peru brought European migration on any scale to these countries only much later.[1] On the other hand the territorial changes which resulted from wars during the nineteenth century set in train population movements of considerable volume.

Two main types of *colonization* are usually distinguished: the exploitation colony and the settlement colony. Colonization of the latter type occurs "when a well-established, progressive and

[1] See Chapter II, p. 16.

I

vigorous State sends out bodies of citizens, officially as a rule, to settle in certain specified localities. The regions chosen are newly discovered or thinly settled countries, where the native inhabitants are so few, or on such an inferior stage of culture, that they offer slight resistance to the entrance of the colonists." [1]

Colonies for exploitation, also, owe their existence to the initiative of the State or its substitutes. Their establishment involves only the transfer of a relatively small number of business men, administrators, and soldiers from the mother-country. Such colonies have been developed mainly in tropical and subtropical regions where climatic conditions do not favour the settlement of white colonists. The import of slaves, and later of indentured labourers, provided the necessary labour supply for colonizing sparsely populated regions.

In the twentieth century the distinction between population movements in the form of colonization and of *migration* has lost much of its significance. Many colonies have evolved into independent or semi-independent States. Moreover the principle of exploitation is being replaced to an increasing extent by that of trusteeship. Colonization, in its present-day form, is either concerned with the settlement of native populations or may be regarded as a special case of migration.

2. DEFINITION OF MIGRATION

Migration, as distinguished from invasion and conquest, may be either *forced* or *free*. Forced migration may take many forms, such as: slave trading, the sale of serfs, the deportation of undesirable aliens or nationals and of convicts. Three categories of forced migration account for the vast movements of civilians which have occurred in recent years:

A. REFUGEES

In the years before the Second World War these were mainly people who had to leave their home country because of political, racial, or religious persecution. Escape from the foreign invader is the dominant motive of the war-time refugee.

B. MODERN SLAVE LABOUR;

an institution produced by the Second World War. Millions

[1] H. P. Fairchild, *Immigration*, p. 19, New York, 1933.

of civilians from all parts of Nazi-occupied Europe were transported to Germany and forced to work for German war industry
and agriculture. It is still uncertain to what extent "reversed"
slave labour will be called for as part of the reparation terms
imposed on the Axis powers. Slave Labourers and War-Refugees,
pending their repatriation are regarded as *Displaced Persons*.

c. POPULATION TRANSFERS

The first large-scale population transfer in modern times was
that between Greece and Turkey and Bulgaria in 1923.[1] An
agreement between the Italian and German Governments in
1939 made provision for the compulsory transfer from South
Tyrol to Germany of all German nationals and of those Italians
of German origin who were not prepared to become "full-
fledged" Italians. This agreement, owing to war-time difficulties,
was only partly implemented. Germany concluded similar
arrangements before the outbreak of the 1939 war with the
Governments of Estonia and Latvia. The alleged object of these
measures was "the establishment of a new order of ethnographic
conditions—that is, a resettlement of nationalities which would
ultimately result in the fixing of better dividing lines than in the
past".[2] The Germans carried out this repatriation policy during
the war on a very large scale; the expulsion of the new settlers
followed immediately on Germany's defeat. The idea of using
population transfers as a means to secure a lasting peace has
been accepted by a number of the United Nations, in particular
by Poland, Czechoslovakia and the U.S.S.R., and far-reaching
population redistributions have taken place after Germany's
surrender. The economic consequences which such changes
are bound to produce will not be discussed in this book.

Our inquiry will deal mainly with certain economic and
social aspects of the *migration of free individuals*—that form of
migratory movement which became a determining factor in
moulding the social structure of the Western World during the
century between the Napoleonic Wars and the first World War.
If we exclude forced migration as belonging to a different
category, migration may be defined as the movement of free
individuals with the intention of effecting a lasting change in
residence. This definition needs elucidation and qualification.

[1] See below, p. 105.
[2] E. M. Kulischer, p. 17 ff, *The Displacement of Populations in Europe*, International
Labour Office, Montreal, 1943, Series O. No. 8.

Migration, so defined, has a twofold aspect; it covers both *emigration* and *immigration*. An emigrant is a person who leaves his abode with a view to giving up his old residence; the immigrant takes up a new residence with a view to becoming settled there. Emigration and immigration are not merely the same act seen from different points of view; they are two different phenomena. Emigration may occur without subsequent immigration; an emigrant who has given up his old residence may not be willing or allowed to become settled elsewhere. But such cases of incomplete migration are only exceptions, and in the normal course of affairs migration consists of emigration and immigration.

Our definition postulates that the migrant has the status of a free man; hence the slave, the deported convict, or the refugee cannot be regarded as emigrants. But the freed slave, the released convict and the refugee obtain the status of immigrants as soon as they are allowed to settle in the receiving country.

The emigrant may either take up his new residence in another region of the same State, or his movement may be from one State to another. The former is *internal migration*, the latter *external migration*. In everyday parlance the word "migration" is usually applied to internal migration alone. This does not correspond to the definition of the Oxford Dictionary or to the use of the word in most publications of the I.L.O. In agreement with the I.L.O.'s practice, we shall use the term "migration" to cover only external emigration and external immigration. Movements of people within the boundaries of a single State will be called "internal migration". This distinction is not so clear-cut in practice as it may seem in theory, for the reason that the notion "State" has become a rather uncertain one. Political development, mainly during the last few generations, has brought into existence political entities which possess only some of the characteristics of independent States, and in various other respects are dependent on other States. Movements of population between a dependent and a dominating State, or between two equally dependent States, are borderline cases, which may be considered either as migration (i.e. external migration) or as internal migration.

The change of residence involved in modern migration is intended to be lasting. This excludes all travellers for business or pleasure. We should not, however, go so far as to exclude every change of residence which ends in another change of residence. As will be seen more clearly later, a considerable proportion of all migrants take up their new residence with a view to returning to their original country after achieving certain aims. This may take scores of years, as in the case of the settler who wants to return to his old country after having made enough money to live there in independence, or of the Chinese who returns only in order to die on Chinese soil. It may take only a few years, as with the student who returns after having learnt and practised his profession abroad.

Definitions are always relative to specific purposes. A general definition intended to cover all the different aspects of migration would appear in some cases to be incongruous. If, for example, we try to find correlations between the growth of a population and its rate of migration, we are more concerned with permanent immigrants and their offspring than with temporary immigrants who are not likely to make a permanent contribution to population growth. On the other hand those of the migrants who will probably not become permanent settlers are relevant to an investigation of the effect of migration on the balance of trade and the balance of payments. Discussion of the wages and unemployment problems must include the case of the alien seasonal worker and the frontier worker.

Other problems arise out of the demarcation between migration and internal migration. This distinction is somewhat meaningless in relation to those conditions which prevailed before the rise of the national State, and even under present conditions a uniform demarcation is of little use. For migration within the British Empire, considered with regard to most economic aspects, it is irrelevant whether the immigration country is a colony, a mandated territory, or a dominion, while for problems connected with the restriction of immigration this distinction becomes significant. In examining the effect of migration on capital disposal it is important whether the receiving and the sending countries have a common currency or not.

We shall therefore, when dealing with each particular problem, concentrate our attention on those types of migrants which are relevant to it.[1]

---

[1] Various definitions used in migration statistics will be discussed in the Note appended to Chapter III.

CHAPTER II

THE HISTORICAL BACKGROUND

1. THE SIGNIFICANCE OF MIGRATORY MOVEMENTS TO THE END OF THE EIGHTEENTH CENTURY

Until the beginning of the nineteenth century the conditions for large-scale migration did not exist. Economic development in earlier periods, therefore, was only to a small extent affected by migration; population movements mainly took the form of conquest, invasion, or colonization, or of borderline cases between colonization and migration, as already defined. To understand the present position, however, it is necessary to review the migratory movements of the past in the context of the conditions which gave rise to them, and to study their effects in the economic field.

A. ANTIQUITY

In antiquity the social structure was generally not favourable to free migration. Serfdom, bondage and slavery were institutions which permeated the whole of the ancient world. Nevertheless migrations as we have defined them were not uncommon at this stage. Migrations of priests, artisans, free agricultural labourers and mercenary soldiers occur in the ancient oriental monarchies and in archaic Greece.

i. *The Greek city-state*

The notion of the optimum size of population for the ideal city-state, as expressed by Aristotle, played an important part in determining the volume of Greek migration. The optimum number of inhabitants is that which allows of *autarkeia*, self-sufficiency. Ten thousand adult citizens are considered as the optimum number for a city-state; a smaller community is not equal to its tasks, and in a State whose members are too numerous the Greek constitution (*politeia*) cannot work adequately.

The *polis* is a community of free citizens: non-citizens and slaves do not count, though a suitable numerical relation between the free citizens and the other classes of the population is desirable.

There are various means of preventing over-population in the city-state. Birth-control by abortion was known, but it was more usual for children to be exposed[1] or to be sold as slaves. Another method of adjusting over-population was emigration. The form it took is a reflection of the Greek political system, centred in the notion of the city-state. The individual derived all his values from his community, to which he owed entire allegiance. This relation was not necessarily severed by emigration. The State established colonies overseas which, though autonomous and independent, were linked with the mother-state spiritually and by intensive mutual trade, a relation similar to that between Great Britain and the Dominions since the Statute of Westminster.

The period of the foundation of colonies in ancient Greece begins at the end of the second millennium B.C., perhaps even before the invasion of the Doric tribes. It was the continuation of a trade policy which the Phœnicians had successfully pursued earlier. The driving force behind Greek emigration was not only over-population or the need for extension of trade, but also the dissatisfaction caused by unequal distribution of wealth within the city-state, which prevented the majority of the free population from holding property.

Many Greeks left their home town in order to earn a better living elsewhere, or for political reasons. As immigrants into another city-state they were allowed to pursue gainful occupations on sufferance. They had no civic rights, and were not even allowed to own land; their status was that of a "metic". The metics consisted of Greek and barbarian immigrants, of freed slaves and their descendants. They were usually the second largest group of the populace—the most numerous and lowest being the slaves; naturalization was granted them or to their descendants only in very exceptional cases.

In the post-Aristotelian Hellenistic period this attitude was entirely changed, because of the decay of the city-state and its disappearance as a political ideal. Citizenship lost its exclusiveness and its importance for the spiritual development of the individual. But colonial emigration received a new momentum through Alexander the Great. The colonies founded by him or his successors extended over all the East as then known. Their population consisted mainly of Greek mercenaries, Greek and barbarian settlers and Macedonian veterans. Normally these

[1] Cf. A. M. Carr-Saunders, *The Population Problem*, p. 258, Oxford, 1922.

came as voluntary settlers and were transferred without any compulsion. The native population of the old cities in the neighbourhood of these colonies very often moved to these new and prosperous settlements. Babylon, for instance, lost all her importance because many of her inhabitants moved to Seleucia on the Tigris. Gradually, as many Orientals became assimilated to Greek civilization, the distinction between Greek and Barbarian lost its meaning. By the beginning of the first century B.C. the whole world around the Mediterranean had become a melting-pot as a consequence of migration and the intermingling of the many nations living there. The city-state had lost all its importance, and the various peoples did not possess enough self-consciousness to create national States which might have prevented such a development.

ii. *The Roman state*

By this time Rome had become the leading Mediterranean power. She was interested in maintaining this state of affairs and in preventing the formation of any power which might become dangerous to her. So the growing Roman republic did not greatly interfere with her subjects' choice of residence, and continued this liberal attitude towards migratory movements and intermingling of population when the whole Mediterranean territory was eventually turned into a series of Roman provinces. During this period we know of but very few restrictions of migration, and these temporary and regional.

More than in Greece, migration in the *orbis Romanus* was determined by its system of slave economy. Migration of labour, nowadays the most mobile element in the population, did not play any conspicuous part when Rome became industrialized at the end of the Republic. Labour in Rome was largely servile, and industry could offer no incentive to the foreign workman. On the other hand, to live in Rome in semi-idleness on governmental grants was a privilege reserved to Roman citizens, and at this time citizenship could seldom be acquired by foreigners. Thus but little free immigration took place. When the native population rapidly decreased, the scarcity was relieved by a kind of indirect immigration, by manumitting slaves and giving them citizenship with their freedom. This was accompanied by a wholesale importation of slaves. Victories brought numberless prisoners of war as slaves to Rome; many more were supplied by the Greek market. It has been estimated that at the advent of the Empire the majority of the plebeians in Rome were sons of slaves, while during the Empire persons of foreign extraction became almost ninety per cent of Rome's total population. Broadly speaking, Rome was throughout her history more liberal in granting citizenship and admitting immigrants than were the Greek city-states. In 89 B.C. all free inhabitants of Italy had become citizens of the city of Rome. Eventually in A.D. 212 citizenship was granted to all free inhabitants of the vast Roman Empire.

It is of no particular interest from our point of view to pursue the history of Roman *emigration*. The expansion of the Roman State accounts for some necessary and extensive emigration movements. Colonies founded for military reasons attracted emigrants. Proscription, land distribution, settlements of veterans, and periods of over-population were often the cause of extensive emigration from Rome. Under the Empire opportunities in the new provinces in Africa, Spain, Britain, Asia Minor, Syria and Mesopotamia induced many Romans to emigrate, particularly when the Roman economy began to decay. This emigration was one reason for the depletion of the native stock in Rome which altered the composition of the population in favour of the freed slaves, as already mentioned. The tendency to emigrate increased when anarchy reigned in the Empire of the third century A.D., and the whole system became disorganized, partly owing to a continual influx of German and Oriental barbarians. The burden of taxes became so heavy that colonists abandoned their property and the artisans ceased working. So for fiscal reasons the State had to apply compulsion to tie the people to their occupations and places of residence. The details of this process, which represents the origin of the serfdom of the Middle Ages, are not always clear. But there is evidence that serfdom existed already before A.D. 332. During the subsequent period—the Middle Ages—serfdom acted as a check to migratory movements.[1]

B. THE MIDDLE AGES

In the Middle Ages, before the advent of the capitalist outlook, the material welfare of the individual was not regarded as the determining factor in economics. It was mainly the doctrines and interests of the Church which ruled economic life. To the

---

[1] On migration in antiquity compare M. Rostovtzeff, *History of the Ancient World*, Vol. I; T. Frank, *An Economic History of Rome;* M. Rostovtzeff, *The Social and Economic History of the Roman Empire.*

Church belonged the first and most important place in medieval society, and her control was at once economic and moral. According to her teaching this hierarchical order had been established by a divine plan in the Universe. To each individual was allotted his special place, and to seek to rise above it would mean interference with the divine plan. Land, the sole foundation of social order, was given by God to men to support their earthly life before they were called to eternal salvation. "The object of labour was not to grow wealthy, but to maintain oneself in the position in which one was born until mortal life should pass into life eternal." [1] To seek for riches was to fall into the sin of avarice. Poverty was of divine origin and was ordained by Providence.

These doctrines harmonized completely with the system of feudal society. The hierarchical principle was regarded as its foundation. Men's worldly inequality was recognized and accepted without question. The activities of every individual were regulated according to his status; his place in society, his duties and privileges were carefully defined. Needless to say, this rigid system did not provide a setting conducive to individual mobility. Both the teaching of the Church and the restrictions on personal freedom inherent in feudalism made it difficult for the individual to improve his economic position by migration.

But this general statement needs qualification for several reasons. The Middle Ages cover, roughly speaking, one thousand years of history. It would be wrong to think of the whole of this period as static and stagnant, and to disregard various dynamic forces which were in operation. Growth of population and progress in science called forth changes in the structure of medieval society which might be delayed but could not be prevented by a body of static doctrines. The lack of a strong central authority with power to enforce these rigid doctrines helped to bring about the individual mobility necessary for these changes. The Church also had to adapt her theories to the new conditions. The traditional economic system of the Middle Ages which was sponsored by the Church did not take account of the growing claims of those who aimed at greater freedom of movement. A distinct tendency to adapt doctrine and theory to these needs can be traced throughout the reforming movement in Christendom from its very beginning in the eleventh century.

Migration in this epoch, therefore, was largely determined by two counteracting forces—the brake provided by the feudal

[1] H. Pirenne, *Economics and Social History of Medieval Europe*, p. 13.

system and the doctrine of the Church on the one hand, and concessions to economic progress on the other. It was inevitable
that these movements should often have been directed to points
of least resistance and not to those which offered most economic
advantages.

In the earlier Middle Ages the propensity to migrate was
only slight.[1] The land was owned by a comparatively small
number of lay and ecclesiastical proprietors, who were free and
possessed the right of free mobility. But all social existence was
founded on property or the possession of land. As movable
wealth then played no conspicuous part in economic life, a
change of residence implied for most of those who were free to
move, a serious loss of wealth and reputation. This does not
apply to the younger sons of the lesser nobility, for example the
Norman adventurers who conquered Southern Italy or followed
Duke William to England. The majority of the soldiers of the
first crusade were recruited from younger sons of noble origin.
Most of them did not leave their old country for a mere temporary
military campaign, but in order to settle in a new country
for good.

The rise of the towns meant considerable migration from rural
districts. The original migrants were mainly landless men,
whom the manorial system was unable to support. The peasant's
holding was often so small that it could provide labour and living
only for a few members of the family, so that the younger sons
were often forced to leave their fathers' homes in order to enable
them to pay their feudal dues. They swelled the army of vagabonds and mercenaries or settled in towns.

The desire to move from the land to the new towns became
greater when the towns developed favourably and provided for
their inhabitants relative freedom and wealth. The serfs ran
away from their manors to become artisans or employees in the
towns. They were often pursued, but the lords seldom succeeded
in laying hands on them. The lack of a central power limited
the possibility of enforcing feudal rights. And as the towns grew
stronger it became even dangerous for the lords to seize fugitives
who were under their protection. So at the beginning of the
twelfth century the townsman was usually free, while the inhabitant of the manorial community was a serf. To obtain freedom
it was enough to have resided for a year and a day within the
walls of a town. "City air makes a free man."

[1] Cf. H. Pirenne, *op. cit.*, *passim*, esp. pp. 67 ff., 46 ff.

This freedom of the town-dweller implied in theory free mobility, but this mobility was in fact very restricted. The spirit of medieval urban economy was epitomized by the guilds. Their ideal was to create stable conditions in a stable industry. They tried to secure for their members an adequate existence, by establishing a *numerous clausus* system. It therefore became inadvisable and very often practically impossible for a guildsman to move from one town to another. He had to forsake the privileges he had enjoyed as a member of his guild and to cope with great difficulties before he could find admission elsewhere.

The expanding medieval economy found a third and important outlet for its surplus population in the bringing of fresh land into cultivation. The Church, especially the Cistercian monks, took the lead in this movement. Serfdom was almost entirely unknown on Cistercian lands. Lay brothers worked there as free men side by side with the monks. These new "immigrants" were either vagrants or inhabitants of the big estates, who thus rid themselves of their serfdom.

The expansion of the medieval economy came to an end at the beginning of the fourteenth century. As a consequence the trend of the migratory movements entirely changed. Pressure of over-population, which had been the main reason for medieval migration, was now followed by under-population. The famine from which Europe suffered from 1315 to 1317 and the Black Death carried off between them perhaps one-third of the population of Europe. The political anarchy in Germany, the Hundred Years' War between France and England, tended in the same direction; they made for a decline of population and for the cessation of all economic expansion and initiative. Emancipation of the serfs proceeded more slowly.

The contracting economy of the late Middle Ages with its declining population called forth movements different in their character and scope from those typical of the expanding economy of the earlier part of the epoch. During the fourteenth century the industry which had developed in North-West Europe began to decline. Guild exclusiveness and monopolistic price policy, which were mainly responsible for a relatively high level of wages and costs of living, made it impossible to adjust production to the conditions brought about by the external factors above mentioned. So about the year 1350 workers began to migrate from the urban industrial centres in Flanders to Florence and also to England, whose kings at that time were encouraging the establishment of a native cloth industry.

The same fourteenth century which saw urban particularism at its height, also saw the advent of royal power in the sphere of economic activity. Hitherto it had intervened there only indirectly, but from the latter part of this century the kings were able to pursue for their territory the same policy of protection which had hastened the decay of the medieval town economy. It was the beginning of a process which eventually overthrew medieval internationalism and transferred the particularism of the towns to the relationship between States. The decay of feudalism enabled the kings to consolidate their power and to establish national States. This development was associated with a new economic system, Mercantilism, which is characteristic of the rise of commercial capitalism. What changes did mercantilist policy bring about in the position which the individual had held during the Middle Ages?[1]

c. MERCANTILISM

The characteristic feature of medieval society had been a blending of two ideas: universalism and particularism. Neither was compatible with the claims of the State on the individual. Church and Empire were considered as essentially universal. In its effective economic and political organization, however, medieval society was almost wholly local. Owing to the lack of means of communication a rigidly centralized government could not provide and enforce efficient administration over a large territory; thus local units became almost independent. Trade was mainly of local importance. Improvements in communication gave rise to an expanding trade, extending far beyond the limits of locally controlled markets. Merchant adventurers took advantage of this new development and a new class of men came into existence, who had both money and enterprise. The interests of this class demanded the removal of local trade barriers: and this was largely achieved by the formation of larger State units.

At the beginning of the sixteenth century absolute monarchy had practically superseded both feudal institutions and in great measure the free city-states on which medieval economy had rested. Political thought adapted itself to these new conditions.

[1] On conditions in medieval times, cf. G. H. Sabine, *A History of Political Theory;* W. Sombart, *Der Moderne Kapitalismus,* Vols. I and II; E. Roll, *A History of Economic Thought.*

The ideological justification for the monarch's claim to absolute power was provided by Machiavelli. For him the State in its own territory is a supreme force, with the right and the obligation to control and direct all individuals and institutions with a view to promoting its own interests. To this end the power of the monarch is unlimited. The individual is nothing; he has no rights of his own. In the interest of the State whole populations may be transplanted, and the State is even supposed to influence the character of its subjects by force, so that they may best serve its ends.

The medieval system had accorded no greater rights to the individual. But the universalism which underlay the whole medieval world-concept, combined with the particularism represented by local units of power and the lack of a central authority, had left a wide margin for individual mobility, so that, as we have seen, considerable migratory movements took place during that period in spite of all obstacles. The attitude of the absolute State was entirely different. It had the power to direct the movements of its subjects and was prepared to use it.

The Mercantilists held that the wealth of a State depends on a favourable balance of trade, particularly if this results in an influx of the precious metals and an increase in the stock of money. Mercantilist writers were mainly concerned with the wealth of the State as a basis of State power; the individual was merely the raw material of which the State was built. Migration policy, therefore, was regarded only as a means of increasing the export surplus of the State. The Mercantilists did not fear rapid increase of population; to them it was a source of military strength and of economic wealth.[1] A small labour force meant a low output until the large-scale introduction of machinery became a determining factor in production. As foreign trade was largely dependent on home manufactures, population increase could be associated with an increase in the supply of labour at low wages and thus in the potential power to export. The migration policy was, broadly speaking, consistently to prohibit emigration and to attract immigrants whose labour was likely to increase exports, or to replace imports by new home production. Skilled foreign workers who could establish new industries became the most desired immigrants. England, Holland and other Protestant

---

[1] "Fewness of people is real poverty; and a Nation wherin are Eight Millions of people, are more than twice as rich as the same scope of Land wherin are about Four. . . ." (Petty, *A Treatise of Taxes and Contributions*, Vol. I, p. 34, quoted by E. Whittaker, *A History of Economic Ideas*, p. 325.)

countries competed with one another for refugees when religious persecution in France, Spain and other Catholic countries expelled many highly-skilled workers. Many new industries and the development of foreign trade in England, Holland and various German States were largely due to the immigration from Catholic countries of persecuted Huguenots and Jews. When these immigrants met with opposition from craftsmen and traders organized in guilds—the remnants of feudalism—the State intervened in their favour, not for humanitarian reasons, but in order to keep them at work. As this policy of prohibiting emigration and encouraging immigration was pursued generally in Europe during the Mercantilist period, an opportunity for international migratory movements on a larger scale arose only when religious intolerance proved stronger than economic or political considerations.

Even then State authority attempted to safeguard its economic interests. When in 1685 intolerance triumphed in France and the Edict of Nantes was revoked, only the ministers of religion were exiled. Lay Protestants were not allowed to leave the country. To attempt to do so was a criminal offence, for which a great number of Huguenots were actually sent to the galleys. The fact that in spite of these measures about 300,000 Protestants left France indicates the French State's lack of authority and efficiency at that time.

The prohibition of emigration was a quite common measure of mercantilist policy. In Britain, after 1720 a series of laws restricted the emigration of artificers and skilled workmen; the Acts were not repealed until 1824, but had never been very effective.

This restrictive attitude seems incompatible with the fact that during the Mercantilist period European powers expanded their economic activities to cover new continents. The beginning of Mercantilism approximately coincides with the discovery of America and of the new route to India by way of the Cape of Good Hope. A race for colonial possessions between the Great Powers followed, with the result that America eventually became a white man's land. But that was not the original end for which these colonies had been acquired. In accordance with mercantilist policy the newly-discovered countries were at first utilized merely for plunder and for the establishment of trading posts. This policy required only a small amount of migration. Later, when the stock of precious metals in the conquered countries was depleted and the commodities produced by the native population appeared insufficient, factories and plantations were established with a view to making exploitation more efficient. This was the main purpose of migration at this period. At this stage of merely commercial exploitation, officials, bankers, merchants or soldiers after years of service overseas returned home and did not settle permanently in the new world. Spain's colonial policy was almost entirely restricted to this commercial relationship. Immigration was directed mainly to Mexico and Peru. Only a limited number of Spanish subjects went overseas, and for a long time they were allowed to stay there only for specified brief periods. Non-Spanish immigrants needed special permission and were subject to very severe restrictions. This lack of Spanish settlements was one of the reasons why Spain later lost a great part of her empire. The new great colonial powers, Holland, Great Britain and France, recognized the right of Spain and Portugal only to those colonies which they had actually settled.

It was not mercantilist principles alone which accounted for this merely commercial policy. Spain's surplus population was not large enough to people with her own stock the huge territories she had conquered. Portugal, and later other countries, had the same difficulties to meet. Holland with her colony on the Hudson from 1610 to 1674, Sweden with hers on Delaware Bay from 1637 to 1655, and even France in Canada and Louisiana could supply relatively few settlers. Conditions in Britain were more favourable in this respect, as we shall see later. But the main object of British colonization also was mercantilist expansion of trade and not settlement. The English settlements developed in the course of the seventeenth century owe their existence mainly to the immigration of refugees from religious or political intolerance who left Britain before the Toleration Act of 1689. Puritans founded the first successful settlement in New England in 1620. English Dissenters established settlements in Massachusetts, where the Massachusetts Bay Company had been granted a charter in 1629. Refugee immigration also brought about the founding of Connecticut in 1633 and of Rhode Island in 1636. At about the same time discontented Catholics turned to the West Indies, where the Earl of Carlisle had received a charter.

Most of these settlements did not contribute to the aim of English policy, which was to improve the mother country's balance of trade. The southern territories, Virginia, Maryland and the West Indies, though for climatic reasons less suitable for white settlers than New England, served much better for this purpose. The production in these territories provided England with raw materials for her industry, with consumption goods which she would otherwise have had to import from foreign sources, and with goods she could export to other countries by reason of her trade monopoly in her colonies—tobacco in Virginia, rice in Georgia, indigo in Carolina. A large labour supply was essential for production in these plantation colonies. Native labour did not cover the demand and proved inefficient, so foreign labour had to be admitted. It was provided mainly in two ways: by the importation of Negro slaves from Africa and by the immigration of white indentured labour from the mother country.

Though production in these colonies became generally based on slaves, the share of white labourers was quite considerable. It has been estimated that between 1635 and 1705 about 100,000–140,000 indentured labourers were brought to Virginia. During the seventeenth century many more white servants than Negro slaves were at work in Virginia. In 1671 there were about 2,000 slaves and 6,000 white servants; in 1683, 3,000 slaves and 12,000 servants. The status of the indentured workers was not much better than that of the slaves. But their servitude was usually limited to seven years, and after reimbursing their masters for the cost of the passage they generally obtained cheap land and became free farmers. The composition of this immigration was very diverse. A great part of the indentured labourers was brought to the colonies by mere compulsion. Political criminals, prisoners of war, vagabonds, children of vagabonds were carried to America by merchants under contract with the government. Others were kidnapped, or induced to go under false pretences. But there were also many genuine immigrants who could not afford the passage money, at that time about £80; they were prepared to endure servitude for seven years in order afterwards to become free settlers.

Britain could afford to send so many emigrants overseas without endangering the ample supply of cheap labour for her home industry. The changes in agricultural organization, particularly enclosures, had created in England a surplus rural population which brought wages down to subsistence level, and provided a large reserve in the labour market. But not even widespread unemployment could greatly alter the hostile attitude of the mercantilists towards emigration, or their conviction that there never could be too large a population. They calculated that for every person who emigrated the country lost £6 through the decrease in the sale of home-produced goods. Unemployment, they held, was not caused by over-population, but could be overcome by a protectionist policy directed against the import of foreign consumption goods, by an increase in the stock of money and the promotion of home production. Apart from this, poor relief in a very rudimentary form, the supervision of vagrancy, the provision of workhouses and restriction of the mobility of the rural population were the usual reaction of the State to unemployment. Emigration, it was thought, could relieve unemployment only under certain conditions. These were defined and developed in Child's theory of colonial economy, which he put forward in 1669 in *A New Discourse of Trade*. He held that colonization in general had harmful effects through loss of population on the part of the motherland as a result of emigration to the colonies. Loss of population was for him equivalent to a decrease in labour supply. But the disadvantages of emigration could be mitigated or avoided if overseas colonies were compelled to confine their trade to the mother country, and if emigration could be directed only to those colonies where the labour of the English immigrant provided work for Englishmen at home. Thus English emigration to the Antilles, to Jamaica and Barbados was useful, because an Englishman with ten natives working under him in the plantations there, provided work for four Englishmen at home. On the other hand emigration to New England should be discouraged, for ten Englishmen there did not give employment to even a single one in England. Child's theory was consistent within the general framework of mercantilist policy, but he did not recognize that an emigration of free and loyal subjects from the motherland was the best guarantee of retaining the colonies, and that colonial prosperity might in the long run be more important to the motherland than particular trade advantages.

The number of emigrants who left the British Isles in order to become settlers in the New World increased considerably in the course of the eighteenth century. The new settlers came mainly from Ireland and Scotland. Scottish emigration was largely due to changes in the agricultural structure of the country in connection with the break-up of the clan system. In the case of the Irish settlers the motive was economic distress or religious prejudice at home.

Generally speaking emigration was more encouraged by the government in the eighteenth century than it had been in the previous century. Lands for settlement were granted on a larger scale to companies and individual entrepreneurs. The main reason for this growing interest on the part of the government was the wish to strengthen its hold on the overseas possessions by actual settlement as a reply to French activities. Its positive share in the development of the overseas settlements was very limited. The transportation of convicts to America, already mentioned, had been sanctioned as early as 1666. After the recognition of the independence of the American colonies, the transportation of convicts was directed to Australia with a view to establishing settlements there. The settlement of the Loyalists and disbanded soldiers at the conclusion of the War of Independence was another problem which necessitated direct State intervention.

The traditional attitude of the United States towards the problem of migration has been quite different from that of Britain. Discontent with the migration policy of the motherland had been one of the reasons for the alienation of the colonies from England.[1] The migration policy pursued by the United States immediately after the attainment of their independence reflects the new liberal spirit which put on end to the mercantilist period and subsequently became general.

We have tried to explain the migratory movements of the three centuries prior to the French Revolution in the context of mercantilist policy. Migration during this time had been by no means uniform in character or volume for the many different European countries. We must bear in mind that Mercantilism was no clear-cut, consistent system. Its principles were developed gradually, and their acceptance in the several European States depended largely on their different economic, cultural and political conditions.[2]

2. LIBERALISM AS THE BASIS OF MIGRATION IN THE NINETEENTH CENTURY

Changes came about in every sphere of life in the course of the seventeenth and eighteenth centuries which made mercantilist axioms obsolete and obstructive, and paved the way for the

[1] *Declaration of Independence*, Grievances against the King of Great Britain: "He has endeavored to prevent the population of these States, for that purpose obstructing the laws of naturalization of foreigners; refusing to pass others to encourage their migration hither and the conditions of new appropriations of land."

[2] On migration during the Mercantilist period, cf.: E. Heckscher, *Mercantilism*; I. Ferenzy, "Modern Migrations," in *Encyclopædia of the Social Sciences*.

emergence of the era of liberalism. They brought about the end of the mercantilist system and tended to remove all the barriers which in previous epochs had limited the field of free individual migration.

The claim of the State to regulate the movements of its subjects had been derived from the absolute authority of the monarch. Belief in the divine right of the monarch began to decline in France about the end of the seventeenth century, when the failure of Louis XIV's reign became apparent. He brought his country after failure in war to the verge of bankruptcy, and the consequences of the Revocation of the Edict of Nantes were felt all over the country. Similarly 1689 saw the end of absolute monarchy in England.

Social and political theory, as developed mainly by Locke in the second half of the seventeenth century, and by the French philosophers in the eighteenth century, set up a system of natural law, a body of inalienable individual rights which limited the competence of the community to interfere with personal liberty and personal property. This system of natural rights, though soon refuted by Hume, became the programme of the progressive and revolutionary forces of the eighteenth century. The Declaration of Independence appealed to it. It was embodied in the constitutions of several States of the American Union, and eventually in the constitution of the French Republic. The French Rights of Man guaranteed *le droit de libre séjour et libre circulation;* the French constitution of 1791 spoke of *liberté d'aller, de rester, de partir.* These new ideas spread over the whole of Europe and America in the course of the nineteenth century. In spite of reactionary tendencies one State after another was compelled to abolish serfdom and to remove other legal obstacles to free mobility.[1] The same ideas are reflected in the economic theory of Adam Smith. He believed in the existence of a natural harmony in the economic order which could be preserved only by the system of natural liberty. Man, in following his own interest, will at the same time be serving the interest of mankind, though perhaps quite unconsciously. It is therefore for the general benefit to allow the greatest freedom to the working of individual self-interest. Intervention

---

[1] In England a Parliamentary Committee of 1819 on the Relief of the Poor expressed the opinion that "all obstacles to seeking employment wherever it can be found, even out of the realm, should be removed" and that emigration into the Colonies should be encouraged. As mentioned before, the Act prohibiting the emigration of artisans was repealed in 1824. Cf. W. Cunningham, *Growth of English Industry and Commerce,* Part II. p. 756.

on the part of authority should be reduced to the minimum indispensable to the safety of all. Consequently Adam Smith stressed the necessity of removing all obstacles to the free mobility of labour. He was concerned but little, it is true, with the international mobility of labour; it is rather the development of international trade which he regarded as necessary in order to increase the general welfare through an international division of labour.[1] But it is patent that the principles outlined in his *Wealth of Nations* implied the advantages of international free mobility of labour. They had a decisive influence on economic policy during the greater part of the nineteenth century, when the *laissez-faire* system was accepted as a leading principle in England and to a lesser extent in most other countries of European civilization.

The *laissez-faire* principle was readily accepted in England as the shortcomings of the Mercantilist system and its lack of adaptability to the economic conditions created by the agrarian and industrial revolutions became apparent. Extreme protective measures in one country incited other countries to retaliate, so that early competitive advantages were soon lost and only the contracting effect of this "beggar-my-neighbour" policy remained. England especially became interested in abandoning the old mercantilist principles which led to isolation in favour of an international division of labour. The agrarian revolution rendered a great part of the rural population destitute. Many found new openings in the towns as industrial workers, and overseas emigration offered another outlet for the rapidly increasing population. But industry could absorb only a small part of the surplus labour. In the manufacturing districts pauperism was widespread, mainly owing to utterly inadequate wages. It has been estimated that in the early nineteenth century about a fifth or sixth of the population existed in a state of destitution and depended in a great measure on charity or crime for a part of their support.[2]

[1] McCulloch in his edition of Adam Smith's *Wealth of Nations*, regards the effect of external emigration as negligible. "Voluntary emigration is never carried so far as to occasion any sensible diminution of the numbers of a people or to raise the rate of wages. If it did this would immediately stop. No considerable emigration takes place from this country, or indeed, any country in prosperous years; it is only when there is a slack demand for labour, or when provisions are unusually dear, that it is carried on upon a pretty large scale; at other times it is but trifling" (Note IV, p. 457), (Ed. 1863).
  The classical theory of international trade entirely ignored the problem of migration by assuming international immobility of labour. The bearing of Malthus' population theory on the migration question will be dealt with in the following chapter.
[2] S. Laing, *National Distress: The causes and remedies*, pp. 164–166.

The England of the Industrial Revolution was interested in international economic co-operation. Raw materials and corn had to be imported, manufactured goods exported. New settlements in America meant to her both new suppliers of raw materials and new customers for her export industry. She, more than any other nation could dispense with protectionism, as her industrial development gave her technical advantages amounting almost to a position of monopoly. Since the supply of labour for her expanding industry was abundant, and could be expected to remain so as a consequence of the growing rate of natural increase of her population, she had only to gain by an increase in the volume of overseas emigration. The inventions and new processes of production developed during the first half of the nineteenth century created the technical conditions for mass migration. They reduced the costs of transport and made the crossing of the Atlantic less hazardous, and thus stimulated the prospensity to emigrate.

By the middle of the nineteenth century, then, all the conditions were in being which could make for an increase in international migration. The acceptance of liberal principles was bound to bring to an end that form of migration which had been typical of the mercantilist period—emigration as a result of religious persecution. The rational and materialistic reasoning of the liberal period recognized the disadvantages of religious intolerance, and the new conception of individual freedom could leave religious persuasion to the conscience of the individual. Emigration for political reasons did not cease, but it chiefly occurred where an anti-liberal, reactionary opposition came into power. The new liberal ideas, however, opened the way to a new kind of international migration, to the greatest migration history has ever witnessed. It was in harmony with the wishes and interests of the migrants and constituted at the same time a vital part of the economic system. The rapid rise in total numbers and the still more rapid rise in total wealth which were associated with the capitalist system during the century between the Napoleonic wars and the First World War could not have occurred without the migration which took place during this period.

CHAPTER III

FACTORS DETERMINING VOLUME AND DIRECTION OF MIGRATION

In the first chapter Migration was defined as the movement of free individuals from one country to another with the intention of effecting a lasting change in permanent residence. This implies that no migration can occur against the will of the migrant, or in the case of persons under age against the will of their parents or guardians. It is the object of this chapter, firstly, to inquire into the motives which may induce free individuals to leave the country of their permanent residence and which determine their choice of the country of immigration; secondly, to discuss the various counteracting forces which limit the scope of migratory movements in real life. Outstanding among these forces during the inter-war period were restrictions of immigration. Their effect was a marked contraction not only in the volume of migration, but also in the choice open to the individual emigrant.

1. PREDOMINANCE OF THE ECONOMIC INCENTIVE

The decision to emigrate may obviously result from a number of motives, which may differ in each individual case. But, generally speaking, among these motives an economic consideration, the desire to become better off, has been predominant. The liberal theory of the economic effects of migration is, as we shall see in the next chapter, based on this assumption, on the abstraction of the "economic man" who always wants to act in accordance with his best economic interests and also knows how to do so. This simplification may be regarded as a fairly realistic first approach to the problems of migration. Of course, not every individual who has the opportunity of becoming better off through migration has the desire to migrate, and not every would-be emigrant has the opportunity to do so—this will be elaborated in the third part of this chapter; but the movements which actually took place were mainly due to economic reasons.[1]

---

[1] This does not apply in the case of refugee immigration, which also during the latter part of the nineteenth century accounted for substantial migratory movements. But as such migrants generally moved from countries where they had been badly off to countries which offered better economic opportunities, these movements had the same economic effects as if they had merely been for economic motives.

Assuming that migration is governed by economic considerations on the part of the migrants, it is likely to occur when people are in a position to increase their real income by moving into another country. The real income of an individual is determined by two factors: his net income in terms of money, and the purchasing power of this money income at the place where it is spent. If the purchasing power of money is low in the country of immigration and high in the country of emigration, a substantial rise in money income through migration is not necessarily associated with a rise in real income. It is therefore important for the potential migrant to know the purchasing power of his future money income in the immigration country.

A. COST OF LIVING DIFFERENTIALS

International differentials in the purchasing power of a given money income are reflected in international cost of living indices. Such indices, however, give only a rough idea of the gain in the level of comfort which may be associated with a relatively low cost of living in the new country. Unfortunately the whole index number problem, especially that of interspatial comparability of indices, is far from solution, and it has been suggested that any attempt to compare the level of income of two individuals or of the same individual at different places is futile. It seems appropriate to give a short outline of the problems involved, since they illustrate the shortcomings of a merely economic approach to the problem of migration.

The formula for the index number of prices is derived from the concept that if a series of commodities in identical quantities and weights are priced at different prices, and expressed in terms of the same currency, the ratio between the two costs is the price index with respect to these commodities. The main difficulty in computing an interspatial comparable cost of living index lies in the impossibility of finding one single set of commodities and services which is representative for more than one country and one income level. We need not dwell here on the relative merits of the various existing methods. All have to meet the fact that under different conditions different commodities and different weights are representative. A difference in the relative prices of the commodities in two countries must affect the relative weights even for the same income level, expenditure over the different items being so distributed that the marginal utilities of each final dose of expenditure are equal; hence no single index can claim general validity. It is therefore necessary to have for each country a different set of weighted representative commodities and services. The migrant will be able and willing to distribute his expenditure in the new country exactly as he did in the old country, if conditions in both countries are very similar and if the scale of his preferences is inelastic. If conditions are dissimilar he will necessarily have to readjust the distribution of his expenditure, e.g. as to fuel, clothing, etc., if climatic conditions have changed. It seems reasonable to assume that after his migration he will compromise between the unaltered maintenance of his old budget and the full acceptance of a budget typical for his income level in the new country. The results of an enquiry conducted by the I.L.O. on these lines are in this respect very instructive. The enquiry was suggested by the Ford Motor Co., Detroit; its object was "to find how much would be spent by employees in certain European cities in order that these employees might have a standard of life approximately equivalent to that of a Detroit employee whose expenditure in 1929 was about $1720".[1] The following results are expressed in a common currency basis: Detroit expenditure = 100; prices and conditions as at January, 1931.

Berlin .	. 83–90	Paris .	. 80–87	Cork .	. 85
Frankfurt	. 89–93	Marseilles	. 75–81	Warsaw .	. 67
Copenhagen .	83–91	Antwerp	. 61–65	Barcelona .	. 58
Stockholm	. 99–104	Rotterdam	. 65–68	Istanbul .	. 65
Helsinki	. 83	Manchester	. 71–74		

Broadly speaking we might conclude from this table that it would have been most advantageous for an American living in Detroit in 1931 on a fixed income of $1720 to move to Barcelona. He could have saved 42 per cent of his income while enjoying the same standard of living which he had in Detroit without saving, or he could have improved his standard of living by buying additional goods and services to this amount.

The authors of this enquiry are well aware that their answer gives approximate values which only correspond to the particular problem put before them, and that any generalization would be a fallacy. The approximate nature of the answer is due primarily to the inherent difficulty of a quantitative measurement of satisfactions, and to the fact that the price data available are not always comparable. The computation of indices of this kind has not been continued and data for later periods are not available.

[1] I.L.O. *Studies and Reports*, Series N, No. 17, p. 3.

International cost of living indices, in spite of their deficiencies, might provide potential migrants with valuable information and often influence their decision. This is especially so if conditions and habits in the old and new country are similar and if the migrant's rate of substitution is inelastic, i.e. if he is conservative in his preferences; for instance, the budget of a workman's family in Naples and in "Little Italy", the Italian quarter of New York, would offer a fair measure of comparability. Would-be migrants who are interested in a comparison of the relative standards of living usually rely on information from friends in the new country or draw their own conclusions from the data available. Information from friends may often meet the individual case much better than any index, but it is limited to conditions in the country where those friends happen to live, and other countries with more favourable conditions will not be considered for lack of information. The national cost of living indices at present published register only changes over time, and are therefore useless for interspatial comparisons. Conclusions based on the relative prices of those budget items which are easily comparable, such as bread, meat, etc., provide rough approximations. The same applies to the International Comparison of General Price Levels, computed by Colin Clark as an average for the period 1925–1934. It shows the order of the main countries of immigration and emigration as to their relative costs of living (expressed in terms of the general price level, U.S.A. = 100).[1]

Australia	126	Ireland	96	Holland .	. 79	Belgium	70
Norway	120	Finland .	94	Turkey .	. 79	Austria	64
S. Africa	119	Gt. Britain	93	Latvia .	. 78	Spain .	62
Sweden .	108	Switzerland	93	Estonia .	. 75	Greece .	53
Denmark	104	Canada .	88	Czechoslovakia	. 75	Poland .	52
U.S.A. .	100	Hungary .	86	Japan .	. 75		
Italy .	97	Germany .	86	France .	. 70		

These figures, naturally, have been rendered entirely out of date by the political events which have since occurred, but they show a remarkable correlation with the figures for the 14 cities in the I.L.O. enquiry given above, if we compare the countries dealt with in both tables as to their rank (ρ = .83), though the assumptions for the two are entirely different.

The publication of comparable international cost of living indices at regular intervals would be useful—in spite of all the necessary qualifications—for a rationalization of migration from

[1] Colin Clark, *The Conditions of Economic Progress*, p. 51.

the viewpoint of the migrant. Various ways of refining the methods for computing these indices have been suggested, but so far no practical use has been made of them.[1] International comparisons of food costs have been published by the International Labour Office since 1940. But since the expenditure on food varies between 30 and 64 per cent of the total expenditure of the average wage earner in different countries, no conclusions as to relative costs of living can be drawn from the figures.

Under stationary conditions the cost of living comparison, as we have seen, is of importance for a migrant with a fixed income. His income in terms of a common currency being unchanged, he is interested only in the relative purchasing power of this income in different countries. As a rule, however, both income and purchasing power will be changed by migration. The percentage of migrants without any income at all, children and aged people, is and in the period of free migration, has always been considerable. But their costs of living constitute only an item in the budget of the income-earning members of the family. The family has therefore to be taken as our unit in respect of both income and expenditure.

In the normal case the emigrant has to take into account changes both in money income and in cost of living in order to ascertain his future real income. Certain types of migrants, however, can disregard possible changes in money income and in making their decision are mainly concerned with a favourable cost of living index. This applies for instance to a considerable number of re-migrants. They emigrate by preference to countries with a low cost of living and a high level of money income with a view to returning to their country of origin as soon as they can live there on the savings made in the new country. For them the decision *when* to return is mainly determined by the purchasing power of their savings in the old country. Similarly, retired persons with independent means are inclined to set up residence in places with relatively low costs of living. Before the war a considerable percentage of British nationals living on the Continent consisted of retired people who were attracted by the relatively low costs of living in France and Italy.[2] It is true that neither the re-migrant nor the emigrant with independent means tends to choose the countries with the lowest cost of living, for

---

[1] H. Staehle, *Review of Economic Studies*, 1936–37, p. 205, "A General Method for the Comparison of the Price of Living," R. M. Woodbury, *International Comparisons of Food Costs*, I.L.O. *Studies and Reports*, N.24.

[2] Cf. R. S. Walshaw, *Migration to and from the British Isles*, p. 19.

their decision is also affected by non-economic motives, but their migration depends largely on international differentials in costs of living.

B. REAL INCOME DIFFERENTIALS

The second factor which determines the future real income of the immigrant is his prospective money income. If this is known to him—if, for instance, if he has obtained a contract for an engagement abroad—he can estimate whether his new money income means an increase in real income in the same way as in the previous case, by comparing the relative costs of living in both countries. Normally the migrant relies on finding a suitable job *after* his arrival. Being without a contract is even an essential condition for admission to the United States. The prospects of finding a job in the new country are then of equal importance for the decisions of the migrant; they will be discussed below.

A study of national wage statistics and of average money income per head combined with the corresponding cost of living indices shows that wide margins exist between the standards of living in different countries, which would indicate possibilities of large-scale migration. Average weekly earnings for comparatively skilled labour (which correspond in many cases to the average income per head of the occupied population)[1] were, expressed in $ in 1930 (money incomes):

U.S.A.	. $42.02	Germany .	. $13.8	Jugoslavia	. $7.1
Canada .	35.00	Czechoslovakia .	11.0	Bulgaria .	. 3.7
Australia .	26.00	France	. 10.5	Estonia .	. 5.2
Gt. Britain .	17.3	Italy	. 7.1		
Eire. .	17.3	Poland	. 8.0		

Comparable international statistics of real wages are not published owing to the practical difficulties already discussed. But if we allow for temporary currency fluctuations and for errors in the computation of the various existing cost of living indices, it remains obvious that the margin between the average real earnings of countries with low and those with high real earnings is very wide indeed.

A comparison of the average real income per head of the occupied population in various countries yields similar results. Colin Clark has computed these incomes for the average of 1925–1934 in International units. (An International unit is defined as the amount of goods and services which one U.S. dollar would purchase in U.S.A. over the average period 1925–1934). Owing

[1] Cf. C. Clark, *op. cit.* p. 46.

to the deficiencies inherent in indices of this kind, his table is not intended to give valid absolute figures, but it provides fairly reliable information as to relative standards of living.

The list is headed by the U.S.A., with 1381 international units, followed by Canada, New Zealand, Great Britain, Argentina, Switzerland, Australia, all with an average real income of about 1,000 I.U. At the lower end we find South Africa with 276 I.U., and Rumania, Lithuania, British India and China with 100–120 I.U. The countries with high real income all enjoy either an abundant supply of capital or of natural resources, or both. U.S.A., Canada, New Zealand, Argentina, and Australia belong to the "new countries" which are immigration countries by tradition. The countries with the lowest average real incomes all suffer from a scarcity of capital or of natural resources relatively to their large population, and are—within the limits set by restrictive measures—countries of emigration. Great Britain, and to a certain degree Switzerland, in spite of their relative high income level, may also be considered as countries of emigration. In both countries, however, migration is mainly directed to countries with a higher real income level, and on the other hand both are receiving countries for immigrants from lands with a lower standard of living. South Africa, in spite of her low average income, is an immigration country. Her average appears unduly low owing to the fact that the vast majority of the population consists of coloured people with a very low income. From the fact that the margin between the lowest and the highest income level is more than 1,000 per cent, and that even between neighbouring countries of similar structure like Austria and Switzerland the standard of living differs widely, we may conclude how effective in pre-War days were the obstacles to the free mobility of mankind.

c. SHORTCOMINGS OF INDICES AS SOURCES OF INFORMATION FOR THE MIGRANT

The information provided by comparing national cost of living indices or national average incomes and wage earnings may be significant in determining the decision of the prospective migrant only under certain conditions. In periods of wide and sudden fluctuations in the price or wage level such data are obviously of little value, even if they represent averages of different phases of the cycle. Moreover it would be unwise to draw any

2*

conclusions as to future prospects from pre-war or wartime statistics. We have already pointed out that the use of average values and the notion of an individual migrant whose only characteristic is that he is a wage-earner imply dangerous generalizations. They are legitimate if the values for which the average is taken are not widely dispersed, but closely concentrated around the average. The mechanism of a free system tends to smooth out differentials in the prices of all commodities, including labour, owing to free mobility of capital and labour and to free competition. This tendency, however, is not effective enough in real life to prevent large disparities in the standard of living for the same type of labour, even within national boundaries, where mobility of factors and goods is least hampered by restrictive measures. Disparities in regional cost of living indices would cancel out, so far as real-wage income is concerned, if the differences in the regional money-wage levels were proportionate to the cost of living differences. This is only very seldom the case. The differences are particularly evident for the standards of unskilled labour in large States whose economic structure is not uniform; e.g. in the United States for the highly developed States, such as New York, Massachusetts, California on the one hand, and the "backward" Southern States on the other. It would be fallacious therefore to apply average figures for the U.S.A. or any other State to a particular region within that State, without additional information as to regional or local conditions.

A similar qualification is necessary for the concept of an average wage earner. The figures of average earnings and incomes actually refer only to a fictitious average wage earner. Their usefulness for the individual depends on how closely the averaged values are concentrated around the central value and on his position relative to that value. A uniform factor of production called "labour" does not exist in the sense that each physical unit of this factor—each wage earner—has equal abilities or can expect an equal rate of remuneration. Only if every worker could find employment in whatever occupation he pleased, would individual real income tend to equal average real income. In fact "labour" as a factor of production consists of numerous not directly competing groups and sub-groups of unskilled, skilled and technical labour. Each of these groups has a different demand and supply schedule. A skilled worker, therefore, who intends to migrate, is interested not only in the general real income level in the new country, but also in the margin between the average income and the income prevalent in his group or sub-group. This margin is, broadly speaking, wider in countries with a low than in those on a higher standard of living. Skill is at a premium, as Prof. A. G. B. Fisher has pointed out,[1] in countries in an early stage of economic development. The income differences between qualified and unqualified labour tend, however, to narrow in countries with a high standard of living where technical training and apprenticeship is comparatively easy to obtain. For a skilled worker in a country with a comparatively low standard of living the advantages of a favourable ratio between the wages of skilled and unskilled labour may outweigh the advantages offered by the high standard of living in economically more developed countries. The standard deviation of the wage rates for skilled workers in the various professions expressed as a percentage of the average wage, computed for different countries, lends support to this suggestion. Colin Clark gives the figures for eight countries as follows:[2]

Sweden	13.7	Australia	14.7	Canada	24.5
France	14.0	Great Britain	17.7	Jugoslavia	40.0
Switzerland	14.5	Spain	24.3	Japan	42.0

It is therefore not astonishing that skilled and unskilled labour often move in opposite directions. Countries which are in transition from primary to secondary production as a consequence of increasing density of population, may have a surplus of unskilled labour which cannot be fully absorbed by the gradually developing industry and which is prepared to emigrate. On the other hand new industry gives rise to an additional demand for skilled labour which in countries of predominantly primary production and low standard of living is usually not available. This new demand can be satisfied only if wage rates are high enough to attract foreign skilled workers from countries with a higher standard of living but with a smaller margin between skilled and unskilled labour wage rates. Switzerland, which has a surplus of skilled labour, until lately sent many workers abroad, but employed many thousands of foreign workers in manual work.[3] Bank clerks and technicians emigrated in large numbers from Austria and Germany to the Balkans in spite of the lower standard

---

[1] *Intern. Labour Review*, Vol. 25, p. 758 ff.
[2] *Op. cit.* p. 251. The exception provided by Canada's wide margin is explained by the comparative weakness of Trade Unions in Canada.
[3] P. Sorokin, *Social Mobility*, p. 234.

of living there.[1] Movements of similar character, from highly capitalised to less developed countries, occur also in the course of industrial expansion; they are often accompanied by wage discrimination between foreign and native workers in favour of the foreigners.

A comparison of the real income of agricultural and industrial workers shows that there is practically everywhere a considerable margin between both, though it differs in extent for each country. This is of less importance for the decision of the migrant, as it is comparatively easy for an immigrant to shift from rural to unskilled industrial work. The large-scale shift of immigrant peasants and landworkers to industrial occupations in the U.S.A. was noticeable even in periods when American agriculture was comparatively prosperous. It is explained partly by the attraction of the town and partly by the peculiar structure of American farming. It is in many respects highly specialised and provides little work for farm-labourers outside the harvest season. Farm work in the Southern States of the U.S.A. used to yield so low a real income that even immigrants from East and South-East Europe could not compete with native labour. Only about ten per cent of the workers employed in agriculture are foreign-born or of foreign or mixed parentage; the corresponding proportion in mining and similar industries is about fifty per cent. In South America conditions are different: in the Argentine, for instance, the Italian immigrant labourers usually find employment in agriculture, and many of them later become small farmers.

Migration and change of occupation and status are often simultaneous. Such changes are usually much easier of achievement in new countries than in old countries where the tiers of the economic structure are more marked and rigid, and transition from one to another more difficult owing to tradition and vested interests. A farm worker may emigrate with a view to becoming an independent farmer. He will leave a country where farm land is scarce and therefore expensive for a country with an abundant supply of land, preferably a "new" country—thinly populated and with unexploited natural resources. The skilled worker, the employee or technical expert in a dependent position, who wants to improve his standing by becoming an entrepreneur, will find more scope for his initiative by emigrating to a country which is not yet industrialised, where labour or factors of production other than entrepreneurship are easily

[1] John W. Brown, *World Migration and Labour*, p. 194.

obtainable, or which provide a favourable market for their product.

D. SIGNIFICANCE OF THE TIME ELEMENT

So far we have assumed that the migrant is motivated only by comparison of his existing opportunities with contemporary opportunities elsewhere. But clearly a static treatment of so essentially dynamic a process as migration cannot yield adequate results, and qualifications in this respect are necessary. By his decision to migrate the migrant links his own prospects permanently with opportunities in the new country. His migration would be a failure if conditions were to deteriorate in the new country or improve in the old, so that he would eventually be better off had he not moved at all. His decision therefore will depend largely on his judgment of his future prospects in both countries; on his preference for satisfactions in the near future to those expected in the distant future, on the probability of expectations being realized, and on his valuation of risk. In order to bring his expected future satisfactions to a common denominator, he will consciously or unconsciously discount them and reduce them to their present value to him. This rate of discount, however, differs with different persons. Elderly people are mainly interested in near future prospects, while younger ones will take a longer-term view. Individual temperament and character have their bearing on this valuation. Many migrants are prepared to work harder, to forgo present satisfactions for a better life in a distant future. They may even be satisfied if they can provide this better life only for their children, without being able to enjoy it themselves. Others will prefer higher security at a lower standard of living in the new country to a higher standard in the old country associated with uncertainty and risk.

It might seem, therefore, that it is for psychology rather than for economics to analyse the reasons of migration, even if the inquiry be limited to material satisfactions. Experience shows, however, that comparisons of present conditions have largely determined the trend of migration. In the U.S.A., during the period of free migration, immigration followed closely the fluctuations of the business cycle.[1] A similar reaction to obviously temporary changes of prosperity can be found in practically all countries of immigration, so that our approach has some justification. This tendency of migration to adapt itself to temporary

[1] Cf. below, Chapter VI.

changes of prosperity has several causes. We shall deal later with
the costs of migration, but in this context it is necessary to mention
that migration is to a large extent financed by assistance from
friends or relatives in the new country. This help can be given
more liberally in times of prosperity. Expectations—apart from
periods of political or social unrest—are based on present conditions, and it is usually presumed that the present trend will not
change. On the other hand a great deal of migration is caused
by an attempt to escape immediate destitution, so that long-term
expectations are only of secondary importance.

A distinction has been made between "push" and "pull"
migration. It may safely be assumed that the migrant who is
driven from his country by adverse conditions of life or by other
circumstances is more concerned with his present lot than with
more or less vague expectations for the future. The migrant who
has lived under tolerable conditions but who expects to become
better off by migration will attach more importance to future
prospects. He will often be prepared for a considerable lowering
of his standards of living during the first years after his immigration, if he is convinced that this loss will be atoned for by later
gains. The settler in an undeveloped region is usually well aware
that conditions for himself and his family will be very hard and
that he will live much less comfortably than before his emigration,
until he has become settled and paid off his debts. In the same
way other categories of immigrants are prepared to sacrifice
present satisfactions. They will not be discouraged by the fact
that they will have to become acquainted with the language,
customs, and habits of the new country before they can expect
to receive their fair share of its benefits. Such reflections will
affect their decisions only in so far as they will take account in
their calculations of the losses which may occur during the period
of transition. They will leave their country only if the margin
between their present standard and the corresponding standard in
the new country is wide enough to allow for their handicap as
newcomers. This includes provision for unemployment, likely
to occur during the first stage after their arrival. If the labour
market is ruled by free competition, especially in an expanding
economy—as in the chief countries of immigration up to the last
war—the individual immigrant will soon find some kind of
employment if he sells his services below their market price. He
is more mobile than his native competitors, who are already
settled, and his inferior standard of living enables him to work

at a wage rate low enough to overcome the bias of employers against foreign labour. Even if below the general subsistence level, this rate may be still attractive for him. This margin between the general wage level and the level of wages for immigrants' jobs has been very considerable during the pre-restriction period of U.S.A. immigration. In 1905–07—a period of extensive immigration comprising various phases of the business cycle— wages of a single man immigrant in comparison with the American worker's wages were as follows:[1]

Italian	.	.	.	.	79.49 per cent
Hungarian	.	.	.	.	68.23 ,, ,,
Other European	.	.	.	53.85 ,, ,,

These differentials are partly due to the fact that the foreign worker was paid a lower rate than the native worker for the same job, partly to the fact that openings for immigrants were mainly confined to unskilled labour.

It is when competition on the labour market becomes imperfect and wage rates are rigid, that the immigrant cannot avoid unemployment by undercutting the normal wage rate. Under these circumstances the higher standard of living in the new country is irrelevant for the immigrant before the problem of finding a job is solved. Relative prospects of employment will then be the main criterion for the prospective migrant in making his decision.

E. THE PROBLEM OF UNEMPLOYMENT

Between the two World Wars competition on the labour market has become increasingly imperfect. The invisible hand of the free system has been replaced by the visible hand of government interference or by other measures backed by State authority. In many countries wage rates are fixed by law, by collective agreements or by wage boards or courts of arbitration. This policy prevented wage rates from falling during the great depression to a level which would have been undesirable for social reasons, and combined with unemployment assistance and more productive emergency measures it had in a great many countries the effect of maintaining a standard of living which would otherwise have fallen more rapidly during the depression period. But the relative standard of living no longer reflected the

[1] Royal Institute of International Affairs, *Unemployment an International Problem*, p. 255.

true equilibrium between demand for and supply of labour. Marginal productivity of labour was kept artificially high at the cost of increasing unemployment. This does not imply that interference with the free system has produced unemployment. The causal nexus may have been the other way round. In our context it is only important to state that the intending immigrant cannot draw any conclusions as to his prospects from the general standard of living in the new country, if this standard is maintained or achieved only by means which are likely to prevent him from sharing it.

We have seen that in a free system the problem of unemployment is for the immigrant mainly a transitional one, though it has a great bearing on his decisions; the result being that during periods of unemployment in countries of immigration the number of immigrants is markedly reduced. The immigrant's position is much worse if there are minimum wages, which prevent his undercutting the normal wage rate, trade unions, which do not admit foreigners as members and pursue a closed shop policy, or State regulations which exclude foreigners without special labour permits from the labour market or from any other occupation. In such circumstances any immigration on chance becomes so risky as to be justified only in exceptional cases. On the other hand this immigration on chance, especially during a slump, is considered by the receiving country to involve so many risks that practically every State which has to cope with unemployment has restricted immigration, and admits an immigrant only if satisfied that he will not become a public charge. Admission does not of course imply any guarantee of finding employment in due course, but the immigrant may take it as a guide to his chances of succeeding in the new country. The use of statistics for measuring these chances is still more questionable, if the labour market and the admission of foreigners is regulated, than under conditions of free mobility. It would be fallacious to rely on unemployment or employment statistics. In many countries, public works, compulsory labour service, and other emergency measures which are not open to foreigners, have kept unemployment figures at a comparatively low level. For example in France in 1938 the percentage of workers unemployed amounted only to 8.5, though industrial production and demand for labour had considerably shrunk. This low figure can be accounted for by shorter hours of work, large-scale repatriation of Polish workmen, and immigration restrictions. In the U.S.A., in spite of a 130 per cent higher unemployment rate, prospects of an early recovery were much better and thither migration appeared to be more promising than to France.

2. SIGNIFICANCE OF POLITICAL AND ECONOMIC CHANGES FOR THE OCCURRENCE OF MIGRATION

Migration governed by the economic interests of the migrants tends in a free system to equalize real income for persons of equal capability.[1] If international economic and political conditions remained fairly stationary, that is to say if no shifts in real income were to occur, other than those caused by migration, it might be presumed that the incentive to migrate would gradually decrease, the rate of migration decline, and migratory movements eventually come practically to a standstill. This does not occur in real life, because changes in political and economic conditions, affecting different countries differently, continually bring about new differentials in real income and therefore provide new incentives to migration.

Such changes—often reacting on each other and producing a cumulative effect—which have caused migratory movements, are:

A. DIFFERENCES IN RELATIVE GROWTH OF POPULATIONS

If a population increases out of due proportion to the capital, technical knowledge and natural resources at its disposal, the return per head is likely to diminish, and the surplus population will tend to migrate to countries where conditions have not deteriorated or have even improved.[2]

B. OPENING UP OF NEW COUNTRIES

Unexploited territories offer new opportunities. Though no new continents or regions are now left to be discovered, not all are as yet thoroughly explored. New finds of oil, gold or other valuable natural resources still occur, and call forth, if not hindered by restriction, a rush of immigration.

[1] Cf. below, Chapters IV, V.
[2] Cf. below, Chapter IV. At the time of the Napoleonic wars the population of France represented 50 per cent of the population of Europe outside Russia, now it is scarcely 10 per cent of the population of the same region. The proportion of the Slavonic nations to the European population, rose between 1910 and 1930 from 42 to 46 per cent.

C. EXHAUSTED NATURAL RESOURCES

These may make it necessary for a population to move. Soil erosion drives the farmer to less exhausted lands. Coal and metalliferous mines are abandoned if their yield becomes too poor. Such exhaustion is often not absolute. Exploitation may be discontinued in response to the discovery of new and richer resources which make the productivity of the older ones extra-marginal. Low costs of production for the growing of corn and the breeding of cattle overseas made these occupations unprofitable for many farmers in England, inducing them and their labourers to resume farming overseas or to change their occupation or residence, or both.

D. NEW TECHNICAL PROCESSES

Many inventions and scientific discoveries have resulted in the development of new technical processes. These have called forth corresponding dislocations and adjustments in the distribution of population. Changes in the sources of power in connection with new inventions have greatly influenced relative standards of living and hence the propensity to migrate. The steam engine, the application of electricity to industry, the transformation of water power into electricity, long-distance transport of power, have all brought about changes in the marginal productivity of labour and consequent migratory movements as means of adjustment. It would be easy to show that the general adaptation of any new technical process of economic importance has also provided new incentives to migration. To mention a few instances: The machine loom brought hunger to the districts which specialized in hand weaving. The production of synthetic dyes in Germany had its effect on those who derived their livelihood from indigo plantations in India. Other synthetic materials such as artificial silk, plastics, synthetic oils, etc., affected the producers of the materials for which the new products were substitutes. It cannot as yet be foreseen whether rubber, sugar and other commodities, before the war mainly primary products, will soon be displaced by synthetic products produced elsewhere. Progress in the harnessing of atomic energy may provide the setting for a redistribution of world population on an unprecedented scale. Utopias of yesterday, the irrigation of the Sahara, the thawing of the Arctic and Antarctic, may become realities in a not too distant future.

E. CHANGES OF TASTE,

though of minor importance, may have a similar effect on migration. It was not until the nineteenth century that people began to take up mountaineering, and only in the twentieth that winter sports became fashionable. The hotel industry of Switzerland, which attracted wage earners, waiters, and entrepreneurs from other countries, owes its existence mainly to such a change of taste. The decline in the demand for oriental spices, for straw hats and many other commodities affected the standard of living in the regions where they were produced. Dislocations caused by changes of fashion and habit are often adjustable within the same region by a shift of occupation if the reduced demand for one product is balanced by an increased demand for another which can be produced in the same region. Migration will then occur only if mobility between occupations is more imperfect than between regions.

F. THE DEVELOPMENT OF NEW TRADE ROUTES

is closely connected with the exploitation of new countries. The centre of gravity of world trade has shifted since the sixteenth century from the Mediterranean to the Atlantic. Trading centres such as Venice, Genoa, Pisa and Florence lost importance and wealth, and enterprising people living there were induced to emigrate. When the Cape route to the East was discovered, the trade of the East began to pour into Lisbon. The Dutch succeeded the Portuguese as masters of the Eastern trade, and they in turn were followed by France and Britain. The discovery of America brought wealth and trade to Spain and later to Holland and England, and emigrants were consequently attracted to these countries, but it was only in the nineteenth century that such changes brought about large-scale migrations (Chap. I). The American transcontinental railways, the Trans-siberian railway, the opening of the Suez and Panama Canals, all led to new migratory movements.

G. POLITICAL CHANGES

may actuate migration in different ways. Maladministration may lead to high and unproductive taxation, currency manipulation, default on external loans, loss of confidence, and an undue lowering of the general standard of living. The same is likely to happen after an unsuccessful war. Payment of war debts, reparations, and the reconstruction of the whole economic apparatus during the period of transition from war to peace conditions are bound to lower the standard of living. Territorial changes are usually followed by migration. There will be an inflow of nationals from the country which has acquired the territory and an outflow both of those who prefer change of residence to loss of nationality and of those who are compelled to leave. Political changes of a revolutionary character practically always give rise to emigration. The former ruling class, if deprived of its privileges, may find better opportunities elsewhere. Its members may emigrate for idealistic reasons or from resentment. Again, persecution by the new rulers may compel its victims to leave the country. Immigration on this ground has become increasingly important since the 1914–1918 war. Estimates of the number of refugees from communist Russia vary between two and three millions.[1] From 1933 to the end of 1938 350,000 persons had left Germany and Austria to escape from Nazi rule. At that time there were about 340,000 Spanish refugees in France. Early in 1938 the number of Italian refugees amounted to 30,000. The political events of 1938–39 led to a daily increase in the number of refugees, so that even before the outbreak of the last war it was extremely difficult to estimate their number. In his book, *The Refugee Problem*, published in February 1939, Sir John Hope Simpson estimated the number of "potential" involuntary Jewish emigrants for the next few years at five million. Events during the war have belied this estimate. A considerable number of Jews from Eastern Europe have become integrated in Soviet Russia during the war, and it seems doubtful whether they will have the wish or the opportunity to emigrate after it. But of the 9.6 million Jews who lived in Nazi-occupied Europe, "it is conservatively estimated that 5.7 million disappeared, most of them deliberately put to death by Nazi conspiracy."[2] Even so an enormous number of people displaced as a result of the war will have to settle in new countries. Most refugees, it is hoped, will soon be repatriated and resettled in the areas whence they came.[3] This work, organized and financed by the United Nations, is being carried out by U.N.R.R.A. (United Nations Relief and

[1] Sir J. H. Simpson, "The Refugee Problem" and "Refugees."
[2] Nuremberg Trial Indictment, November, 1945.
[3] About 1,675,000 displaced persons were receiving assistance in March 1946. The hard core of "irrepatriables" has been estimated at 500,000.

Rehabilitation Administration). A discussion of the problems involved is beyond our scope. It has become the responsibility of the Inter-governmental Committee on Refugees (established in 1938) to take care of the "irrepatriables". The activities of this Committee were originally confined to aiding refugees from Germany, Austria and the Sudeten areas. Its mandate was extended in 1943 "so as to include, as far as practicable, also those persons wherever they may be who, as a result of events in Europe, have now to leave or may have to leave their countries of residence, because of the danger to their lives or liberties on account of their race, religion or political beliefs."[1]

3. OBSTACLES TO MIGRATION

The permanent flow of migration from regions of low to those of higher prosperity, which should in theory be the consequence of any major change in relative standards of living, is in real life greatly reduced by the effect of friction. The individual will make use of this outlet only when the incentive to migrate has become so strong as to overcome his natural disinclination to leave his old environments and sever his links with his milieu. Moreover he has to cope with many objective obstacles to migration, such as costs of transport, government regulations, and the like. The ability of a locality to hold its population is likely to exceed its original ability to attract it. Many people prefer to endure, within limits, a deterioration of their living conditions, rather than leave their country. They can accommodate themselves by spending less, by working harder, by checking the size of their families by birth control, etc. This inertia is due to lack of initiative, to ignorance of opportunities, to fear of uncertainty and risk, and to the influence of tradition and social heritage.

A. CULTURAL LINKS BETWEEN THE INDIVIDUAL AND HIS NATIVE COUNTRY

Emancipation from links with the past is a problem mainly affecting those advanced in years. Prejudice, national customs and habits, social codes, and the real values of their national

---

[1] A special committee of the Economic and Social Council of U.N.O. recommended in June, 1946, the setting up of a new International Refugee Organisation (I.R.O.). The resettlement of about 200,000 Polish armed forces who do not wish to return to Poland has become the concern of the British Government.

civilization exert a much firmer hold on them than on persons who are still in the formative years. In the course of the last thirty years or so we have experienced simultaneously two conflicting cultural trends: the revival of long-forgotten national traditions and languages and a tendency towards a homogeneous Western civilization. The effect of the latter development is to facilitate international mobility. The pattern of America's way of living has permeated all other nations. National and local theatre traditions have been displaced by Hollywood films of world-wide circulation. Donald Duck, Deanna Durbin, Gary Cooper enjoy almost the same popularity all over five continents, and the migrant, wherever he may go to, can be pretty sure of meeting his old idols on the screen. The picture-goer has become quite familiar with conditions in other countries and continents. There is practically no country in the world which has not formed the background for more than one popular film, though the information derived from such a source is usually incorrect or at least incomplete. Documentary films convey a less distorted impression of conditions in foreign countries and may be regarded as an important incentive to emigration.

In many other respects the economic expansion of the U.S.A. has created a common standard for the whole civilized world; Ford motor cars, Woolworth chain stores, etc., have become household words far beyond the United States. The technical achievements of the past twenty years have in still another way mitigated the effects of dislocation and up-rooting usually connected with migration. The immigrant is now able to listen to the wireless programmes of his former country exactly as he used to do before his emigration. It has also become much easier to maintain direct contact with people in other countries. Air-mail, cheap cable rates, transatlantic telephone, opportunities for faster and cheaper travelling by air, sea and land have increased the propensity to migrate.

The conflict between the reluctance to give up one's old way of life and the desire for a higher standard of living can often be solved by a compromise. In this case migration is not directed to the country which offers a maximum of economic advantages, but for practical and sentimental reasons a country is preferred which is similar to the former homeland, even if from the merely economic viewpoint it appears less suitable. A similar climate, a common history and language, the existence of friends or relatives in the new country may influence the emigrant's decision, and must be taken into account in order to make individual migration successful.

B. RELATION BETWEEN STATE AND INDIVIDUAL

The relation between the individual and society is another factor which affects migration. In the era of *laissez-faire* and liberalism the individual was attached to State and society only very loosely. Men were considered during the early liberal epoch as separate individuals, each seeking only pleasure and relief from pain. Social well-being was judged in terms of individual happiness, and social and political relations as mere means to this end. As each individual knows his own interest best, he should be left as much freedom as is compatible with public order; the less the restraint put on his activities, the better for society. The activities of the State were therefore confined to four directives to maintain order, i.e. to protect the security of persons and property, to defend the members of society against external attack, to provide redress for individuals against injury and to enforce private contracts. It was beyond the scope of this "negative" or "night watchman" State to establish any restriction on migration. To do so would have been incompatible with the general principle that men should be allowed to act as they please, provided they do not interfere with the liberty of others to do the same. Moreover, in the nineteenth century State property was a condition of full membership. "The Nation belonged to the middle class," as E. H. Carr[1] has put it; the working class from which emigrants were mainly recruited "had no fatherland". They had little access to the cultural heritage of their country; social services were reduced to a minimum. Clearly such a State could neither claim from the potential emigrant any allegiance for irrational reasons, nor could it offer material advantages which might have induced him to forego better prospects abroad. It was only in a later phase of liberal development that State activity was turned to social services. The "social service State" which was to mitigate the shortcomings of orthodox *laissez-faire*, reduced the incentive to emigrate by providing old-age and unemployment benefits and similar social services.

The trust in a natural harmony of individual interests, which had to be kept free from State interference, appeared to be unjustified. The State's coercive power was extended to wider fields. A revival of authoritarian ideals gained increasing

[1] E. H. Carr, *Nationalism and After.*

influence on public life after the turn of the century. Such a tendency is opposed to the individualism and rationalism of the liberal concept. It emphasizes the immaterial links between individual and nation, the feeling of loyalty to a common land and the unity of national culture. By monopolizing or regulating the whole educational system of the country, the State has an efficient means of inspiring the whole people with these ideals, and exerts a powerful influence on the economic and spiritual life of its subjects. The individual has then to overcome strong inhibitions before he is able to sever the links with his nation for mere economic reasons. The new nationalism which has replaced the cosmopolitan tendency of liberalism has undoubtedly affected migration both in democratic and authoritarian countries. It is one of the motives for those movements of re-migration which have been seen in recent years, e.g. for the tendency of Irish emigrants in the U.S.A. to return to Eire.

c. IMPERFECT KNOWLEDGE OF OPPORTUNITIES

We have already pointed out that, given an objective reason for migration and the subjective willingness of the individual to migrate, ignorance of the opportunities existing and of the costs of movement are further obstacles to free migration. In discussing the various methods of computing internationally comparable standard of living indices, we saw how difficult it is to find an objective measure of interspatial standards of living, mainly because of the subjective element inherent in any valuation of satisfactions. Moreover, no statistical data on which such indices could be based are available, so that the attempts made in this direction are still in the experimental stage. Unbiassed publications on conditions abroad are not easily accessible to the general public. To make individual migration a success, information as to where the highest standard of living is obtainable has to be supplemented by information on the cultural, social and climatic conditions in the countries concerned. During the period of free migration one of the major technical problems was how to provide the prospective migrant with unbiassed, reliable information on his prospects abroad.[1] The liberal State was reluctant to do this, lest it should interfere with the free play of self-interest.

[1] "The desire to get cheap labour to take the passenger fares and to sell land have probably brought more immigrants to this country than the hard conditions of Europe, Asia and Africa have sent." Prof. Commons in Carlton, *History and Problems of Organised Labour*, Chapter 8.

The main source of information has always been the letters and visits of friends and relatives who have already emigrated. Optimistic reports from them and evidence of their prosperity in the form of money remittances to their old country are very effective incentives to those who have stayed at home. It has been often observed in rural districts of emigration countries that a considerable number of the population from one village has emigrated to a particular country or town, while in neighbouring villages practically no such migration has occurred. The usual reason is that the reports of one or a few emigrants have made this village more migration-minded than others which had no such pioneer migrants. Information so obtained is generally unselfish and reliable, and covers both the economic and the irrational concerns of the would-be emigrants. It comes from persons whose problems resembled those awaiting the new emigrant. Its disadvantage is that it depends on the chance occurrence of some previous migration and is restricted to the conditions in one particular district, so that better opportunities in other countries remain unknown. The haphazard information available from previous emigrants was supplemented by the activities of transport companies and labour agents. The job of the labour agent was to recruit persons for work abroad. He was prone to give too optimistic an account of conditions in the new country in order to promote his own ends. He stimulated migration by advancing the passage money, often against a mortgage on the property of the emigrants on unfavourable terms. The emigrant had to agree to work for the agent or the agent's employer in the new country for a certain period, and, ignorant of the real conditions, he usually agreed to terms which were very profitable to the agent. This kind of exploitation of the ignorant has been practically abolished in the case of the U.S.A. since the Act of February 1885, "prohibiting importation of laborers under contract". In more recent years labour recruitment from abroad has in many countries of emigration been supervised by the State in order to prevent abuses. There is now scarcely any State that does not subject such activities at least to licensing and supervision.

During the period of free migration all transatlantic shipping companies maintained a large and ever-extending net of agents in the emigration countries. One line, the Inman Steamship Company, in 1892 had 3,500 agents in Europe.[1] The growth

---

[1] Mayo-Smith, *Emigration and Immigration*, p. 46.

and prosperity of these companies was largely based on the income from steerage emigrants. The rapid development of the two leading German steamship lines since the last quarter of the nineteenth century was almost entirely due to their success in securing for themselves the main flow of transatlantic migration from Eastern Europe. The agents were not all accredited representatives of particular companies. Free-lance agents, connected only loosely with the companies, proved in many respects more useful, especially after U.S.A. legislation in the eighties and nineties of the last century took the first step towards regulating immigration. "Encouragement or solicitation of immigration by steamship or transportation companies, except by means of regular advertisements giving an account of sailings, facilities and terms" was declared illegal.[1] The unofficial agents were easily tempted to exploit the ignorance of their customers, and to misrepresent opportunities abroad in order to earn commissions on as many passages as possible. They had no interest in the welfare or success of the emigrant after his immigration. On the contrary, it has even been maintained that the steamship companies had a certain interest in the misfortune of their passengers, and preferred immigrants likely to return to the old country, as this meant a traffic both ways. This backward movement was made up both of successful migrants who preferred to return after having secured the means for a higher standard of living and of immigrants who returned disappointed, their venture having proved a failure.

While it is not possible from the available statistics to compute the percentage of unsuccessful returning migrants, it is undoubtedly considerable, and is to a certain extent due to the migrants' ignorance of conditions in the new country. But the number of failures is by no means equivalent to the number of migrants returning for this reason. Many cannot afford the return passage, and continue to live in the new country in a state of destitution or at a lower standard than their pre-emigration one.

On the other hand causes other than ignorance may be responsible for unsuccessful migrations. Lack of adaptability unforeseeable changes in the relative conditions, etc., are other factors leading to re-migration. The harm done by shipping companies and their agents in exploiting the ignorance of emigrants would seem to have been somewhat exaggerated,

[1] Federal legislation, Act of March 3, 1891.

perhaps to supply an argument for the restrictive legislation of the U.S.A. In order to make immigration more successful, many immigration countries made provision in countries of emigration for the dissemination of information as to the opportunities offered to newcomers. Canada maintained paid agents in several countries of north-western Europe for this purpose. Advertisements in newspapers, pamphlets, exhibits of Canadian products were used to attract suitable immigrants. South American States, particularly Brazil, widely advertised the privileges and opportunities awaiting their immigrants. Information services open to all intending emigrants are maintained by the consular and diplomatic representatives of the immigration countries in the countries of emigration. This information is of course limited to conditions in the particular countries, and is not always uninfluenced by each country's general attitude to the desirability of immigration.

The information services which the governments of emigration countries have developed within their own territories have much more effective means of spreading knowledge of opportunities abroad, of preventing false information from being disseminated, and of checking any enlightenment of the population in this respect. In most emigration countries shipping companies are forbidden to carry on propaganda in favour of emigration by publishing circulars, etc., or to give any information to this end. This applied to Greece, Hungary, Italy, Lithuania, Poland, Portugal, Spain, Rumania before the last war.[1] In Great Britain any person who by any *false* representation induces or attempts to induce any person to emigrate or to engage a steerage passage in any ship is liable to fine or imprisonment (Merchant Shipping Act, 1906, Section 24). A similar provision, also restricted to false information, exists in Norway. In Great Britain the Government established an "Emigrants, Information Office" as early as 1831. The purpose of this office was to give reliable information regarding opportunities in the British Overseas Dominions and in certain foreign countries. Valuable handbooks were issued and information was given by correspondence and personal interviews. In the inter-war period the work of the Emigrants' Information Office was taken over by the Overseas Settlement Department of the Dominions Office. Its service is supplemented by that of many private, commercial and philanthropic associations, but such activities have declined

[1] I.L.O. *Studies and Reports:* Series O, No. 5, p. 60 ff., Vol. I, Chapters IV, V.

with the decline of British emigration. The Ministry of Labour Employment Exchanges had special arrangements for supplying information on oversea settlement and employment, and special officers were employed on this work.[1]

The official employment exchanges are in most countries entrusted with the task of advising prospective emigrants. Several countries have established special emigration offices. In pre-Hitler Germany the "Reichsstelle für Auswandrungswesen" in Berlin, with branches in other cities, was just such a governmental organization for the information of the public. Private information in return for a fee was prohibited. The giving of advice free of charge was permitted only to licensed associations.

We shall have to deal later with the restrictions on migration, applied by both emigration and immigration countries, which have reduced migration to a fraction of its former volume. The State regulation or prohibition of private propaganda may have had a certain restrictive effect on emigration; but by eliminating wrong and spreading correct information, State interference has contributed to the relief of frictional obstacles to migration which are due to ignorance of the opportunities available. Improvement of information services together with a higher standard of education and the growing knowledge of conditions and achievements in other countries have brought it about that free mobility is no longer seriously affected by ignorance.

D. DIFFICULTIES OF TRANSPORT

Progress in transport has made it easier for nations to know and understand each other and so has indirectly stimulated migration; the direct bearing of this development on the volume of migration remains to be discussed. Up to the second half of the nineteenth century the crossing of the Atlantic, and still more the voyage to Australia or New Zealand, was a hazardous venture for the emigrant. The appalling conditions on board the emigrant vessels have often been described and investigated by State commissions. Mortality on the voyage, mainly due to privation and to ship-fever—a severe form of Irish typhus—was extremely high.[2] The average length of the passage from Liverpool to New York in 1849 was about thirty-five days, from London forty-three days. But voyages often took up to twelve weeks, and in

---

[1] Cmd. 5766, *Report on Oversea Settlement*, p. 33.
[2] Fairchild, *op. cit.*, pp. 84–87.

such cases insufficient water and food added to the hardship of the passengers. Before 1850 steamships played no part in the transport of emigrants, and even in the eighteen-sixties about fifty per cent were still carried in sailing vessels, but by 1873 this proportion was reduced to 3.6 per cent. In the steamships, too, conditions were far from satisfactory, but at least the voyages took less time. Owing to government regulations and to competition, facilities on the emigration ships were gradually improved, and eventually a new type of steerage was developed which provided some comfort and eliminated unnecessary hardship and dangers for the passengers.

The decline of migration since the First World War has made the voyage much more comfortable for the emigrant. Ships are not overcrowded, competition has become keener in spite of traffic agreements, and the old type of steerage has practically disappeared. The cost of steerage passages had varied but little during the century before 1914. In 1820 the approximate cost of emigrating to Canada was about £6. In 1850 the London–New York passage cost £4 10s.; Liverpool–New York £3 10s. The whole expense for emigrating Irishmen in 1855 averaged £5 10s. per head. In spite of the better facilities and the lower purchasing power of the £, the rates did not rise much higher until the 1914 war. In 1913 steerage rates were £5 10s. and £6 15s., second cabin from £8.[1] Since 1918 international traffic agreements, contraction of migration and the provision of better facilities have made for a considerable rise of the rates. By 1939 the cost of a passage from England to New York third class was about £20, to Australia and New Zealand £37–£40.

The passage-money is only one item in the migrant's expenditure. Others are: the fare to his final place of destination, the transport of his belongings, the loss caused by the liquidation of his property and the transfer of his money, and special taxes levied in the countries of emigration and immigration. These are mainly the concern of wealthier migrants, except for the entry fees collected in certain countries in the form of a head tax or of a fixed amount to be deposited before admission to the new country.

E. CLIMATIC CONDITIONS

Wide differentials in climatic conditions between sending and receiving countries have an adverse effect on the volume of

[1] St. C. Johnson, *Emigration from the United Kingdom to North America*, Chapter V.

migration in various respects. Countries with an extremely hot or extremely cold climate offer little attraction to the migrant from Europe even when prospects of economic success are favourable. In the past, however, adjustment to the new environments proved so difficult that economic success could be achieved only in exceptional cases.

Generally speaking congenial climatic conditions are an important factor of success in any migration. Their absence accounts for the failure of many attempts by European emigrants to settle in the tropics or in the arctic regions of Canada as well as for the limited scope of Japanese and Korean immigration into Manchuria.

There is little doubt, in spite of the incompleteness of the existing surveys, that sub-tropical, sub-arctic and arctic regions offer enormous potentialities for immigration provided that the immigrants can become acclimatized and preserve their vitality and health. Technical and scientific progress during recent decades makes it possible—at least in theory—to overcome some of these difficulties. Reluctance to immigrate into these regions is likely to become less marked as such adjustment is facilitated.

A. Grenfell Price in his book *White Settlers in the Tropics* is mainly concerned with three questions: Why have white settlers in general failed in the tropics? Are they beginning to make progress? Can they hope for ultimate success? He concludes that "the early history of White settlement in the tropics was a story of wasted lives, wasted efforts, and wasted resources, but the recent years glow with achievement. The scientific world has at last glimpsed the vastness and complexity of the problem. In the hands of scientific workers lies the solution." [1]

F. STATE INTERVENTION

The period of a hundred years from the end of the Napoleonic wars until the outbreak of the First World War is generally associated with the idea of free migration; but though during this period the policy of most immigration and emigration countries was largely influenced by the *laissez-faire* concept, migratory movements were never entirely free from State intervention. Only during the inter-war period did the State intervene

---

[1] *White Settlers in the Tropics*, A. Grenfell Price, American Geographical Society, 1939, p. 238.
Pioneer Settlement in the Asiatic Tropics, K. J. Pelzer, New York, 1945, deals with agricultural colonization for natives in the Philippines and Netherlands Indies.

mainly with the intention of reducing the volume of migration. Previously its intervention had been chiefly directed to promote migration, at least so far as European migrants were concerned. New countries tried to attract immigrants by propaganda abroad, by the promise of cheap public land to immigrant-settlers, and by giving immigrants various other kinds of financial assistance. The U.S.A. Homestead Act of 1862 gave the right to obtain 160 acres of land against a nominal fee to any citizen or person over the age of twenty-one, who had actually settled upon and culti-vated the land.   Similarly after the Dominions Act of 1872, homesteads of 160 acres in Canada were offered free to all persons over 21 years of age.   In most immigration*countries, especially in the South American republics, provision was made to assist certain types of immigrants by giving them financial support or by helping them to acquire farm land.

State authorities in the emigration countries, by the use of coercion and by financial assistance, promoted the emigration of those whom they considered as surplus population.   In England the Poor Law Amendment Act of 1834 and several later amend-ments to this act allowed for the raising of public funds in order to finance the emigration of poor persons.[1]   Moreover, under the auspices of the Colonial Land and Emigration Department, founded in 1840, numerous schemes to help emigrants to proceed to the colonies were devised.   This department sent out 339,000 emigrants to Australia and other parts of the Empire between 1847 and 1869 at a cost of £4,864,000, of which 89 per cent came from public funds, mainly colonial, the rest from the emigrants or their friends.

After the eighteen-fifties the British Government rendered little assistance to its emigrants; an active policy was resumed only in 1922.   The Empire Settlement Act of that year permitted of an annual expenditure, not exceeding three million pounds, on schemes for assisting emigrants.   It authorized the government to participate (up to 50 per cent of the total costs) in such schemes in co-operation either with a Dominion government or with any public or private body in the Dominions or at home.   From 1922 to 1931 403,902 out of a total of 1,070,277 emigrants from

---

[1] During the years 1836–1846 the Poor Law Commissioners provided assistance in England and Wales for 14,000 emigrants; a sum of £80,000–90,000 being awarded by the parishes for this purpose. (Evidence before the Select Committee of the House of Lords, quoted by Johnson, *Emigration from the U.K. to North America*. The same source, pp. 68–100, gives further details of emigration assistance in the U.K. before 1914.)

the U.K. to overseas' parts of the Empire received assistance.[1] Not all the assisted emigrants can be considered as representing additional emigration brought about through State intervention; many of them would have migrated in any case, though possibly not within the Empire. It seems certain "that, if the Act had not been passed, the British emigration to the Dominions would have been far less between 1923 and 1929 than has in fact been the case."[2] Other emigration countries were less active than Great Britain in promoting the emigration of their nationals, but even her emigration policy remained during the inter-war period confined to the assistance of migration within the Empire.

Though the great majority of all emigrants migrated without any direct State assistance, there can be little doubt that the measures of the countries of immigration to attract immigrants and of the countries of emigration to assist their emigrants, taken together, have in the past greatly contributed to reduce friction and to increase the volume of migration. On the other hand through the imposition of restrictions both in emigration and immigration countries State intervention gradually became the most effective obstacle to the international mobility of mankind.

Let us first consider restrictions on emigration and their effect on the volume of migration. These appear still more incompatible with the principle of individual liberty of liberal political theory than restrictions of immigration. The would-be migrant who has to meet with restrictions in various countries of immigration may find that it is not possible to emigrate to the country of his preference, yet since such restrictions apply only to particular countries, he may be able to move to a country where conditions are less favourable but restrictions less severe; but if emigration restrictions prevent him from leaving his native country, no alternative choice is left him and he cannot exercise his "natural" right. Governments influenced by liberal and democratic ideas remained therefore generally reluctant to prohibit the emigration of their nationals, but they made it subject to various conditions. They held that the right of the individual has its limitation in the State's right of self-preservation; in other words: "keeping in view the idea of the State's

---

[1] Report to the Secretary of State for Dominion Affairs of the Interdepartmental Committee on Migration Policy, 1934. The Empire Settlement Act was renewed in 1937.

[2] Carr-Saunders, *op. cit.* p. 201.

right of self-preservation, the liberty of the individual must be reconciled with a system of regulation of emigration."[1] The nature of this "reconciliation" depends, of course, largely on the weight which the government gives to the respective interests of the individual and of the State in the case of a conflict.

Before nationalistic ideas become predominant, the imposition of emigration restrictions affected the total volume of migration but little; they were generally confined to the protection of the State's interest in three respects:

(1) Emigrants had to fulfil their legal obligations before being allowed to leave the country. When dependents were left behind, a guarantee for their support might be required. In countries with military conscription the emigration of nationals within the ages of active military service was subject to the consent of the military authorities.

(2) In order to protect the family as one of the chief bases of society, minors were allowed to emigrate only with the consent of their parents or guardians, married women only with that of their husbands.

(3) In order to protect the would-be emigrant, it was considered desirable to prohibit emigration in cases where he was unable to comply with the immigration laws of the country of his destination. Moreover his compulsory return to his native country might involve the State in unnecessary trouble and expense. It is also in the interest of the prospective emigrants that they should be prevented from leaving their home country if it seems obvious that their emigration will be a failure—that they are likely to be exploited or to become destitutes abroad.[2]

In the countries which have denounced the liberal conception of the State, the position of the would-be emigrant is entirely different. He is allowed to leave his country only if it is in the political or economic interest of the State; his own interests are of only secondary importance or of none at all. The result of this attitude is that emigration from Russia is practically prohibited. Emigration from other totalitarian countries such as Italy and Germany was greatly reduced, apart from clandestine migration—it was mainly confined to the victims of racial and

---

[1] P. Fauchille, "The Rights of Emigration and Immigration," in *International Labour Review*, Vol. IX, p. 320.

[2] For example, the government of India has imposed various restrictions on the emigration of indentured labour in the interests of the emigrants, and since 1915 has prohibited any emigration under indenture.

political persecution, many of whom were allowed to leave. Moreover, in particular cases these countries promoted the emigration of such nationals as might be expected to remain loyal to the political associations of their native country and after their emigration to pursue its interests. It was this latter category which was considered by the countries of immigration as endangering their national unity and which increased their hostile attitude toward immigration.

Even if we take into account the fact that the restrictions in the countries of immigration and other circumstances, to be discussed later, would in any case have brought about a contraction of the volume of emigration from their countries, it seems obvious that such restrictions have markedly reduced international mobility. If the immigration countries were to abandon their restrictionist policy, the peoples of countries which were formerly among the main countries of emigration would in any case remain excluded owing to the isolationist attitude of their governments.

The same argument—the right of the State to self-preservation—which serves to justify restrictions on emigration, is used in favour of immigration restrictions. In this case the State is not confronted with a conflict between its interests and the individual interests of its own nationals who propose to leave their native country, but it has to reconcile its interests with those of aliens whose welfare before their admission is not its immediate concern. It is therefore almost unavoidable that the governments of the receiving countries should incline to interpret this right of self-preservation in their own favour, and be ready to stop any type of immigration which might be harmful to them or to powerful groups within the State.

The U.S.A. adopted the principle of selective immigration as early as 1882 by discriminating against oriental immigrants. The Burlingame treaty of 1862, which had allowed Chinese to enter, was replaced in 1880 by a treaty which gave the U.S.A. full liberty in handling Chinese immigration. By the Chinese Exclusion Act of 1882 Chinese immigration was suspended for ten years.[1] This act was extended in 1892, and Chinese immigrants have remained practically excluded ever since.[2] Japanese

---

[1] There were in 1882 39,000 Chinese arrivals, making a total of 130,000 with those already in the country.

[2] A nominal quota of 100 immigrants per year has been allocated to China as a token recognition of her contribution to the war effort as a member of the United Nations.

immigrants had entered the country since 1869, but it was only after 1899 that they came in numbers.[1] This movement was stopped in 1908 by the "Gentlemen's Agreement" between the U.S.A. and Japan. Inhabitants of India and the East Indies have been excluded since 1924.

Restrictions against European immigration remained relatively ineffective until the Quota Act of 1921. The first federal Act prohibiting the entry of undesirable immigrants dates from 1875. It refers only to professional prostitutes and to criminals convicted of a crime involving moral turpitude. The Act of 1882 was more far-reaching. Its main provisions were: a head tax (of 50 cents) to be levied on all aliens landed, the exclusion of non-political convicts, lunatics, idiots, and those likely to become a public charge. About this time the various labour organizations began to fight against the increasing competition of foreign labour,[2] and to agitate for more restrictive immigration legislation. Anti-immigrant tendencies had shown themselves previously at various stages in American history,[3] but the rapid increase in the volume of migration and the transition from the "old" to the "new" immigration, which set in at that time, gave a new impetus to this hostile attitude. The old immigration had come almost exclusively from north-western Europe, the British Isles, Switzerland, Holland, Germany and the Scandinavian countries; it carried with it a relatively high standard of living and civilization. The new immigration consisted of emigrants from southern and eastern Europe, mainly from former Austria-Hungary and Tsarist Russia, from Italy, Greece, Portugal, Spain and Syria, all countries with a relatively low standard of living.

Attempts to restrict European immigration to the U.S. by means of legislation were not very successful for the next forty years. Various acts and amendments added to the classes of excluded immigrants, and the head tax was gradually raised to $8. Numerous bills of wider scope were either rejected by one House or were vetoed by the President. The Burnett Bill, which in 1917 was passed over the veto of President Wilson, among other restrictions introduced the literacy test; it excluded in principle illiterate immigrants over the age of sixteen; but this

---

[1] Japanese arrivals in 1899: 2,844, average 1893–1899: 1,730; Japanese arrivals in 1900: 12,635, average 1900–1907: 15,987.
[2] Cf. Chapter VI, p. 292 ff.
[3] Cf. Chapter V, p. 202 ff.

law had not the expected restrictive effect.[1] The number of immigrants, after the interruption during the war, had in 1921 again reached 805,000. It was only the Quota Act of 1921 which led to a drastic limitation, especially of the new immigration. This Act provided that the number of aliens of any nationality who might be admitted into the U.S. in any year should be limited to 3 per cent of the number of foreign-born persons of such nationality resident in the U.S. as shown by the census of 1910. The total number admissible under this quota law was 358,000 per year. This Act was superseded by the Act of 1924, which is still the basis for the admission of non-oriental immigrants into the U.S. It made further discrimination against the new immigration, and reduced the total annual number of immigrants from countries outside the American continent to about 165,000 from 1925-1929 and to 153,774 since 1930. However, after the crisis of 1929, the immigration authorities were instructed to make a much wider use of the public charge clause.[2] Only a very few immigrants without substantial means were admitted, and actual immigration remained far below the quota.

The same tendencies which are evident in the history of American restrictive legislation may be found in the immigration policy of almost all important immigration countries. They all tend, either by legislation or by administrative measures, to tighten immigration restrictions and to discriminate against certain types of immigrants. Immigration into the British Dominions is strictly controlled, and these controls have been used in favour of British immigrants and to a certain extent of immigrants from other countries of the old emigration. All the Dominions had at a relatively early date provided for the practical exclusion of oriental immigration. Legislation with a view to preserving a "White Australia" was introduced as early as 1855 in Victoria and 1861 in New South Wales. These Acts were later repealed, but new Acts prohibiting Chinese immigration were passed in Queensland in 1877 and in other States in 1881. Since the federal Immigration Act of 1901 the "Dictation Test"

---

[1] Illiteracy had been widespread among the new immigrants. According to Fairchild (op. cit. p. 198) immigrants over 14 years of age during the ten-year period 1899–1909 included persons who could neither read nor write when entering the U.S. in the following proportions: among Scandinavians 0.4 per cent, English 1.1 per cent, Irish 2.7 per cent, Italian (North) 11.8 per cent, Hebrews 25.7 per cent, Greeks 27 per cent, Poles 35.4 per cent, Italians (South) 54.2 per cent, Portuguese 68.2 per cent. It was therefore presumed that the literacy test would greatly reduce the volume of new immigration.

[2] Executive Order of September, 1930.

has been used to exclude oriental immigration. This Act provides that an immigrant must pass before disembarkation a test which consists in writing not less than fifty words dictated to him in any prescribed language. By choosing a language which the applicant does not understand the immigration authorities can reject any immigrant they think undesirable. Canada imposed on Chinese immigrants a prohibitive poll tax until the Chinese Immigration Act of 1923, which prohibits practically any immigration from China; while a "Gentleman's Agreement" with Japan prevented Japanese immigration of any amount. Legislation in New Zealand and South Africa provides in a similar way for the exclusion of Oriental immigrants.

During the inter-war period restrictions in the Dominions were gradually extended to cover various types of European immigrants, and during the "Great Depression" even British nationals became subject to severe selection. In Canada, for example, a distinction was made between "preferred", "non-preferred", and "other" countries. Immigrants from the "preferred" countries (Belgium, France, Germany, Holland, Switzerland, Denmark, Norway and Sweden) were admitted on similar terms to British nationals, that is to say they had to show on arrival evidence of assured employment or of sufficient funds to maintain themselves during a period of transition during which they might be expected to find employment. The "non-preferred countries" included Austria, Czechoslovakia, Poland, Hungary, Yugoslavia, Lithuania, Esthonia and Russia. Their nationals were admitted only as agriculturists or domestic servants. Immigration from "other countries" was subject to a special permit in each individual case. The distinction lost much of its significance in the years of depression, since immigration from Britain and other preferred countries was also reduced to a minimum by an extensive use of the clause in the Immigration Act which excludes persons likely to become a public charge.

In the countries of Central and South America immigration is subject to a strict control of visas and to a number of legal restrictions. In Brazil immigration for each nationality is limited to 2 per cent of the number of immigrants of that nationality who have settled in Brazil during the last fifty years.[1]

[1] Certain exemptions have bee nprovided for by two Legislative Decrees of May 4 and August 20, 1938. Very comprehensive information on migration restrictions in all countries of emigration and immigration can be found in: I.L.O., *Studies and Reports*, Series O, No. 3; *Migration Laws and Treaties*, 3 Vols., 1928–1929. Changes which have occurred since then are outlined in the I.L.O. Yearbooks.

Similar tendencies towards restriction are characteristic of the immigration policy of European countries. In Britain immigrants became subject to certain restrictions with the Aliens Act of 1905. This Act, amended in 1914 and 1919, provided the legal basis for the issue of the Aliens Order, 1920. According to this Order an alien is permitted to land only if the immigration authorities are satisfied that he can support himself and his dependents or if he has a labour permit issued by the Minister of Labour. The admission of alien immigrants to practically all European countries is governed by Acts or administrative regulations on similar lines. They all have it in common that the decision whether an applicant is regarded as undesirable is largely left to the discretion of the immigration authorities.

There is, however, one significant difference between the policy of the new countries, whose nationals are practically all former immigrants or of immigrant stock, and that of the "old" European countries of emigration. Broadly speaking, in the new countries the immigrant once admitted is regarded as a future citizen. It is largely left to his initiative to find the best way to become settled in his country of adoption. In most old countries the immigrant has become during the inter-war period subject to strong supervision. He needs a labour permit for taking up or changing employment; to be granted naturalization is rather the exception than the rule, and he has always to face the possibility of deportation if in periods of general unemployment his labour permit is withdrawn or if for any reason he is regarded as a public liability.

Generally speaking until the 1914 war restrictions on immigration had a marked effect only on the volume of non-European migration, but during the inter-war period they affected also the mobility of potential European emigrants to an ever-increasing extent.[1] It is safe to say that without the policy of restriction and selection the volume of migration would have been much larger, and that the almost complete cessation of normal migratory

---

[1] A certain mitigating effect arose from bilateral treaties which were concluded between a country of emigration and one of immigration with a view to regulating migratory movements between them. They were developed by France immediately after the 1914 war, and a number of other countries have followed her example. Most of these treaties are mainly concerned with temporary and seasonal migration; they are designed to regulate the technical measures necessary for this type of migration. Only a few affect migration from Europe to overseas countries. Such agreements have been concluded, for instance, by Argentina with the Netherlands, Switzerland and Denmark, by Bolivia with Poland. The International Labour Office has encouraged such treaties as a means of reviving international migration. Moreover, the I.L.O. had planned before the war the establishment of a Permanent

movements to the countries of immigration after the great depression is due to this policy.

On the other hand, as outlined at the beginning of this chapter, various economic and non-economic forces which tended to reduce the propensity to emigrate were in operation during the inter-war period. It would therefore be a mistake to assume that in the absence of restrictions emigration from Europe would have had the same volume and effect in that period as it had before the First World War. The existence of such forces is entirely disregarded, for instance, in a statement made in 1941 by the Chairman of the Cunard Company in his annual report. Sir Percy Bates suggested that the building programme of the Cunard Line had been dislocated by the restrictions which were placed by the U.S., Canada, Australia and the rest of the world upon immigration. "But for these restrictions there would by 1939 have been some twenty million fewer people in Europe." In the different economic and demographic setting which prevailed during the two wars the effects of large-scale migration would probably have become much less favourable and would almost automatically have led to a contraction of migratory movements. This point will be elaborated in later chapters.

4. VOLUME OF MIGRATION

The numerical effects resulting from the many counteracting forces which either stimulate or hamper migratory movements are reflected in the statistics of migration. The shortcomings of these statistics, especially those referring to earlier periods, are discussed in the appendix to this chapter (p. 67). The figures and percentages given below are based on national statistics or on more or less accurate estimates. They are therefore subject to a considerable margin of error and cannot claim to do more than convey a rough idea of the trends of international migration during the past century.

International Committee on Migration for Settlement—"in order to facilitate co-ordination between emigration countries, to study in detail the problems of international finance involved in the development of migration for settlement, and to carry out many other duties in connection with international credit operations which might be found necessary". The outbreak of the 1939 war put an end to all these attempts at international regulation under the sponsorship of the I.L.O. and the League of Nations. Their effect on the volume of migration was only small, because of the limited power of these two international institutions.

INTERCONTINENTAL EMIGRATION FROM EUROPE

The number of emigrants from Europe to the new continents from 1815 to 1932 has been estimated at more than 60 millions. In spite of wide fluctuations, the volume of migration showed a tendency to rapid increase between 1846 and 1914. Fluctuations during the inter-war period were on a much lower level. There was a slight rise in the number of emigrants during the three or four years preceding the Second World War, which is, however, not reflected in the average figures of the table below.

TABLE I

Intercontinental Emigration from Europe, 1846–1937 (Estimates)
Annual Averages (thousands)

1846–1850	.	260	1896–1900	.	600
1851–1855	.	340	1901–1905	.	1,050
1856–1860	.	200	1906–1910	.	1,390
1864–1865	.	220	1911–1915	.	1,350
1866–1870	.	350	1916–1920	.	430
1871–1875	.	370	1921–1924	.	770
1876–1880	.	280	1925–1928	.	580
1881–1885	.	690	1929–1932	.	290
1886–1890	.	780	1933–1937	.	150
1891–1895	.	730		

COUNTRIES OF EMIGRATION

Of the 52 millions who emigrated from Europe between 1846 and 1932, about 18 million, or more than one-third, came from the British Isles. The share of the main countries of emigration in the total is as follows:

TABLE II

British Isles	.	35 per cent	Russia .	. 4.4 per cent
Italy	. .	19 ,,	Portugal	. 3.5 ,,
Austria-Hungary	10 ,,	Poland .	. 1.7 ,,
Germany .	. 9.6 ,,	(1920–1932)	
Spain	. .	9 ,,	France .	. 1 ,,
Scandinavia	. 4.8 ,,	Other Countries 2.4 ,,	

Until about 1880 the majority of all emigrants came from the British Isles. The marked rise in the volume of European emigration since 1880 (see Table I) coincided with a significant shift in the national composition of the emigrant population. During the 33 years preceding the outbreak of the First World War there was a rapid rise in emigration from eastern, south-eastern and southern Europe, while emigration from north-western Europe tended to contract. This is borne out by Table III.

TABLE III

Intercontinental Emigration of Citizens (18 European Countries)
Percentage Distribution, 1846-1924

	British Isles	Germany	Scandinavia	Spain	Portugal	Italy	Austria-Hungary	Russia*	Poland	Other Countries
1846-50	77.9	14.3	1.6	0.1	0.1	0.1	0.2	0.0	—	5.7
1851-55	67.7	21.9	2.0	0.3	1.5	0.2	1.2	0.0	—	5.2
1856-60	61.4	24.6	2.3	0.9	4.0	2.1	1.1	0.1	—	3.5
1861-65	64.3	19.5	4.4	0.8	3.6	3.6	1.0	0.1	—	2.7
1866-70	49.4	24.1	11.3	1.3	2.2	5.4	1.7	0.1	—	4.5
1870-75	52.2	21.3	6.0	1.9	3.9	6.3	2.8	1.6	—	4.0
1876-80	50.1	16.3	8.2	2.0	4.1	10.2	4.2	1.9	—	3.0
1881-85	37.5	24.9	8.5	7.0	2.4	9.3	5.0	1.9	—	3.5
1886-90	32.5	12.5	7.8	9.8	2.6	17.2	6.7	5.7	—	4.6
1891-95	26.8	11.0	6.6	10.7	4.3	20.6	9.3	7.7	—	3.0
1896-1900	25.4	4.1	3.7	13.4	3.7	27.5	12.8	6.7	—	2.7
1901-05	22.2	2.7	5.2	6.9	2.4	30.5	19.3	8	—	2.8
1906-10	24.1	1.9	3.2	10.5	2.8	29.0	19.1	7.1	—	2.3
1911-15	26.7	1.2	2.1	12.4	4	23.2	18.1	10.4	—	1.9
1916-20	29.3	0.6	2.7	22.0	6.1	29.3	2.6	—	2.3	5.1
1920-24	37.1	7.5	3.6	12.7	2.5	21.7	7.4	0.4	4.4	2.7

*Until 1915 this includes Poland.

3*

The table is taken in a slightly simplified form from *International Migrations*, Vol. I, Tables I and II. It does not include emigration from Greece, Turkey and other Balkan States, which was negligible until the nineties of the last century. Nationals from these countries went mainly to the U.S. (see Table IV below). The figures for 1920–24 are not strictly comparable with the pre-1914 figure owing to changes of frontiers, but they clearly indicate the growth in the share of the "old" emigration as a result of the discrimination against immigrants from south-eastern and southern Europe.

The shift from the "old" to the "new" immigration was most marked in immigration to the U.S. This is reflected in the table below:

TABLE IV

Immigration into the U.S. by country of last residence

	Absolute Figures	Percentages				
		Western & Northern Europe	Eastern & Southern Europe	British North America	Mexico	Other Countries or not stated
1821–40	743,000	78.8	1.2	2.2	1.5	16.3
1841–90	14,685,000	81.2	8.2	7.0	0.1	3.5
1891–1915	16,943,000	25.6	66.8	3.2	0.8	3.6
1921–24	2,345,000	25.2	41.3	18.6	8.7	6.2

The share of the Eastern and Southern European countries after 1920 is somewhat higher than is indicated in this table. In order to evade the restrictions a substantial number immigrated clandestinely or took up temporary residence in other American countries.

COUNTRIES OF IMMIGRATION

Out of a total of about 60 million European emigrants roughly 60 per cent went to the U.S.A.; Argentina accounts for 11 per cent, Canada for 8.7 per cent, Brazil for 7.4 per cent. Australia received roughly 5 per cent, New Zealand 1 per cent, and South Africa about 1.3 per cent.

Table V shows the changes since 1856 in the distribution of immigrants between the four main receiving countries which account for more than 87 per cent of the total volume of European emigration.

TABLE V

Intercontinental Immigration of Aliens (from all Continents)
into the U.S., Canada, Brazil and Argentina since 1856.

Period	Percentage				Annual average in thousands
	U.S.	Canada	Brazil	Argentina	
1856–60	78.7	8.6	7.9	4.8	203.3
1861–65	78.9	11.1	5.2	4.8	193.4
1866–70	81.9	9.6	2.5	6.0	377.4
1871–75	80.4	7.7	4.2	7.7	384.1
1876–80	73.3	5.9	11.5	9.3	240.6
1881–85	81.4	6.2	4.3	8.1	633.3
1886–90	66.4	4.8	11.6	17.2	683.3
1891–95	67.3	4.1	21.1	7.5	631.1
1896–1900	60.8	4.6	18.6	16.0	513.7
1901–05	76.8	6.8	5.8	10.6	994.7
1906–10	67.1	9.7	5.7	17.5	1,415.0
1911–15	61.9	13.1	9.4	15.6	1,229.0
1916–20	56.5	15.2	13.8	14.5	266.2
1921–24	59.7	11.4	8.5	20.4	713.5
1925–28	33.5	22	18	26.5	513.1
1929–32	31.4	20	18.5	30.1	288.3
1933–37	28.0	6.9	32.7	32.3	100.8

RETURN MOVEMENTS

The percentage of immigrants who did not settle permanently
in the receiving countries but returned to their home country or
re-emigrated has been considerable throughout the history of
migration.   The magnitude of the return movement is very
uncertain until recent times and only a few figures can be given.
It is believed that 30 per cent of the U.S. immigrants between
1821 and 1924 and 47 per cent of the immigrants into Argentina
(1857–1924) have returned to home again.   Willcox estimates
for the U.S. that the net increase from alien migration amounted
for the period 1908–1930 only to 63 per cent of the number of
immigrants admitted.   This percentage rose from 61 for 1900–
1907 to 65 for 1891–1900 and by 5 for each earlier decade up to
100 in 1820–1830).[1]

Recent developments are illustrated by the table below,
which gives the net balance of migration between 1927 and 1941
in various countries of emigration and immigration, and shows
the small volume of intercontinental migration during the whole
period.   The reversal in the direction of migration during the
years of the "Great Depression" is reflected in the figures for

[1] *International Migrations*, Vol. II, p. 89.

1931–1934. In this period the main receiving countries, such as the U.S.A., Argentina, and Australia, had virtually become countries of emigration, while in the traditional sending countries the number of returning nationals exceeded the number of emigrants. It is noteworthy that the figures for 1935–1938 indicate the resumption of the normal trend—the result partly of the beginning of economic recovery in the new countries, partly of refugee movements out of Germany and other European countries.

TABLE VI

Net Intercontinental Migration, 1927–41 (in thousands)
Annual Averages

I. Movements of Aliens from and to countries of immigration

Country	1927–1930	1931–1934	1935–1938	1939–1941
United States	+ 107.5	− 25.7	+ 18.1	+ 31.9
Argentina	+ 79.2	− 4.6	+ 21.4	+ 3.2
Brazil	+ 40.3	+ 14	− 0.5	+ 0.7
Australia	+ 20.4	− 4.2	+ 4.7	+ 7.8

II. Movements of Nationals from and to countries of emigration

United Kingdom	− 67.3	+ 34.9	+ 12.9	
Poland	− 51.9	− 10	− 24.3	
Italy	− 17.3	+ 2.5	− 13	
Spain	− 8.1	+ 25.6	—	
Czechoslovakia	− 10.1	± 0	− 2.7	

INTENSITY OF MIGRATION

The intensity of migration can be measured by the proportion of immigrants to the population of the receiving country and by the proportion of emigrants to the population of the sending country.

In the period 1846–50 about one per 1,000 inhabitants emigrated every year from Europe; there were 2.5 emigrants per year per thousand inhabitants in 1901–1905; 4.3 in 1913, and less than 0.4 in 1933–1937. The ratio is, of course, much higher for particular countries of Overseas emigration. The highest recorded intensity of gross emigration is that of Italy: between 1906 and 1910 11.6 persons on the average emigrated every year per 1,000 population. Peak periods for the United Kingdom are 1853–55 with 8.4 emigrants per 1,000, 1881–85 with 7.4 and 1911–1915 with 7.9 emigrants per 1,000 population. As to net emigration, according to I. Ferenczy,[1] Sweden holds the

[1] *International Migrations*, Vol. I.

record with 7 per 1,000 in 1886–1890. Then follows Italy with 6.3 for 1901–1905 and Finland with 5.5 for the same period. Among the American countries Argentina has had the greatest annual intensity of immigration, with 22.2 for 1881–1890 and 29.2 for 1901–1910. Canada had for 1901–1910 17 immigrants, the U.S. 10 and Brazil 3.4 per 1,000 population. During the inter-war period immigration had no appreciable effect on population growth in the receiving countries except in the case of Jewish immigration into Palestine.

CONTINENTAL MIGRATION

Migration within Europe before the 1914–1918 war had largely a seasonal character. The main countries of emigration were Italy and the Polish regions of Austria. The annual average for 1906–1910 amounted to 249,000 for Italy; 210,000 for Austria; Belgium and Hungary followed with 15–16,000. The Italians went mainly to France, Austria, Germany and Switzerland, the Belgians to France, and the Poles to Germany. During the inter-war period seasonal migration of unskilled labour lost its former importance, while France, particularly until 1930, admitted large numbers of immigrants from Poland, Italy, and other European countries for more or less permanent settlement.

Immigration into France in 1930 was as high as 220,000 (net immigration 178,000). In 1932 emigration or repatriation of aliens exceeded immigration by 39,000 persons. Between 1933 and 1939 average immigration of aliens into France amounted to 55,000, emigration to 44,000. A considerable amount of continental migration occurred during the past century on the North American Continent. Between 1820 and 1940 about three million persons immigrated into the U.S. from Canada (1,775,000 since 1911) and 780,000 from Mexico. The volume of continental emigration from the U.S. has been much lower.

ASIATIC MIGRATION

The total volume of Asiatic intercontinental emigration has been estimated at about three million persons.[1] The movement started after the abolition of slavery. Indian migrants, mainly indentured labourers, went to the West Indies, Mauritius, South Africa, South America, and to a small extent to Australia and North America. The peak of the movement was reached in 1858

[1]Excluding the middle east with Jewish mass immigration into Palestine and native emigration from Syria and Lebanon.

with 46,000 emigrants. Though statistical evidence is lacking it seems that Chinese intercontinental emigration (as in the case of India mainly indentured labour) was on a considerable scale between 1848 and 1873. Its destination was broadly speaking the same as that of Indian emigration. Chinese immigration into the U.S. practically ceased from 1884, after having reached its peak in 1882 with 40,000 persons (only 116 of whom were females). As the result of rigid restrictions by all countries of white immigration and by the Indian government, the volume of Asiatic intercontinental immigration had become negligible by the turn of the century, while a considerable number of earlier immigrants were repatriated.

Movements of Chinese and Indian emigrants within Asia were impeded by restrictions to a much lesser extent. They went to the undeveloped monsoon and tropical lands in Asia; the Chinese penetrated also into the undeveloped temperate zones in the north of China. The following table shows the numbers of Chinese and Indians settled in these regions and gives a rough idea of the scope of the underlying migratory movements

TABLE VII

Chinese and Indians settled in underdeveloped Asiatic countries[1]

Region	Total Population	Number of Chinese settled	Number of Indians settled
Temperate Region: Manchuria, Mongolia, Asiatic, Russia . .	— .	40,000,000	—
Monsoon Lands:			
Burma . . .	16,000,000	193,000	1,400,000
Malay Peninsula .	5,300,000	1,275,000	624,000
Siam . . .	14,500,000	2,500,000	120,000
Indo-China . .	23,900,000	700,000	6,000
Philippine Islands .	16,400,000	117,000	unknown
Formosa . . .	5,800,000	4,500,000	—
Equatorial lands:			
Ceylon . . .	5,900,000	—	900,000
Netherlands East Indies	68,000,000	1,800,000	28,000

Chinese emigration to Manchuria increased to more than a million between 1927 and 1929, but Chinese settlement on the land seems to have been barred since Japan established control over Manchuria. A quota was fixed for the immigration of Chinese coolies; 986,000 were admitted in 1939.[2] The volume

[1] Figures from: R. Mukerjee, *Population Problems in South-east Asia*, 1945.
[2] Mukerjee, *op. cit.*, p. 13.

of recent Chinese and Indian immigration into the under-
developed monsoon lands is epitomized by the following figures:

TABLE VIII

Continental Migration of Aliens in various Asiatic Countries (in 000's)
Annual Average

| Year | Indo-China | | | Malay Peninsula | | |
	Immi-gration	Emigra-tion	Balance	Immi-gration	Emigra-tion	Balance
1927–29	72.7	42.0	+30.7	427.2	234.0	+193.2
1930–33	51.4	54.4	− 3.0	127.6	250.8	− 123.2
1934–36	45.9	33.7	+12.2	195.3	108.5	+ 86.8
1937	71.4	36.4	+35.0	361.7	—	—

It is noteworthy that the recovery after 1934 occurred in
both countries in spite of a restrictive immigration policy.

5. NOTE ON MIGRATION STATISTICS

For the student of population statistics "migration" has a
meaning entirely different from that accepted in this book; for
him "migration" is merely the difference between total population
growth and natural increase during a given period of time. For
instance, England and Wales had according to the 1921 Census
a population of 38 million (in round figures); according to the
1931 Census a population of 40 million. The excess of births over
deaths during this decade, as reported by the Registrar General,
amounted to roughly 2.2 million, indicating an outward balance
of migration of about 200,000 persons during the Census period
June 1921–April 1931.

This method of subtraction is based on two assumptions:

(i) It assumes that both, census returns and registrations of
births and deaths are accurate. This is undoubtedly unwarranted
in the case of earlier censuses and vital Statistics, but significant
inaccuracies can be found also in those of recent date. There is,
for instance, in the U.S. Census of 1930 an apparent discrepancy
of more than a million between the figure for the native population and that expected on the basis of the 1920 returns and the
natural increase during the interval, which is apparently due to
greater under-enumeration in 1920 than in 1930. It has been
estimated for the U.S. that about 5 per cent of all children under
5 years of age are usually not enumerated.[1] Non-registration of
births is frequent, and in certain areas in the South and West of

[1] National Resources Committee *The Problem of a Changing Population*, p. 256.

the U.S. probably as high as 10–20 per cent.[1] Statistics of the actual movements from and into the Census area are therefore invaluable as an indication of the inaccuracies contained in the Census or vital statistics returns.

(ii) The net balance of the inward and outward movements during the period under consideration is alone relevant to the interpretation of total population growth; that is to say that those who emigrated and re-immigrated during that period are left out of account. On the other hand temporary visitors present in the census area on the day of the census have to be counted as immigrants. It is easy to see that such measurements of the volume of migration, derived from census figures and vital statistics, are of little value for the study of migratory movements as defined in Chapter I.

Official migration statistics of some kind were introduced by various countries of immigration and emigration soon after the end of the Napoleonic wars. The methods and criteria applied by the various countries were subject to frequent changes during the last century with the consequence that figures for immigration compiled by the receiving country and figures for emigration compiled by the sending country referring to the same movement often show important discrepancies due to the heterogeneity and inaccuracies of the national statistics. A considerable margin of error must, therefore, be allowed if such information is used for international comparisons or for a discussion of fluctuations in the volume of migration over time. Broadly speaking records of immigration are more complete than those of emigration. Relatively reliable information is now available for most countries of immigration and emigration. But its usefulness for international comparisons is still impaired by the diversity of the criteria on which national statistics of migration are based. Some States only have adopted their legal definition of a migrant for statistical purposes, and even the national legal definitions vary greatly. In some countries different administrative authorities make use of different definitions in the statistics they compile. The definition may be based (1) on personal characteristics of the migrant, (2) on conditions of transport, (3) on the migrant's future plans, or (4) on a combination of the three criteria. Some examples only of each category need be mentioned.

Personal characteristics: Only own nationals emigrating to America are considered as emigrants (France). Only persons not belonging to the coloured

[1] *Ibid.*, p. 128.

races or only including special coloured races, are immigrants (French and British Colonies, South Africa). Only manual workers or only the holders of a contract of employment or only transatlantic passengers entering the country for the first time are immigrants.

Conditions of transport: All Transatlantic passengers but cabin passengers are considered as migrants; so are passengers arriving on board a special kind of ship or paying a fixed rate; travellers holding a single journey railway ticket for a foreign destination.

Future plans: Immigrants are only those in search of livelihood or only those who intend to settle for a certain time, usually at least twelve months.[1]

The International Labour Office has since 1920 worked on the problem of drafting a uniform definition and having it generally adopted. These attempts have so far been unsuccessful, as no agreement in this respect has been yet concluded. To be sure, recently, national statistics of migration have become somewhat less discordant as a result of the suggestions issued by the I.L.O. and of the increasing awareness that migration is an international problem. In compiling international migration statistics, the I.L.O. has to rely mainly on the figures provided by the national statistics, whose results are interpreted so as to fit into the various general tables. Constant care is exerted to examine as closely as possible all the figures received by studying the administrative measures under which they were compiled and the definitions used in making the returns.[2] International migration statistics should be based, according to the suggestions of the I.L.O., mainly on three principles:

(1) Every international act of removal for a certain length of time from one country to another should be considered as migration.

(2) A distinction should be made between permanent migration (more than one year) and temporary migration (more than one month, but only for the purpose of carrying on an occupation).

(3) Migration between a home country and its colonies or between different colonies of the same home country should be dealt with by analogy to international migration properly so called.[3]

[1] These distinctions are not only of theoretical interest but may become a practical issue; e.g. in certain countries it was possible until recently to avoid existing restrictions for the admission of immigrants by entering as a first-class passenger.
[2] International Labour Office, *Studies and Reports*, Series O (Migration), Nos. 1, 2, 4, p. 7.
[3] I.L.O., *Studies and Reports*, Series N (Statistics), No. 18, Statistics of Migration, p. 69.

CHAPTER IV

MIGRATION AS A MEANS OF ADJUSTING A DISHARMONIOUS DISTRIBUTION OF POPULATION

1. THE OPTIMUM THEORY OF POPULATION APPLIED TO MIGRATORY MOVEMENTS

In discussing the occurrence of individual migration in a free system, we have already mentioned that the liberal attitude towards migration is based mainly on two propositions: (1) Individual free migration is determined by the economic self-interest of the migrant. (2) The economic self-interest of the individual coincides with the general interest. The corollary is that any interference with free migration would be against the general interest. It implies that the State or any other authority should refrain from either restricting or promoting migratory movements. This argument gives rise to several questions which will now be dealt with. We shall first give an account of the liberal concept of the theory of migration, based on the theory of marginal productivity. We have then to ask ourselves whether (1) the conclusion drawn from this theory, viz. the claim that migration should not be interfered with, is consistent with itself, and (2) whether or how far it is applicable in real life when allowance is made for the over-simplifications implied in its assumptions.

A. UNDERLYING PRINCIPLES

The whole liberal conception is, as we have seen, based on the principle that the State ought to be only a means of promoting the welfare of its individual members. Proceeding from this proposition liberal theory maintained that in the long run national and international interests coincide.

For the smooth working of the *laissez-faire* system the State is only considered as the "sublimated check or hindrance".[1] States are artificial entities; they have no natural rights, nor do they as such prosper or suffer. The real entities behind them, those with whose welfare we must be concerned, are the human

[1] Cf. League of Nations (Internat. Inst. of Intellectual Co-operation), *The State and Economic Life*, p. 194.

beings who do suffer and do prosper.[1] If we follow this line of approach, we have to ignore all problems connected with the claims of sovereign States and of nations as such, and the end of any State policy can only be to secure for its individual members a maximum amount of welfare. It is therefore not the aggregate national income but the average real income per head with which we are concerned. A policy which would increase the aggregate national real income by increasing the supply of labour in such a way that it would lead to a reduction of income per head would be opposed to this principle. Moreover, the theory is limited to the mere economic aspect of the problem by identifying maximum real income per head with the maximum satisfaction per head. Accepting this criterion, the optimum theory of population considers that size of population as an optimum which provides the greatest real income of commodities and services per head. When this optimum has been reached, any increase through immigration or natural growth, or any reduction through emigration or natural decrease, is presumed to lower real income per head. In terms of the marginal theory of production: the optimum point for a population *with a given amount of capital and natural resources* is reached under conditions of free competition when the marginal product of labour is equal to the average output per head. So long as the marginal product of labour is greater than the average output an increase in the working population would raise the output per head, and conversely so soon as the marginal product has fallen below the existing output per head, a population increase would cause output per head to fall. Such changes in the marginal productivity of labour as a consequence of changes in population size are explained as the resultant of two opposing forces:

If the population is small relatively to natural resources, there is but little opportunity for specialization, for economies brought about through division of labour. Moreover, with a small population the scope for economies by large-scale production must necessarily remain limited. With modern methods of production the optimum size has markedly grown until relatively lately for many industries and for transport and for the firms in such industries. Their capital equipment can be fully utilized only if there is a fairly large total demand for their products. Under these conditions population growth may be associated with a rise in real income per head.

[1] Cf. I.I.I.C., *Peaceful Change*, 1938, p. 273.

This tendency of population growth to raise real income per head, which is due to large-scale economies in the production of goods and services, is counteracted by the effect of the law of diminishing returns. With a given volume of natural resources and capital equipment and a given state of technique, an increase in the numbers of the working population means that the amount of other factors of production available for co-operation with each unit of labour becomes smaller and that output per head will tend to fall. "The larger the population, the less important will the advantages of large-scale production become and the more important will be the fact that there is little capital and land to use with each worker, so that at some point output per head would be reduced by a further growth in numbers."[1] Definitions of "over" and "under" population can be derived from this theory. A country is considered as over-populated when its population has increased beyond the optimum point and as "under-populated" when it falls below it.[2]

B. PROCESS OF ADJUSTMENT

It is obvious that no immediate changes in marginal productivity can be expected from changes in numbers as a consequence of a fall or rise in the birth rate, since a time lag of about fourteen years has to be taken into account before the newly-born babies have reached working age. It is different in the case of migration. Changes in total numbers through migration represent normally gains or losses to the working population and therefore alter the ratio between labour and other factors of production at once. If we apply the optimum theory to the effects of migratory movements on changes in real income per head in the countries concerned we can see that migration from one country A to another country B may affect the position of these countries relative to the optimum point in four different ways:

(1) A is over-populated, B under-populated.
(2) A and B are both under-populated.
(3) A and B are both over-populated.
(4) A is under-populated, B is over-populated.

Under conditions of free migration all these four cases may

[1] J. E. Meade, p. 266, *An Introduction to Economic Analysis and Policy.*
[2] The term "over-population" is used in current literature with very different meanings. They are discussed in: F. C. Wright, *Population and Peace*, pp. 65-71.

occur, even if migration is determined only by the economic self-interest of the migrants.

(1) has been the most frequent case in the past, when free migration has prevailed. Migration from densely populated European countries to the undeveloped new continents is presumed to belong to this category. Migration brings both the emigration and immigration countries nearer to the optimum point.

In case (2) migration would occur only if B were nearer to the optimum point than A. It would be disadvantageous for A, but would improve the position of B.

Case (3) would occur only if B were less over-populated than A. A would gain by this migration, but B would lose.

Case (4) is likely to occur if the effect of under-population is more marked than the effect of over-population in B. Migration is disadvantageous for both the emigration and immigration countries. In the years of the "Great Depression" Australia, Argentina, the U.S.A. and other traditionally immigration countries experienced a considerable emigration. It is probable that these movements from overseas countries to the old continent belong to a large extent to category (4). (Cf. Chap. VI.)

Only in case (1) does free migration appear to be advantageous for both countries concerned; in case (2) restriction of emigration is useful for A, in case (3) restriction of immigration would be in the interest of A, in case (4) a restriction of emigration and immigration appears to be advisable for both the countries concerned.

From the international point of view, migration should be free, according to this argument, in cases (1), (2), (3), though in (2) and (3) only one of the two countries improves its position thereby. Migration is in accordance with the assumptions which we have made only if it increases the total productivity of A plus B. In the long run, however, it may be wise for the State to adopt the international point of view. In a world-wide *laissez-faire* economy free trade enables all countries to profit indirectly from any increase of productivity; on the other hand restrictions on migration in these cases are likely to lead to excessive pressure of population with repercussions on the economic welfare of the restricting country, by disturbances of the international price and currency equilibrium, and to result in political friction and war.

c. MARGINAL PRODUCTIVITY AS A CRITERION FOR THE OPTIMUM
SIZE OF A POPULATION

It has been suggested[1] that this theory provides a method of judging whether a population with a given amount of land and capital is greater or less than optimum. Since if the marginal product of labour were greater than the average output per head an increase in population would raise output per head, and conversely if the marginal product of labour were less than output per head a fall in population would increase average income per head, changes in the marginal productivity per head of the population of a given country may be correlated with changes in the size of its population, and it is claimed that changes in this correlation indicate whether the population is moving nearer to or away from its optimum point. Applied to the migration problem: in the former case immigration, in the latter case emigration, is the desirable policy for the countries concerned in order to promote economic welfare. The test is "simply" this: "if the payment of wages to labour, equal to the marginal product of labour, would not absorb as much as the total output of the community because output per head is greater than the marginal product of labour, the population is greater than the optimum. If, however, output per head is less than the marginal product of labour so that there would not be a sufficient output to pay labour a wage-rate as great as its marginal product, the population is too small."[2]

Such a test can in practice be made only if the marginal productivity of labour is measurable. For a small and uniform community it is comparatively easy to ascertain the production function, which gives us the average and the marginal product of labour if the supply of labour is taken as variable and all other factors are fixed. For instance, an agricultural settlement run on collectivist lines which has a population of, say, ten members or families, can find out from its production plan or, by experimenting with nine and eleven members, can determine from its production figures whether an increase or decrease in its population is likely to increase income per head. It is assumed that any new member would have the same efficiency as the rest of the population. Similarly it may be possible to make fairly precise calculations for countries of predominantly agricultural character and with little developed foreign trade.

[1] J. E. Meade, *op. cit.*, p. 268.
[2] *Ibid., loc. cit.*, p. 268.

Measurements of the marginal productivity of labour, however, allow hardly any significant practical conclusions when the labour force and all other factors under consideration are so composite and continually varying as in the case of whole industries and highly developed countries, so that the results arrived at have admittedly to be based on unrealistic assumptions. This objection applies to the method used by Professor P. H. Douglas in measuring the marginal productivity of labour and capital in the U.S., in Massachusetts and in two Australian States. His assumptions include: Perfect mobility of labour and capital, perfect competition on the labour market, equal bargaining power of labour and capital, full employment of the factors of production, and the absence of State intervention.[1] Measurements of the optimum size of a population based on the marginal productivity of labour or similar criteria such as the real income per head, would certainly not make much contribution to the solution of either the population problem in general or the migration problem. This will become apparent after a fuller discussion of the optimum population concept.

Such a discussion appears to be the more pertinent as until recently experts and international conferences have tried to approach the population and migration problem from this viewpoint. The concept of optimum population was first suggested by Edgeworth, Sidgwick and Wicksell, and re-invented by Cannan. Since then many suggestions have been made in order to find a satisfactory criterion for the distinction between over- and under-population.[2] But it was not claimed that any of these criteria would provide a method for determining the exact numbers of the optimum population for a given territory.[3] The criticism which blames the optimum theory for its inability to do so[4] seems therefore unjustified so long as no alternative method can be proposed. What this theory mainly sought to achieve was to show the fallacies and shortcomings of the two extremist theories of population which had previously prevailed. There was on the one hand the mercantilist proposition which,

[1] Cf. P. H. Douglas, *Theory of Wages;* G. T. Gunn and P. H. Douglas, "The Production Function for American Manufacturing in 1919," in *American Economic Review,* 1941, p. 70 ff.

[2] Cf. I. Ferentzy, *The Synthetic Optimum of Population,* 1938.

[3] Fairchild in *Proceedings of the World Population Conference,* Geneva, 1927: "I believe that commonsense and logic are just as useful implements for human improvement as mathematical and statistical treatment. Once the concept of optimum population is fully established. results of immense value can be obtained by an intelligent matter of fact survey, and sound public policies may be based on the conclusions" (p. 83).

[4] G. Myrdal, *Population.*

not concerned with the social welfare of the masses as an end in itself, suggested that the supply of labour and hence of population should be as large as possible, and that therefore emigration should be prohibited and immigration encouraged (see Chapter I). On the other hand were Malthus and his followers, who tried to prove that every country was doomed to become over-populated, as the natural increase of population would every-where continue until subsistence level was reached. The corollary was that all population increase is to be deplored. Migration appears but a "slight palliative".[1] It is implied by Malthus' theory that under ordinary conditions migration does not decrease the size of the population of the emigration country or relieve the effects of population pressure, just as little as immigra-tion influences the rate of growth of the population of the immigration country if it has passed the primary stages of settle-ment. So he concludes that migration can but give temporary relief to the emigration country in periods of transition, when the standard of living of the population is below subsistence level until the rate of increase has adapted itself to the new situation (see Chapter VI).

It was the main contribution of the optimum theory of population to refute both these theories by showing that the standard of living is dependent upon two opposing forces: the effect of the law of diminishing returns and the economies of large-scale production (other factors such as capital and state of technical knowledge being taken as constant). The implication was that neither Malthus' axiom that the standard of living under practically all circumstances would be higher with a smaller population, nor its opposite, holds good. The possibility that the *total* income and wealth of a population might increase with an increase in its numbers, even if average income decreased, did not need any special discussion for the liberal economists who developed the theory of optimum population. It was obvious from the liberal point of view that only the average welfare of the individual which, again from this standpoint, was not signifi-cantly different from the average real income, could provide the standard for the optimum point of population. Thus the attitude towards the migration problem was self-evident: to recommend free migration which would shift population from over-populated

---

[1] Malthus, Revised Edition, Book III, Chapter IV. Malthus' attitude toward emigration as a means of relief is more positive in 1827 in his evidence before the Second Select Committee on Emigration.

to under-populated countries, and when under-population in one country is only relative to the size of population and standard of living in other countries. The theory of migration which resulted from this argument has been outlined more comprehensively at the beginning of this chapter.

D. THE OPTIMUM THEORY COVERS ONLY ONE ASPECT OF THE PROBLEM

But the liberal economists were fully aware that their static analysis had only covered *one* aspect of the population and migration problem.[1] A definite optimum point of population can be expected only if other factors remain constant. If technical knowledge and the supply of capital increase as a result of increase of the population, it is likely that the production curve or income curve per head will have over large spaces a level course or even several maxima at different population sizes. Before we can apply the optimum theory to the migration problems in real life, we have therefore to inquire how far the state of technical knowledge and the supply of capital is affected by migration in both the emigration and immigration countries (Chapters VI, VII). The static treatment also could not consider the effect of migration on the rate of growth of the population in the countries concerned. Moreover, it cannot be assumed that a change in population size will equally affect the production of the variety of goods and services of which the income of a community consists. Some kinds of goods and services will be harder to get, some easier. In order to decide whether these changes can be associated with a rise in real income per head, we have to decide whether the shift is advantageous or not; this remains often a matter of personal opinion which cannot be eliminated by any index-number method.[2] Such changes in the relative availability of goods and services are likely to be greater when population increase or decrease is the result of emigration or immigration than when it is the outcome of changes in the rate of natural increase.

Other and, as it appears, still more important aspects had to be neglected by the optimum theory. "The effects of population on economics are not determined chiefly by the total number nor by its age distribution, but by changes in these factors. It is the

---

[1] L. Robbins, *London Essays in Economics*, p. 132. *The Optimum Theory of Population.*
[2] Cf. Hicks, *The Social Framework*, p. 158.

rate of change in a population during a dynamic process in time, and not the quantities at any particular point of time, which are of importance."[1]

2. BEARING OF POPULATION CHANGES ON THE MIGRATION PROBLEM

A. THE POPULATION TREND IN EUROPE

Before we go on to apply the argument developed in the previous section to conditions in real life, we have to examine population trends in the main countries of potential emigration and immigration. We must consider to what extent present and prospective disharmonies in the distribution of world population call for adjustment. This demographic approach together with our previous discussion of existing international differentials in standards of living will give a rough idea of the magnitude of the problem. We can then consider how migration and other alternative means of adjustment can contribute to its solution.

According to W. F. Willcox' estimate of world population,[2] Europe's population amounted to:

187 millions in 1800
266   „   „ 1850
401   „   „ 1900
519   „   „ 1933 (L.o.N. Estimate)

i.e. it increased by 42 per cent in the first half and by 50 per cent in the second half of the nineteenth century, and relatively less, by only 28 per cent, in the first third of the twentieth century. This "unparalleled outburst of population" probably began about the middle of the seventeenth century, but at a less striking rate; the increase for the whole century 1650–1750 is estimated to have been 40 per cent, and that from 1750 to 1800 about 33 per cent. The figures include European Turkey and European Russia. The following figures show Europe's population growth between 1900 and 1940 if both these areas are excluded:

	Actual numbers in millions	Per cent increase in decade
1900	310	—
1910	339	9.4
1920	345	1.8
1930	376	9.0
1939	399	6.1

[1] G. Myrdal, op. cit., p. 130.
[2] A. M. Carr-Saunders, World Population, p. 30.

Changes in the size of a population are determined by natural increase, i.e. the excess of births over deaths during a given period, and by the effect of migration. Though the loss in numbers by net emigration was considerable in the twentieth century up to 1915, the slowing down of the rate of increase is mainly due to a reversal of the underlying trend of natural increase.

Growing success in avoiding wastage of life through premature death led to the unprecedented expansion which the European population experienced during the nineteenth century.

The progress in control over mortality is indicated in the heavy fall in the death-rates of all age groups during this period. Birth-rates remained generally constant, fluctuating round a high level. Symptoms of a reversal of this trend became apparent by the end of last century. While death-rates continued to fall, the rates of natural increase tended to decline as a consequence of falling birth-rates, indicating progress in the control of fertility. The fall of the birth-rate is entirely due to a decrease of fertility the effect of which on the crude birth-rate is mitigated by a temporary abnormal age structure which at present prevails more or less pronouncedly in all European countries. This age distribution is characterized by a small proportion of infants and old persons and a relatively large proportion of persons of working age; the reason being that the birth-rate was high when those who are now middle-aged were born, and has fallen recently when those were born who are now infants. It is obvious that this present age-constitution can last only for a period of transition provided that fertility and mortality rates remain unchanged. When the present generation of children has grown up, the ratio between infants, adults from 15 to 50, and the old will have significantly changed; the proportion of people in the age groups above 50 will have increased and the proportion of children decreased. This ageing of the population has a decisive bearing on its future natural increase, and hence on its migration problems. At a given rate of fertility the birth-rate depends entirely on the proportion of women in the reproductive ages from 15 to 50. If this proportion is reduced, a falling birth-rate must be the consequence. As the death-rate is lowest in the middle age-groups, an ageing population—mortality being unchanged—will display a rising death-rate.

The decline of fertility in Europe would have had a much greater effect on the growth of its population but for the continuous fall in mortality, which, however, enhances the ageing of the population. But there is evidently a point beyond which the fall of the birth-rate cannot be compensated by a fall in the death-rate.

The measurement of the gross and net reproduction rates, as devised by R. R. Kuczynski, enables us to see those consequences of the decline of fertility on the population trend which are obscured by abnormal age distribution. The net reproduction rate indicates by what percentage a population constantly subject to a certain fertility and mortality will ultimately, i.e. after having reached a stable age distribution, increase or decrease within a generation. The gross reproduction rate eliminates the effect of mortality by assuming that all newly-born children would survive up to the end of the child-bearing age. When the *net* reproduction rate is below unity the population is not replacing itself, and natural decrease must ultimately occur unless fertility rises or mortality falls. When the *gross* reproduction rate is below unity no fall in mortality can ensure replacement. If an abnormally large proportion is of child-bearing age, some natural increase may occur even if the reproduction rate is below unity. But if rates of fertility and mortality remain constant the age composition becomes stabilized, and a population with net reproduction rate below unity will continuously decline.

The European population is still increasing, or at least was increasing up to the outbreak of the Second World War. The rate of increase is, however, constantly and markedly falling. This tendency became evident in Western and Northern European countries with a relatively high standard of living as early as the last decades of the nineteenth century, and it is in these countries that the decline is most marked. But in the countries of Eastern and Southern Europe also, such as Poland, Rumania, Italy, the rate of natural increase has significantly fallen, though the number of births still exceeds considerably the number of deaths. Actually a natural decrease of population has up to now occurred only in France, but an examination of the reproduction rates for the other European countries indicates that the present natural increase may soon give place to a population decrease. This will happen in those countries which still have at present a reproduction rate above unity, if the secular trend of fertility decline continues, and in countries which at present have a reproduction rate below unity even if the present trend could be checked and the fertility rate remain constant. Before the outbreak of the 1939 war it seemed probable that the agricultural

States of Eastern and South-Eastern Europe—the main source of the "new" emigration since about 1880—might in the near future expect a large natural increase in population, in spite of their falling gross reproduction rate, from a fall in the death-rate due to a steady improvement in social conditions and health services. As the population in these countries has been and still is extremely hard hit by the devastation of the war, these expectations will scarcely materialize soon after the war. It may, therefore, be safely assumed that a change in mortality will not significantly alter the prospect of population decline in Europe. According to R. R. Kuczynski, the net reproduction rate was, before the last war, certainly below .9 in Western Europe (excluding Holland and Eire), and in Northern and North-Eastern Europe (excluding Poland and Lithuania). Forty years ago these countries had a net reproduction rate of 1.4–1.5, with the exception of France, whose rate was even then only unity. In Southern Europe: Portugal, Spain, Italy, the Balkan States, in Poland, Lithuania and Eire the pre-war rate did not exceed 1.25. There is no reliable estimate available to show the reproduction rate of these countries forty years ago, but it cannot be doubted that even then it was higher than that of the Western and Northern European countries.

In the years immediately before and during the Second World War birth-rates and reproduction rates showed generally a rising trend. But there is little doubt that this is due to temporary factors which will cease to operate in due course. Available evidence suggests that a temporary rise in marriage frequency as a consequence of the pre-war boom and of war conditions was the main cause of the rise in fertility. But there was no indication that the trend from the medium-sized family to the one- or two-child family had been checked. The population trend characteristic for Europe may be summarized as follows: "While the nineteenth century was a period of rapid population increase due to reduced mortality, future years in many countries threaten to be a period of population decline due to reduced fertility" (L.O.N. Yearbook, 1938–39, p. 154).

If pre-war fertility trends resume their course after the war, a decline in the total population of Europe is likely to begin during the decade 1960–1970 even if vital losses through the war and future losses through emigration are left out of account, and if it is assumed that mortality will continue to fall. This is borne out by the population projections which have been computed by the Office of Population Research at Princeton University on the basis of these assumptions.[1] The figures for Europe in the table below exclude Soviet Russia but include the Baltic States and Poland east of the Curzon line. These, representing in 1939 a population of some 22 million people, were among the "new" emigration countries and still have fairly high reproduction rates. But they and presumably Poland, will cease to be potential sources of emigration because of the restrictive migration policy within the Russian sphere of influence.

Population Projection for Europe and various European Regions, 1940–1970 (in millions)

	Europe		U.K. and Ireland		West Central Europe		Northern Europe		Southern and Eastern Europe	
	Population	Per cent change in decade	Population	Per cent change in decade	Population	Per cent change in decade	Population	Per cent change in decade	Population	Per cent change in decade
1940	399				163		20.1		165	
1950	415	4	50.6	0.8	166	2	20.5	2	177	7
1960	421	1.4	49.4	− 2.5	165	− 0.5	20.3	− 1	187	6
1970	417	− 1	37.1	− 5.1	159	− 3.5	19.5	− 4	192	2.7

As shown in the table below, the tendency towards decline is even more marked in the age-group 15–35 from which the vast majority of emigrants is normally recruited.

Population Projection for the Population 15–35 years of age in Europe and various European Regions (in millions)

	Europe		U.K. and Ireland		West-Central Europe		Northern Europe		Southern and Eastern Europe	
	Numbers 15–35	Per cent of total population	Numbers 15–35	Per cent of total population	Numbers 15–35	Per cent of total population	Numbers 15–35	Per cent of total population	Numbers 15–35	Per cent of total population
1940	130.2	32.63	16.29	32.42	51.3	31.41	6.75	33.61	55.7	33.76
1970	118.9	28.54	12.19	26.04	43.15	27.17	5.17	26.46	58.4	30.48

It goes without saying that demographic trends are only one of many partly interdependent factors which determine the propensity to emigrate. Other factors may have, at least tempor-

[1] Notestein, F. N., and others, "The Future Population of Europe and the Soviet Union." *L.O.N.*, *1944*.

arily, a counteracting effect; but, broadly speaking, rapid population growth in densely populated areas is a powerful incentive to emigration which in most European countries will in due course cease to operate.

It would be unwarranted to base forecasts of the future German population on the projection of past trends. A rapid fall in fertility does not seem unlikely; nevertheless there may be a strong tendency to emigrate while in the near future very few receiving countries will be prepared to admit German emigration of any amount.

B. POPULATION TRENDS IN THE FAR EAST

Asia, excluding Soviet Russia, has 1,150 million people crowded into 21 million square kilometres; whereas in the continents of Western civilization, Europe, America and Australia, 680 million live on 55 million square kilometres. The ratio of population to natural resources and capital equipment is even much more unfavourable to Asia's teeming millions than these figures suggest. Up to now rigid restrictions have prevented any considerable migration from Asia to the white countries, and Asia's population movements are mainly confined to migration within the Continent.

Present demographic and economic trends indicate that India, China and other countries of the Far East may have to expect an outburst of population similar to that which Britain experienced during the nineteenth century. India's population rose in the decade 1931–41 from 338 to 389 millions, that is to say by 15 per cent; that of the Dutch East Indies between 1930 and 1941 by about 18 per cent, from 60.7 to 71.5 millions.

What are the facts which enable us to conclude that populations in Asia are likely to grow at an increasing rate, while those of the white nations shows a declining trend both in Europe and in the new countries (see next section)? Our demographic knowledge of the former countries is' too incomplete to provide a basis for population projections. But we know that their birth-rates and death-rates are both high. The practice of birth-control is very limited. High death-rates are mainly due to insufficient health services and to the operation of the Malthusian checks on population growth. However, "there is no reason to doubt that in the course of some decades many of these countries will achieve more and more adequate control of death-rates and will make a beginning in controlling birth-rates, but the control of the latter is certain to lag by several decades behind that of death-rates."[1] A heavy fall in the death-rate, especially in the rate of infant mortality, would result from improvements in sanitary services and living conditions in general.

But with birth-rates remaining high the resulting rapid population increase must lead in these countries to further overcrowding and, in the absence of outlets for population pressure or of other counteracting measures, to a fall in the standard of living below subsistence level and consequently to a new rise in mortality. The present discrepancy between the relatively great wealth of the white nations and the poverty of the nations of Asia may then become much wider, with possibly disastrous consequences for the welfare of mankind. The question whether such consequences can be avoided by opening the white countries to Indian and Mongol immigration or whether there are more expedient and satisfactory alternatives will be discussed in later chapters.

Japan seems to have reached a later stage in the population cycle than the other Asiatic nations. Urbanization and industrialization were accompanied by a marked decline of both mortality and fertility. Control over fertility, however, lagged behind control over mortality.[2] The result was a rapid population growth, similar to that of Britain during the second half of the nineteenth century—during the two decades 1920–1940 Japan's population increased by 30.6 per cent. The population policy of the Imperial Government sought to check the declining fertility by means of coercion and of economic incentives. If this policy is abandoned after the war a heavy decline in fertility may be expected, otherwise rising mortality would probably slow down the rate of growth. But Japan's birth-rate is bound to remain high because of her favourable age distribution, and the natural increase is likely to remain high for at least one generation after the war.[3]

C. POPULATION TREND IN COUNTRIES OF IMMIGRATION

The prospect of a growing population pressure among the

[1] W. S. Thompson, *Plenty of People*, 1944, p. 95.

[2] This is illustrated by a comparison of changes in gross and net reproduction dates in the period before the war. The former fell from 1.7 in 1925 to 1.6 in 1935 and to about 1.4 in 1938, indicating a fall of 5 per cent during the decade 1925–1935. The gross reproduction rate, which does not take into account the effect of mortality on prospects of replacement, fell by 23 per cent during the same decade, namely, from 2.6 to 2.0.

[3] Cf. *The Demographic Heritage of the Japanese Empire*. I. B. Taeubers. E. G. Beal in *Annals*, Jan., 1945

non-European nations of Asia presents a striking contrast to the population trends in the overseas countries of white immigration. The figures given by Carr-Saunders indicate that the population increase in the course of the nineteenth century was even more rapid in these countries than in Europe. This is largely accounted for by the influx of European immigrants. North America's population increased between 1800 and 1850 from 5.7 to 26 millions (355 per cent), between 1850 and 1900 from 26 to 81 millions (210 per cent), between 1900 and 1933 from 81 to 137 millions (69 per cent in 33 years). The population of Oceania grew from 2 millions in 1850 to 6 millions in 1900 and 10 millions in 1933, an increase of 200 and 67 per cent respectively. The figures in millions for Central and South America are: 18.9 in 1800, 33 in 1850 (75 per cent increase), 63 in 1900 (90 per cent) and 125 in 1933 (100 per cent in 33 years). If we add up these figures representing the population of the two continents which are mainly inhabited by European immigrants and their offspring and compare them with those given above for Europe, we see to what an extent the share of the population of Europe in the total for the three continents has diminished in the course of the last century. It was 84 per cent in 1850, 72 per cent in 1900, and 65 per cent in 1933. These figures suggest that the rapid growth of population in the countries of immigration has considerably diminished the discrepancy between overcrowded Europe and the vast empty spaces in the new continents.

Birth- and death-rates in the immigration countries have the same trend as those in Europe: a constant and in some cases rapid decline of the birth-rates and a constant but much slower decline of the death-rates, making for a considerable fall in the rate of natural increase since the 1914 war. The annual natural increase has fallen (per 1000 total population):

In the U.S.A.	from	11.0	in	1911–13	to	5.8	in	1937
In Australia	„	17.1	„	1911–13	„	7.1	„	1934
In New Zealand	„	17.0	„	1911–13	„	8	„	1934
In Argentina	„	17.4	„	1921–25	„	13.5	„	1934
In Canada	„	16	„	1921–25	„	9.6	„	1937

As mentioned above, the movement of the net reproduction rate gives a more exact account of the population trend than the crude birth- and death-rates. If we examine the data available for immigration countries, we find among the English-speaking countries overseas a distinct general tendency towards a stationary or declining population. The sharp rise of the net reproduction

4

rates in recent years can be attributed to the same temporary factors which account for a similar reversal of the trend in Europe (see above, p. 81). The net reproduction rates for the U.S.A., Australia and New Zealand are now fluctuating around unity. The figures are:

U.S.A.[1] (White population)		Australia		New Zealand (White population)	
1905–10	1.34	1920–22	1.32	1911–15	1.357
1920	1.14	1932–33	0.976	1921–22	1.291
1930–35	0.972	1935–36	0.956	1933	0.978
1935–40	0.957	1937	0.989	1935–36	0.949
		1938	0.976	1937	0.999
		1939	0.986	1938	1.02
		1940–42	1.038	1939	1.07
				1940–42	1.22

The pre-war trend towards stability or decline is reflected in a number of population projections which have been computed for these countries on the assumption that net migration would be nil. As to mortality and fertility, various possible trends have been taken into account.

Assuming a moderate fall in mortality and fertility (starting from the favourable conditions in 1940) the U.S.A. population would reach 151 millions by 1950, a gain of about 15 per cent over the 1940 figure, and 160 millions by 1980, representing a gain of only 6 per cent in two decades. After 1980 the favourable age composition, due to the earlier period of high birth-rates, will have spent its influence, and a decline in total numbers can be expected after 1995. The loss between 1985 and 2000 would amount to about 2 millions.[2]

The situation in Australia is being investigated by the Federal Government. In a statement issued in 1944 the National Health and Medical Research Council arrived at the following conclusions: (a) it is clear beyond any doubt that the birth-rate is falling steadily; (b) the general rate of fall is such that if present conditions continue no hope of a recovery and subsequent continued rise can be justified; (c) the ultimate result of this continued fall must be such as to cause, even now, the gravest anxiety about the future of the Australian people. It has been estimated that even on the optimistic assumption that a net reproduction rate of unity can be permanently maintained after 1950, Australia's

---

[1] These official figures are slightly too low since no allowance has been made for under registration of births, the adjusted N.R.R., 1939–1941 is 1.01, for 1942: 1.19.

[2] *Estimates of Future Population in the U.S.* 1940–2000, National Resources Planning Board, Aug., 1943.

population would not much exceed $8\frac{1}{2}$ million by the end of the century[1] (as compared with 7.138 million in 1941). The conclusion from less optimistic assumptions anticipating a further decline in fertility is that Australia will have reached by about 1960 a maximum population of roughly $7\frac{1}{2}$ million. The following decline is likely to bring her population below the 7 million mark within 20 years, provided that no migration occurs during the whole period.[2] On similar assumptions New Zealand could expect some population increase for the next ten years or so. (White population in 1942: 1.549 millions.) Total numbers would begin to decline after 1955 and would fall below the present level by 1970.[3]

At first sight, the position seems to be rather different in Canada and South Africa. Canada's net reproduction rate in 1931 was still as high as 1.32; it fell to 1.08 in 1938. That of the white population of South Africa fell from 1.42 in 1924–29 to 1.30 in 1937–38. Both Dominions are likely to maintain a fairly high rate of natural increase at least for the next generation or so. But this is almost entirely due to the high fertility of the non-British elements of their population. In Canada differential fertility between French and British Canadians is marked. In 1931 the provinces with a large percentage of French Canadians had reproduction rates about 50 per cent higher than those of the British provinces. Fertility is likely to remain fairly high among the French Canadians; largely owing to this factor Canada's population may increase by about 30 per cent within the next generation.[4] In South Africa too the non-British white population (mainly of Dutch origin) has preserved the large family system, so that a population increase of 25 per cent within a generation does not seem unlikely. But it is widely recognized in both Dominions that a much higher rate of population increase would greatly help their economic development.

Statistical information about population trends in South American countries of immigration is too incomplete as to allow of the calculation of reproduction rates or of population projections. Available data, however, indicate that South America at

---

[1] Cf. Estimates by G. R. Burns, Melbourne University, 1943, *Economic Record*, Dec., 1936.

[2] Cf. S. H. Wolstenhome, *The Future of the Australian Population*, 1936, pp. 195–213.

[3] D. V. Glass, "Estimates of Future Populations in various countries," *Eugenics Review*, Jan., 1944.

[4] The increase would be about 20 per cent if the Canadian fertility trend followed the European. Cf. Enid Charles, "Problems in the British Overseas Dominions", *Annals*, 1945.

present can be regarded as the fastest-growing continent. Both birth-rates and death-rates are high. The former show a declining trend, but there is a wide scope for reducing mortality. Since in these sparsely populated countries the ratio of population to natural resources is favourable, rapid growth is unlikely to produce population pressure and a rise in mortality, as in the densely populated countries of Asia; improvements in health services are therefore likely to have a permanent effect.

D. ECONOMIC EFFECTS OF POPULATION DECLINE

What is the bearing of these population trends on the future volume of world migration? To what extent will immigration policy into the white countries of immigration be effected by the prospect of population decline? Clearly, if these trends take their course, and if the new countries wish to maintain a steady annual increase of their population, they have to rely more than before on immigration.

The rationale of future immigration is therefore closely linked with the economics of a declining or stationary population. If it is true that the transition from an increasing to a stationary or declining population implies economic repercussions which eventually lead to a reduction of the standard of living in the countries concerned, the new countries subject to this trend will have a vital interest in resuming their former policy of attracting immigrants instead of pursuing their present policy of restricting immigration drastically. On the other hand the former European countries of emigration, when they have become aware of the economic disadvantages of the imminent decline of their populations, may be interested in keeping back their prospective emigrants and may even try to attract immigrants. We should experience under entirely different conditions a revival of the old mercantilist proposition, that, generally speaking, immigration is useful and emigration harmful.

The following argument seems at least to a certain extent to justify these expectations. It is based mainly on the economic effects of the change from a growing to a declining population which is characteristic for the present demographic situation in general, and no stress is laid on the distinction between a stationary and a declining population. This can be justified because, as we shall see from the following discussion, the difference between the effect of transition from a fast-growing to a declining population on the one hand or to a stationary or very slowly growing but ageing population on the other, is one of degree only, so that our main conclusions hold good for both phenomena.

Moreover, as indicated in the previous section, the rapid slowing down of natural increase through the exercise of full control over natality must be regarded as a stage in the population cycle of new countries of Western civilization, to be followed by stationariness and actual decline in total numbers, in the absence of counteracting forces which are not yet in operation.

The first sections of this chapter have shown that the optimum theory provides no criterion whether a change in total numbers brings the population of countries with highly developed capitalistic production nearer to the point of maximum real income per head or no. Real income per head in a given economy is determined by a number of interrelated factors. As J. J. Spengler has put it: "The societal universe is a system of mutually interacting variables, acted upon also by external conditions not readily comprehensible within such a system. Each of these variables, of which the population factor is one, is both a cause and effect. A change in any one mode (e.g. natality, mortality) of the population factor, if not counterbalanced by a change in external conditions, will be accompanied by a compensatory change in some other mode of the population factor or by a change in other of the variables composing the system or by a combination of such changes. Modification of the population factor, therefore, will react upon the population factor itself."[1] The effect of migration on other modes of the population factor, i.e. the interaction between mortality and natality and migration in sending and receiving countries, will be discussed later.

In the present context we have to distinguish between (i) densely populated countries at a primitive stage of capitalistic production, with relatively few outlets for international trade and extremely low standards of living, for instance China and India; (ii) densely populated highly industrialized countries with opportunities for international trade and relatively high standards of living (Britain, Belgium, etc.) (iii) sparsely populated countries with high standards of living (Australia, New Zealand, Canada). These three groups represent extreme cases. Many potential countries of immigration and emigration do not belong to either group. For instance, the position in Eastern and Southern Europe

[1] J. J. Spengler, "Population and Per Capita Income", *Annals*, Jan., '45, p. 182.

before the war was partly that of Group I, partly that of Group II. The U.S.A. ranges between Group II and Group III.

(i) As to the first group, it seems that the static approach of the optimum theory needs little correction. Provided that these countries are successful in maintaining a declining rate of population growth, the effect of the decline is bound to be beneficial. Their economic welfare is mainly determined by the ratio between population and land for agricultural and other productive activities. Population growth can be associated with a less favourable combination of these two factors of production, and hence with diminishing returns from land, with dwarf holdings, with increasing population pressure, with less opportunity for capitalistic production, and with lower real income per head.[1]

(ii) It is often thought that the law of diminishing returns from natural resources must come into operation when population increase brings about a less favourable proportion between immobile natural resources and population size. It is, however, only for primary production, such as agriculture and forestry, and for mining, that land as such is required in special qualities and in relatively large quantities. Secondary and tertiary production, which is a much more important income-producing factor at later stages of economic development, is fairly independent of immobile natural resources. In such economies the advantages of population agglomeration often outweigh the adverse effect of the law of diminishing returns. Normally the capital equipment necessary for the expansion of capitalistic production will be available and the terms of trade for the import of raw materials or foodstuffs and the export of manufactured goods and services will be scarcely affected. The efficiency of capitalistic production then largely depends on a large and preferably an expanding internal market. This argument lends support to the suggestion that the most densely populated countries of Western civilization cannot expect any substantial rise in over-all real income per head from a decline in total numbers. In the relatively unimportant sector of primary production a lower ratio of population to natural resources may lead to higher productivity per head. But such changes may have no effect, or an opposite one, in other sectors of production.

Generally speaking, the effect of the population factor on

---

[1] The labour of one male agriculturist in New Zealand is able to supply an optimum diet to forty people, in the U.S.A. to eleven people, in Germany to eight, in Poland to three, in Japan to about two (Colin Clark, *op. cit.*, p. 150).

real income per head is obscured in densely settled areas of highly developed capitalistic production by the short-term fluctuations of the trade cycle. In the U.S.A., for example, the gross national product, adjusted to 1941 price levels, fell from 87.7 billion $ in 1929 to 62.0 billion $ in 1932, and rose again to about 120 billion $ in 1941 and 170 billion $ in 1944. It is obvious that changes in the rate of population growth cannot account for these violent fluctuations which indicate changes in real income per head of similar size.

Economic conditions during the inter-war period led to the belief that even new sparsely populated countries such as New Zealand, Canada and Australia must be regarded as over-populated inasmuch as a higher standard of living could be expected if there were fewer people to share in and to produce the national income. This may have been true during the years of the "Great Depression". But it became evident during the period of recovery after 1933 that the economic development of these countries was greatly handicapped by the fewness of their inhabitants; that if fluctuations due to the trade cycle are dis-regarded and a long-term view is taken, a greater population density in these countries would make for higher standards of living. This argument will need to be elaborated and qualified in later chapters with special reference to the migration problem, and the bearing of non-economic factors on the migration policy of the receiving countries will have to be discussed.

E. ECONOMICS OF POPULATION CHANGE

We came to the conclusion that the countries in Group I would be better off if they had fewer people, those of Group III would be better off with more people, and standards of living in those of Group II would probably be about the same as at present if they had a somewhat larger or smaller population. In the latter case greater weight can be attached to sociological and political criteria; for example, it is widely held that the great density of population in Britain is not conducive to a "healthy social life". If Britain had 10 million fewer people, there would be less overcrowding, and those in urban districts would have easier access to the unspoilt countryside. Much stress is laid on the importance of a harmonious balance between urban and rural life, which is lacking in industrialized Britain. Obviously, a much smaller population would be desirable if opportunities for international or Empire trade were lacking. On the other hand those who think only in terms of power policy would prefer a Britain with 10 million more inhabitants.

We have now to consider the effects of transition from a growing to a stationary or slowly declining population in countries with high standards of living, a process which has already begun in all countries of Western civilization, and which will gain momentum if present trends are to continue their course.

Granted, for argument's sake, that Britain would be better off with a population of 38 than with one of 48 million, we have to face the fact that the advantages of smaller numbers may be outweighed by the disadvantages of population decline. The economic problems arising from decline in population growth have been widely discussed in recent years.[1] It would be beyond the scope of this book to go into details which are still controversial. It will suffice for our purpose to give a brief summary of the main points at issue.

As already outlined, the declining population trend is the consequence of the adoption of the small family pattern. Undoubtedly the individual family greatly benefited from this change. The rearing of a large family meant for practically all strata of the population a lower standard of living, and for the lower income groups a life below the poverty line. The average standard of living, therefore, may be expected to rise with a fall in the percentage of large families. The situation would be similar if the community were to relieve the individual family from the burden of parenthood, e.g. by the introduction of adequate family allowances. Smaller families mean a smaller number of children which have to be supported by the community, and therefore, *other things being equal*, a higher real income per head of the total population.

What is likely to happen if the number of people in the working age-groups is affected by the trend to decline?

Population decline may be associated with a greater amount of income-producing wealth (capital equipment and natural resources) per head of the working population. It is likely to bring about in fairly densely populated areas a more favourable ratio of population to other factors of production over large sectors of production. We should therefore expect that income

---

[1] Reddaway, *op. cit.*; J. M. Keynes, *Some Economic Consequences of a Declining Population;* L.o.N. *Yearbook,* 1938–39; *Glass, Population Policies and Movements;* National Resources Committee, *The Problems of a changing Population,* Washington, 1938, etc.

per head of the *occupied* population would tend to rise with a fall in the total number of people in the relevant age-groups and to fall with a rise in their number.

But we have to take into account that the relatively greater number of ageing dependents makes for a lower real income per head of the *total* population. These considerations, however, are subject to important qualifications. Neither fewer children nor fewer people of working age would have these beneficial effects if people were to become on the average *less successful in making use of the other factors of production.*[1]

Our economic system has developed under conditions of steady population growth, and there are reasons for believing that with the cessation of this growth various forces have come into operation which tend to lower average real income per head by producing "poverty in the midst of plenty", that is to say: (i) a lower volume of production than is consistent with the full employment and full use of other factors of production; (ii) a trade cycle with long periods of heavy depression and not fully developed periods of prosperity.

At first sight the unemployment problem might appear less difficult to handle in a declining population. If fewer children are born, the number of new entrants into the labour market will eventually be reduced. But apart from the time-lag of some fifteen years before the reduction in numbers can ease the competition of labour, this advantage becomes insignificant if unemployment in general is growing.

When a community becomes wealthy, general or involuntary unemployment will tend to rise. A smaller proportion of the total income will be consumed, so that the demand for consumer goods falls, and, as the accumulation of capital becomes larger, the opportunities for further investment become less attractive (unless the rate of interest falls rapidly); the gap between actual and potential production will widen, and this will result in depression and unemployment. Stimulation of capital outlay and of consumption may adjust the discrepancy between income and expenditure on consumption goods, and so mitigate or prevent unemployment. This, however, will be much more difficult if the increase in wealth per head is brought about by a decline in numbers. The demand for industrial capital equipment and for various other capital goods (e.g. houses) is likely to fall when the number of consumers ceases to grow, and the incentive to borrow

[1] W. B. Reddaway, *Economics of a Declining Population*, p. 117.

4*

for capital development will be small, even at a low rate of interest. The problem of structural unemployment becomes more acute with a declining population. Structural unemployment occurs when over-production of particular goods, caused by a shift in the demand for these goods or by other false expectations of entrepreneurs, is adjusted to the real level of demand. Production with a declining population is to a much larger extent subject to shifts of demand than in an economy which expands almost automatically owing to the increase in number of the population. In an expanding community supply can be adjusted to changes in demand with comparatively little friction. The demand for practically all goods and services is likely to grow unless total income is tending to diminish. "If for one reason or another a particular commodity is over-produced, the consequent maladjustment may be rectified simply by refraining from installing more productive plant and from employing more labour until the demand has expanded again with the growth in the number of consumers."[1] In the absence of an expanding population excessive capital and excessive labour has to be shifted into other industries, a process which involves loss of capital and frictional unemployment. Moreover, production is then to a much larger extent subject to shifts of demand. If a population declines, less of its income is spent on basic foodstuffs and other more or less durable necessities such as clothing, but so long as the national income has not decreased, more can be spent on semi-luxuries such as fancy goods and durable consumer goods, motor cars, radio sets, etc. The implication of the drop in demand for basic foodstuffs on the international division of labour and hence on migration will be discussed below. For the national economy it means that production becomes more sensitive; demand is more determined by the whims of fashion, and if economic conditions or expectations become less favourable, it is easy for the public to refrain from buying goods which are not necessities or from replacing durable goods. Business therefore becomes more uncertain, the risk for the entrepreneur becomes greater, the demand for capital equipment falls (though some capital equipment may have become obsolete owing to the changes in demand) and the impact of general depressions will be more severe. Cyclical unemployment in slump periods is therefore likely to be extended with a declining population, as the stimulus of the growing demand for necessities is lacking.

[1] L.o.N., *Yearbook*, 1939, p. 156.

There are two other aspects which make it likely that a decline in population will have an unfavourable effect on prosperity. If numbers fall and demand contracts, capital equipment is not always easily adjustable to the new conditions. If prime costs represent only a small part of total costs, as is the case in many branches of modern capitalistic production electricity supply, railway traffic, etc.) cost cannot fall proportionately with turnover. Eventually it may not pay to apply large-scale production methods for the manufacture of goods, so that prices will rise.

The greater the number of old persons in a declining population which has to be supported by a smaller number of people in the earning ages—it is only during the years of transition that their proportion will continue to increase—charges for old age pensions, health insurance and other social services will rise. On the other hand the costs of public education and other welfare institutions for children will not fall proportionately with the number of children, so that a substantial increase in the net social burden is likely to be felt.

In giving an account of the various forces which tend to reduce the standard of living in a contracting economy, we have drawn a gloomy picture of the economic prospects of a declining population. "The first result on prosperity of a change-over from an increasing to a declining population may be disastrous."[1] Whether the future of all those countries for which a decline of population can be foreseen will be disastrous depends, in the economic field,[2] (1) on the rate of the decline and on whether the decline will be halted by immigration and other demographic measures, and (2) on the possibility of counteracting by State intervention the forces which make for a lower standard of living in a declining population.

There is an increasing confidence that if we are successful in adjusting our economic system to the circumstances of a stationary or slowly declining population, cessation of population increase may on balance be conducive to higher standards of living in the densely populated countries of Western civilization. But we have to realize that if the decline in fertility is not checked in

[1] J. M. Keynes, Galton Lecture, 1937.
[2] Military considerations and national prestige sometimes govern population policies more strongly than economic considerations. The economic aspect is, of course, entirely different, if the decline of population leads to military defeat or to a weaker position in diplomatic negotiations. Granted that "Defence is a magical word used to justify almost any form of economic lunacy", still experience has taught that its neglect may involve great risk.

time, total numbers are likely to fall at a progressive rate. And any optimism as to the consequences of *rapid* decline seems to be unwarranted. Remedies which may be effective at the present stage of the population cycle would then become inadequate. Productivity per head is bound to fall with an over-aged population. When the stage of under-population has been reached, institutional changes, unless designed to reverse the population trend, can only mitigate, but cannot prevent, a heavy fall in standards of living.

F. ALTERNATIVES TO MIGRATION

World population trends, as we have seen, tend to enhance the present unharmonious distribution of population; they suggest, therefore, new prospects for large-scale migratory movements. But is it likely that these prospects will materialize in the near future? It would obviously be fallacious to expect that the nations which are alarmed at their slow rate of natural increase should remove existing restrictions and open their doors to immigrants from over-populated countries. Some countries would regard such a policy as a counsel of despair. In the case of Britain this attitude is reflected in the P.E.P. Report on Population Policies: "To rely chiefly upon the encouragement of immigration as a means of redressing Britain's demographic balance," they suggest, "would be an admission of national defeat. It would imply that the British people are so disatisfied with, or indifferent to, the way of life they have created for themselves that they have no wish to perpetuate it by perpetuating themselves as a people. . . . Nevertheless, as a supplementary measure, here should be certainly scope for the selective attraction of immigrants."[1]

For similar reasons the over-populated countries may be reluctant to lose their most active elements and may try to cope with the problem of population pressure by means other than emigration.

A short outline of these alternatives will indicate how far they are suited to be a substitute for or a complement to emigration or immigration.

Economic remedies alternative to *emigration* are:

i. *A More Equal Distribution of Income*

This is likely to raise the general standard of living. A greater part of the national income, however, may then be spent on

[1] In course of publication.

consumption goods, so that less is available for capital investment. This may diminish the favourable effect of the more equal income distribution, because the prosperity of a growing population depends largely on the supply of sufficient capital for new capital equipment.

ii. *Transition from Primary to Secondary Production*

A densely populated area is favourable to the development of industry. Its success depends largely on the provision of the additional capital equipment and on a market for the new production, either as export goods or as substitutes for imported goods for home consumption. Lack of skilled (and technical) labour may require the immigration of experts from already industrialized countries.

iii. *Expansion of External Trade*

It is much more important for over-populated than for under-populated countries to secure free access to raw materials and to find customers for their products. Invisible exports by rendering services to other nations (merchant marine) may also relieve the pressure of over-population. The efficiency of these remedies, however, depends largely on the geographical situation of the country and on economic and political conditions in the rest of the world.

iv. *Attraction of Foreign Capital*

If the establishment or the expansion of secondary industries is hampered only by lack of capital, it will, under normal conditions, be comparatively easy to borrow for capital construction from wealthy countries with a contracting economy and therefore with a low rate of interest prevailing on the home market.

v. *More Equal Distribution of Landed Property, and Internal Colonization*

In general large estates in Europe, if they were divided up, could support a much larger peasant population. Internal colonization, especially the clearing of waste lands, may often not be a paying proposition from the capitalist point of view, but in industrial countries with increasing populations and increasing demand for foodstuffs each new farm will find a market for its products and at the same time increase the internal demand for the industrial products of the country, provided that no higher tariffs for agricultural protection become necessary.

vi. *Power Politics*

Declining populations are more anxious to avoid wars and the consequent loss of lives. It appears to be a temptation to quickly-growing nations to profit by this anxiety and by the advantage they gain in war through their greater reserves in manpower. The threat of war may improve their bargaining power; they may obtain favourable terms of trade in bilateral commercial treaties and so raise their relative standard of living, or they may be able to acquire colonies for exploitation or as an outlet for their surplus population. Power politics is evidently the most risky and, as to its ultimate success, the most doubtful of all alternatives to emigration.

Economic remedies open to countries with a *declining* population follow easily from the previous discussion of the economics of a declining population. They are mainly:

(i) *More equal distribution of income.*

(ii) *Foreign lending and other invisible exports,*

which require the possession of capital, e.g. international insurance; the establishment of new industries in under-capitalized, densely populated countries.

(iii) *Measures to counteract unemployment.*

These include: Regulation of imports, promotion of internal mobility of capital and labour, old age pensions, the raising of the school-leaving age and the stimulation of expenditure on consumption goods by increased public investment (the effect of the "multiplier"), etc.

The purpose of *demographic* measures is to adjust the size and growth of a population to political or economic requirements and not merely to provide a remedy against the symptoms of the evil. The regulation of migration is but one means to this end.

Birth control, legalization of abortion, compulsory postponement of marriage have been introduced or proposed as means of reducing the birth-rate. For both practical and ethical reasons, the scope and effect of these remedies can only be limited. No attempt has been made in modern times (unless it be by starting a war) to raise mortality by State interference. We may take it for granted that the reduction of the mortality rate is the aim of every civilized nation, irrespective of its effect on the population trend. Population policies designed to stimulate fertility are much more topical. Pronatalist measures fall into three broad categories: the use of propaganda to encourage parenthood, the use of repressive measures to discourage individual control over conception and child-bearing, and the granting of allowances as a reward for raising families. It is controversial whether it will be possible in the long run to exert any significant check on the population trend by any of these policies; their success in Germany and Italy has only been temporary.[1]

G. RAPID POPULATION GROWTH AS THE BASIS OF LARGE-SCALE MIGRATION IN THE NINETEENTH CENTURY

Ample scope still remains for migration from over-populated to under-populated countries, but we must realize that the whole economic setting of migration has entirely changed since—less than a century ago—large-scale free migration overseas became a normal feature of world economics. It was then that the principles of international division of labour, of free trade and free migration became firmly established in England. Population in England increased rapidly. With the increase of population grew the demand for basic foodstuffs, and progress in agricultural technique did not as yet provide for the additional agricultural production required. In a closed economy it would have been necessary to produce food under diminishing returns by cultivating less fertile soil and/or by applying more units of labour or capital to each unit of land; the cost of living would have risen, and the purchasing power and the standard of living of the population as a whole would have correspondingly fallen. The solution suggested by the principle of division of labour and free migration was: to exploit the undeveloped agricultural resources in the empty new continents by emigration of labour and capital. European emigrants supplied foodstuffs to industrialized England cheaper than they could have been produced here, and at the same time these new settlers, mainly in America, became the best customers for English industrial production. In the later period of overseas migration the flow of emigrants from the agricultural countries of Eastern and South-Eastern Europe was largely absorbed without much friction by the growing industrialization

---

[1] Cf. Glass, *op. cit., passim.*

of North America. They either found openings directly in industry or trade or filled the vacancies which were created by the migration of American labourers into the towns. Europe's demand for agricultural products was still rising, as her population continued to grow, and as more European countries turned from agriculture to industry, so the American farming population—allowing for cyclical fluctuations—found on the home market and in Europe sufficient demand for its production, which had continued to grow mainly as the result of technical progress in agricultural methods.

The demand from Europe for essential foodstuffs has rapidly fallen with the slowing-down of the growth of Western European population and with the transition from free trade to a policy of agricultural protection. "Thus the need which was so marked in the nineteenth century for a constant expansion of the world areas of agricultural production has largely disappeared, and the new, and as it would have seemed to thinkers of a hundred years ago, the astonishing phenomenon of redundant productive capacity in many important branches of agricultural production has made its appearance."[1]

H. THE PRESENT SITUATION

The transition from primary to secondary and tertiary production which takes place in the "new" continents and which has been hastened by the decline in the European demand for staple foodstuffs before the war and by the war-time shortage of imported industrial goods, implies an increased demand for labour in the countries concerned.

Before the war, they regarded industrialization mainly as a measure of structural adjustment. Its primary object was to create employment and to become less dependent on the import of manufactured goods. Industrial labour therefore, could be largely recruited from the agricultural surplus population, and immigration came practically to a standstill.

It was only during the War that governments and public opinion in Australia, New Zealand and Canada realized that their economic progress was seriously handicapped by their sparse population, and that the resumption of immigration would promote their future prosperity. "A country that is too sparsely inhabited often encounters a vicious circle. Its industrial costs of

[1] H. D. Henderson, "Economic Consequences", in *The Population Problem*, p. 96, cf. below, Chapter VI, p. 222 ff. The complete breakdown of European agricultural production in 1945/6 must be regarded as a temporary factor.

production are high because its factories cannot employ the methods of mass production that are possible in a country with a large internal market. Costs of local government, of transportation are higher if there are comparatively few people to pay these costs. The consequent burden is a drag on national development and population increases more slowly because it is already too small."[1] Moreover the development of an efficient home industry is likely to provide new opportunities for agricultural development and to check the depopulation of rural districts.

Undoubtedly political considerations have greatly contributed to this change in outlook. The decisive importance of more man-power for the political survival of these countries became apparent. They then discovered that there was no real conflict between their need for a larger population for political reasons and their wish to maintain high standards of living. This argument does not of course apply to the U.S.A. In its case the close relationship between expanding population and economic progress suggests that a revival of immigration may be conducive to higher standards of living. But it might be argued that planning for full employment of both man-power and natural resources, and an expansion of international trade and capital movements, would ensure for a stationary or slightly declining American population a rising level of prosperity. And this alternative might be deemed preferable to an increase in numbers through immigration (see below, Chapters VI and VII).

In this chapter the economic effects of population change due to migration or otherwise have been examined mainly from that national point of view which has governed the migration policy of all countries in the past. It is easy to see that different standards must be applied if migratory movements are to aim at narrowing existing discrepancies in international standards of living and at a higher level of comfort for the world at large. This aspect of the problem can be discussed only after a more detailed examination of the pros and cons of large-scale migration. It seems however convenient to sum up in general terms the conclusions which can be drawn from our preceding examination of world population trends and of their economic consequences:

The demographic setting of future migratory movements will be significantly different from that of the last century, when the new continents were peopled by mass emigration from Europe. Then both sending and receiving countries had rapidly

[1] W. H. Chamberlin, *Canada To-day and To-morrow* 1942.

increasing populations. Broadly speaking, emigration meant for the sending countries relief from population pressure. Their population continued to grow in all age-groups, and the adverse effects of population decline became apparent only in a few exceptional cases (see below, Chapter VI). Similar conditions favourable to emigration are likely to prevail in Oriental countries whose nationals are at present not admitted to the new countries, and to some extent in various countries of Southern and Eastern Europe whose nationals have been the least welcome of all Europeans as immigrants in the new countries. Their admission has been subject to severe restrictions. Western Europeans are generally regarded as the most desirable immigrants. But their countries have little to gain and probably much to lose from a further depletion of their shrinking stock through emigration.

For the receiving countries the argument in favour of immigration is reinforced by their declining trend of natural increase. As long as these nations could rely upon the population trend bringing them a steady natural increase, the desirability of an acceleration of population growth by adding immigration to the natural increase was only a matter of expediency. If no natural increase is forthcoming, immigration (and restriction of emigration)· is not only a means of intensifying a development which would have occurred in any case, but becomes the only means of achieving an increase in numbers.

CHAPTER V

THE CONTROL OF MIGRATION

1. THE CASE AGAINST FREE MIGRATION

In Chapter IV we tried to show that migration has in the past been an important means of adjusting an unharmonious distribution of population, and that migratory movements may have a similar effect in the future, though under different economic and demographic conditions. Obviously, large-scale migrations have never achieved anything approaching a harmonious international distribution of population. In 1914, when the period of free migration from Europe to the new continents ended, there was still a wide margin between the standards of living in receiving and sending countries. A number of factors which were ignored in the previous chapter account for this failure; some of these were mentioned in Chapter II. Costs of transport proved prohibitive in many cases. Lack of information prevented many people from emigrating. And perhaps still more important: the prospect of a better standard of living abroad is not always a sufficient incentive to emigration. Undoubtedly each of these factors had a weakening effect on the tendency to emigrate. But the volume of migration would hardly have been much greater in the absence of these forces. It is more probable that the period of free emigration from Europe would have ended earlier as a consequence of restrictive measures in the receiving countries. It would be a great over-simplification to explain such measures as merely the outcome of an irrational nationalism. International migration is likely to be checked by counter-measures on the part of the receiving countries long before anything approaching equilibrium has been reached. Clearly, so long as the control of migration is the prerogative of sovereign states, receiving countries will object to a volume of immigration which might lower the standard of living of the native population even if it should raise aggregate real income for the receiving and the sending country taken together. The same reaction must be expected if it is not the general standard of living but that of politically influential elements of the population (e.g. unskilled labour) which is adversely affected by immigration (cf. Chapter VI).

Various considerations, which will be further developed below, lead to the conclusion that symptoms which call for restriction are likely to be produced by a much smaller inflow of immigrants, if migration is free, than under conditions of planned migration.

(1) Free migration cannot discriminate against undesirable types of immigrants. There may be, for instance, in the receiving country a surplus of farm labour, but a scarcity of skilled and semi-skilled industrial labour. To exclude criminals and other obviously anti-social elements is not inconsistent with the principle of free migration, but apart from this exception free migration has to rely on the selective effect of the free play of the market. This method is inadequate to meet the demand for immigrants of a modern complex and highly specialized economy.

(2) In order to avoid temporary dislocations in new countries it is important to co-ordinate the inflow of capital with that of immigrants. Such co-ordination was lacking under the free system, though capital imports and migration usually moved in the same direction and were to some extent interdependent.

In the nineteenth century, the "open" frontier in the U.S.A. and other new countries provided an outlet for a surplus population. Temporary scarcity of means of production brought about through large-scale immigration could be largely offset by geographical expansion. In the twentieth century relatively few opportunities are left for such extensive expansion. Broadly speaking, close adjustment of the volume of immigration to the amount of capital equipment available for the newcomers has become more important for the success of modern migration.

(3) Our discussion of the economic effects of population changes showed the unfavourable consequences of *rapid* growth and *rapid* decline, and suggested that migration which might *per se* be desirable would become a failure if it were forthcoming in a rush. It is much easier for a country to absorb a given number of immigrants if their inflow can be regulated according to a plan. This plan must take into account the various factors determining the size and composition of the immigration which can be absorbed during a certain period of time (see below). Friction between nationals and immigrants, and much wastage of human effort inherent in the trial and error method of the free system, can be avoided by controlled migration.

It is important to emphasize that regulated migration does not necessarily mean less migration. On the contrary it seems that migratory movements which are regulated, uninfluenced by political or economic nationalism, would have in the long run a wider scope and larger volume than free migration under the same conditions. This is borne out by the experience of Greece after the First World War. Beginning in 1922, within roughly eighteen months, Greece, at that time with a population of five million, admitted 1,400,000 Greek refugees from Asia Minor and Bulgaria, while only a few hundred thousand non-Greeks had to leave the country. If no plan for their settlement had been made, if each of these immigrants had received in cash his share in the amount of capital which the League of Nations had provided for this purpose, an economic catastrophe would have been unavoidable. The problem could be solved only by planning: 1,400,000 immigrants were absorbed without much friction and brought to Greece a period of relative prosperity.[1]

In the light of this argument, the main objection to control loses much of its strength. The question of free migration *versus* control, however, is as much a moral as an economic and social one; it is true that any restriction on migration or any selective migration is apt to cause hardship in individual cases. Moreover it seems to be incompatible with a fundamental human right, the right of free mobility. Planning in any sphere of human relationship has to face similar problems. It is justified if its contribution to the promotion of human welfare is greater on balance than that of the free play of self-interest. Free international migration can satisfactorily function only so long as full harmony is attained between the interests of the migrants and both the countries concerned. It broke down not because the receiving countries had reached their "optimum" population, but because it gave rise to social and economic disturbances which were mainly due to the lack of control and planning.

2. FACTORS DETERMINING THE DESIRABLE VOLUME OF IMMIGRATION

If it is agreed that regulated migration is preferable to the free migration of the period before 1914 and to the system of general restriction or prohibition of immigration in force before 1939, it becomes of vital importance to find how to determine for any country the desirable volume of immigration or emigration. Two

---

[1] Cf. Sir John Hope Simpson, *The Refugee Problem*, p. 11 ff.

important aids in doing so are estimates of the *carrying* capacity and of the population-absorbing power of a country.

A. POPULATION-CARRYING CAPACITY

In recent years estimates of carrying capacity have fallen into disrepute, and it has been suggested that they are entirely useless or even harmful for practical migration policy.[1] The wide range of existing estimates, which in the case of Australia, for instance, vary from about 20 to about 200 millions, lend support to this view. These figures have been used and abused in popular political discussions as arguments for particular migration policies without their true significance being realized; so that the real issue has become rather obscured by discussions concerning the carrying capacity of a country of immigration.

i. *Meaning of the Concept*

The bearing of the population-carrying capacity of a country on its migration policy can best be demonstrated by comparing it with the bearing of the productive capacity of a firm or an industry on its policy. If an industrial firm utilizes for its current output only 70 per cent of its productive capacity, it is easy to calculate how many hands the firm would employ if it worked at full capacity; but we cannot draw any conclusions as to whether it would be wise or possible to increase present output without knowing *why* the production remained below capacity. This might be due to various causes:

1. The entrepreneur may have been unable to obtain the number of workers necessary for output at full capacity.

2. He may have been unable to secure the capital necessary to pay the prime costs (wages and raw materials) for a larger output.

3. Inefficient management.

4. Market conditions may be such that a larger production would reduce total profits or could be sold only below cost price.

These causes indicate the policy required in order to bring the firm up to full employment. The need in case 1 is simply to attract a sufficient number of workers to make up for the shortage. In case 2 it is a matter of obtaining the necessary capital. This may be possible either by borrowing, or, if the concern is a paying one, by accumulating profits instead of dis-

[1] Cf. Introduction to *The Peopling of Australia* (Further Studies), Melbourne, 1933.

tributing them. In case 3 the reorganization of the firm under a new management appears to be the remedy. In case 4 we have to consider several alternatives. It may be possible to sell the full product if foreign competitors can be excluded from the market, or if the existing capital equipment is used for the production of other articles which can be sold at a competitive price. Full production may depend on a reduction of costs by wage cuts or by adopting labour-saving methods of production. It may, however, happen and in real life very often does happen, that none of these remedies avails, and that the market position is such that any increase in output and in the number of persons employed would reduce the prosperity of the firm, so that there is no alternative but to continue production below capacity. The statement that the production of a firm is 30 per cent below its full capacity and hence that the number of its employees is, say, 20 per cent below its full employment capacity does not imply that the firm would become better off if it changed over to full employment; but it does imply that there are prospects for larger employment and better prosperity as soon as the obstacles which prevent the firm from working at full capacity have been mastered.

The applicability of this concept to the migration problem is obvious. Employment with the firm at full capacity corresponds to the carrying capacity of a country. It indicates the size its population would have if all its resources were fully utilized, without taking account of the reasons why in actual fact they are not so. The natural resources of the country would comprise all arable soil and that which could be made arable by irrigation or other means, provided that the costs of development are not unreasonably high. They may be considered as reasonable if, allowing for a low rate of interest on the initial capital outlay, the soil would eventually produce a yield similar to that of other soil actually under cultivation. The same principle can be applied in estimates regarding unexploited coal, oil, water power, etc.

An element of conjecture is added to our estimate when we take into account secondary employment. If the population increases by reason of immigration which has led to a fuller utilization of the natural resources, demand for manufactured goods and services will also increase, so that additional population is required to supply these goods and services. (The same would happen to our firm if it provided board, lodging, etc., for its workmen and their families.) An estimate of this additional population might be based on the ratio between the population occupied in primary, secondary and tertiary production in fully-peopled countries of similar constitution. The margin of error is, however, wide, as it is not possible to make any assumption which could be substantiated as to the standard of living of this as yet unexistent population.

It cannot be claimed that the difference between carrying capacity and actual population indicates the amount of increase desirable and, allowing for natural increase, the amount of desirable or possible immigration. It is desirable, from the point of view of the immigration country, if the present standard of living at least can be maintained; it is possible only if the capital necessary for the development can be provided and if the market can absorb the new production. So far carrying capacity indicates the upper limit of potential immigration rather than the actual target for a positive immigration policy. But one qualification must be made here. Our definition of the population-carrying capacity of a country assumes that all natural resources are utilized with that amount of labour which corresponds to the present marginal productivity of labour in that country. We have, however, seen (in Chapter III), that marginal productivity differs widely in different countries; estimates of the carrying capacity for different countries, therefore, are not comparable. We might arrive at comparable figures by relating potential full production to a standard marginal productivity of labour. If we accepted such a standard, e.g. the average marginal productivity of labour in Europe, the population-carrying capacity of India and China would probably be much lower than their actual population, in spite of unused resources in these countries, and would indicate a need for emigration.

ii. *Estimates of Carrying Capacity*

We owe to Griffith Taylor "estimates of future white population" which in our opinion are rather estimates of the population-carrying capacity of the countries concerned. His method is best described in his own words: "He tries to take into account standards of living as well as the remarkable diversity of environments in the world. It is clear that Europe offers the only example where white settlers have produced a fairly stable population which has 'saturated' a continent of considerable complexity. The writer took the European distribution as his criterion. He divided the world into seventy-four economic regions and deduced the population which each would support (using criteria of rain, coal and location) under European conditions. . . . It assumes that the standards of living will be like those in Europe, hence if higher standards are required, fewer people can be supported. The future Australian population comes out about 60 millions. If the standard of living in Australia is twice as costly as in Europe then the future Australian population will rest at 30 millions."[1]

Using the present saturation level of Europe as criterion G. Taylor suggests that the future white population will be distributed somewhat as follows:[2]

North American region	.	.	.	610	millions
European	,,	.	.	.	500	,,
Argentine	,,	.	.	.	115	,,
Siberian	,,	.	.	.	100	,,
South African	,,	.	.	.	82	,,
Australian	,,	.	.	.	62	,,

Estimates of future white population based on the present demographic trends were given in Chapter III. They indicate the enormous amount of immigration which would be necessary to bring the population of these regions near to the size envisaged in Taylor's estimates.

There is no reason to expect that the white population will ever have the size or distribution forecast by Taylor, and it is difficult to see why this future population, settled at the present European saturation level, should have the present European standard of living, as his estimate presumes. The present standard of living and the present production in Europe depend largely on the exchange of goods between Europe and overseas countries. If these countries were settled according to the European pattern, demand for European export goods such as coal would fall, and that for European import goods such as wheat would rise. It is evidently impossible to assess the influence of these changes on future production and standards of living, apart from the additional fact that unpredictable changes in the extent of technical knowledge, etc., cannot be taken into account.

These estimates, however, represent a valuable contribution to the problem of the population-carrying capacity of these countries. They indicate that the traditional countries of immigration are still far from having reached the European "saturation point", and that a redistribution of the white population by

[1] G. Taylor, Australia: *A Study of Warm Environments and their Effect on British Settlement*, London, 1940.
[2] G. Taylor, *Environment, Race and Migration*, Toronto, 1937.

resuming emigration to these countries is likely to raise the general standard of living, provided that it is possible to transform potential into actual opportunities. It must be the object of a *long period* migration policy in sparsely populated countries to *create* openings for future immigration. Such plans, like estimates of carrying capacity, should be based on surveys of the natural resources of each country. "It may be thought that our knowledge of the resources of the world is by this time complete. The truth is far otherwise. Some areas have been thoroughly prospected and certain resources, such as oil and tin, have been searched for all over the world. Their existence and reserves have become well known through individual owners, financially interested companies or the scientific departments of governments. But a very large part of the mineral, water power and soil resources of the world are actually unknown."[1]

For a *short term* immigration policy the findings of these surveys are relevant in two respects: they indicate actual openings for immigrants in so far as they refer to natural resources whose immediate exploitation is practicable. Prospects which are less likely to materialize in the near future have also a certain short-term significance in that they may justify an optimistic view with regard to the absorptive capacity of the country.

B. CAPACITY TO ABSORB IMMIGRANTS

It is obvious that if there is a wide margin between actual and potential population, the population cannot at once be brought up to the desirable level without giving rise to friction and serious economic derangement. The capacity to absorb immigration may be regarded as the annual rate at which a country can receive immigrants without being subject to such adverse consequences. The choice of a period of twelve months is merely a matter of convenience, as it comprises one full seasonal cycle; a subdivision according to seasonal requirements has proved to be practical. The process of complete absorption is bound in many cases to take much longer than one year; it takes several years before settlers on virgin soil can become self-dependent, whereas the qualified workman may become settled only a few days after his arrival if there is a strong demand for his services in the new country.

This rate of absorption is not constant for subsequent years,

[1] H. Finer, *The T. V. A. Lessons for International Application*, I.L.O., 1944, p. 222.

but is subject to annual re-assessment, so that the effects of the immigration of the preceding year, changes of economic trend, and changes in the rate of natural increase should be taken into account.

We have defined above the capacity to absorb immigration as that rate of immigration which a country can receive without *serious* derangement. If the rate is fixed by the receiving country, it will normally be such that the eventual effect of immigration is an improvement of the standard of living of the whole population. Temporary dislocation and injury to vested interests are often unavoidable when large-scale immigration occurs; the immigration country will put up with these disadvantages only if it can expect that they will be outweighed by future improvements in the standard of living. Improvement or maintenance of the old standard is not, however, necessarily implied in the concept of absorptive capacity. Governments may be prepared for non-economic reasons to admit immigrants, even if the consequence of their absorption is a general reduction of the standard of living; e.g. sparsely settled countries with an extraordinarily high standard of living, such as Australia, New Zealand and Canada, may deem it advisable for political reasons to fix for their absorptive capacity a target which lies below their present standard of living. The same might happen if the rate were determined, not by the States themselves, but by an interstate agency. The maintenance of a high standard of living might then not be considered essential, and any other criterion might be adopted. A Federal Union, for example, might require its member-states to admit immigrants from other members with a view to levelling out the variations in living conditions over its whole territory, even if the immigration implied a reduction of the general welfare in the countries of immigration. The method of determining the absorptive capacity has to be adapted to these different viewpoints.

i. *Various Methods of Estimating Absorptive Capacity*

Sir Alexander Carr-Saunders's approach to the problem is concerned with the absorptive capacity of the new countries with a carrying capacity much larger than their actual population. He points out that their development cannot proceed at more than a certain speed. "No matter how many people a country could accommodate in time, using existing technical methods for its exploitation, there is a limit to the rate of increase of population which is desirable."[1] This rate of increase cannot be determined theoretically, but experience shows, as Carr-Saunders suggests, that an average annual increase of 2 per cent indicates the rate of population increase desirable for these countries. This 2 per cent rate, representing the average population increase of the new countries for the period 1864–1924, is only to be taken as a broad general guide to the capacity of absorbing population. On this basis, the annual rate of immigration desirable is indicated by the difference between 2 per cent plus emigration and the rate of natural increase. As we have seen in the previous chapter, the rate of natural increase has been continually falling in these countries, and their net reproduction rates show that a further fall must be expected, so that if the countries of immigration are to maintain a 2 per cent average annual increase of their population, they must rely more and more on immigration. Following this argument, an annual average immigration of 2 per cent therefore appears desirable for "new" countries if their population has become stationary, and a correspondingly higher rate if it is declining.

The estimate by Phillips and Wood[2] of Australia's capacity to absorb immigrants is based on slightly different lines. The average net gain from immigration for the sixty-four years from 1860 to 1924 and again for the eight inter-war years until the beginning of the great depression in 1929 was, for Australia 0.55 per cent. These writers conclude from this that an average net rate of migrant absorption of 0.5 per cent could be maintained for a considerable time, corresponding to 35–40,000 migrants per annum. Eggleston[3] is more doubtful, but suggests that if natural increase fell, the migration quota could be enlarged, though not to quite the same figure as the decline of natural increase. These methods, based on past experience, are only intended to yield a rough approximate estimate of the average absorptive capacity of a country, for a period long enough to enable differences between the absorptive capacity in years of prosperity and that in years of depression to cancel out. They cannot take account of any possible changes in the methods of production and in the structure of the world market. It is easy to see that such fluctuations can be greatly reduced in a planned economy, if in the plan priority is given to demographic considerations.

[1] *Op. cit.*, p. 175.
[2] *The Peopling of Australia*, I, p. 53; II, p. 223.
[3] Eggleston, *Population Problems*, p. 13.

Demographic criteria have been accepted for determining the target of Australia's post-war immigration policy. The Australian Government have declared that about two years after the end of the Second World War immigration will be resumed on a big scale. They envisage an annual immigration of 70,000 persons, i.e. 0.5 per cent of the total population, or about twice as much as Phillips and Wood's pre-war estimate. The target figure they have set themselves for their population policy is an annual rate of increase of two per cent, or at present roughly 140,000 per year. They hope that the excess of births over civilian deaths can be kept at the high war-time level of 70,000, leaving a deficit of 70,000 to be made up by the net balance of immigration.[1]

Among the other criteria used to determine the economic absorptive capacity of a country, we have already discussed the carrying capacity. As this reflects long-term potentialities of immigration, it must have also some bearing on any short-term migration policy. Migration, as defined in Chapter I, is a process which by its very nature exerts on the immigration country a permanent effect. In determining the capacity to absorb immigrants we have therefore to take into account that the immigrants and their offspring are presumed to stay in the new country for good. During periods of boom or in wartime, when large parts of the population are engaged in military service and the production of war material is increased as much as possible, immigrants can be easily absorbed even by countries whose carrying capacity is relatively low and which under normal circumstances are considered as over-populated. But as soon as the favourable conditions have come to an end, it will become apparent that the immigration has brought about an undesirable population increase.[2] If the country of immigration has large reserves of unexploited natural resources, adjustment is, and in the past has been, much easier.

It depends partly on the extent of available natural resources whether a country can easily shift from primary to secondary production. The effect of such a transition is usually twofold: (1) an increase in the value of production per head and hence an improvement of the standard of living, and (2) an increase of the absorptive capacity of the country, as a much larger population

---

[1] Statement of the Minister of Immigration in the House of Representatives, Canberra, Aug. 2, 1945.
[2] Seasonal or temporary migration may be the given remedy in this case.

can be supported by secondary than by primary production. The United States was able to absorb for decades many hundreds of thousands of immigrants per year, mainly by expanding her secondary industries.- She had started as an exporter of primary and an importer of secondary goods. The export industries required the establishment of accessory industries and the provision of services. Together they created a home market which offered opportunities for other industries, so that a larger proportion of the primary production could be used for home consumption and after the secondary production had reached the stage of competitive mass production, manufactured goods could be exported; but with the growth of the home market the country became less dependent on external trade. A similar trend is evident in the other immigration countries; its significance in connection with changes of the absorptive capacity cannot be over-estimated. "The natural capacity to maintain and absorb population depends not only upon the resources available, but upon the extent to which the home marker has become large enough to provide opportunities. Natural growth is progressive and cumulative."[1]

A survey of some of the estimates which were made before the war of Australia's economic absorptive capacity conveys some idea of the various criteria and arguments which have been used to determine the absorptive capacity of a country. They all need revision in the light of wartime experience, but they are of considerable theoretical interest. Most of them can also be applied *mutatis mutandis* to the other countries of white immigration, except perhaps the United States, which at the present stage of development has lost most of the characteristics of a "new" country.

As to the prospect of absorbing immigrants by developing primary production opinion is generally sceptical. There is agreement that agricultural development in Australia has vast potentialities. Her agriculture is still producing under diminishing costs, so that physical marginal productivity could be increased by intensification. In many districts suitable for white settlement uncleared land could be developed at lower costs than that at which developed farms on comparable soil can be purchased. The prospects of realizing these potentialities were under pre-war conditions, and still are, very limited. Expansion should be stimulated, but not so much as to increase the volume of pro-

[1] I. B. Bridgen, *The Peopling of Australia*, p. 116.

duction for sale on the world market because of the difficulties which Australia had experienced for a number of years with the export of her present production. Any expansion therefore depends largely on the development of home consumption and on the provision of the necessary capital funds. Similar obstacles prevent a fuller exploitation of mineral resources. Even under the unfavourable pre-war conditions Australia's primary production would have been able to absorb a limited number of immigrants; it is, however, held that an estimate cannot be ventured until a great many more data are accumulated.[1]

L. Withall[2] is mainly concerned with the absorptive capacity resulting from an expansion of secondary production. He estimates that before World War I about £50 kept one inhabitant at the normal standard of living in Australia, so that each £50 increase of production without cost to the community or each £50 increase after the deduction of its cost would have made it possible to absorb one additional inhabitant. According to Withall the manufacturing industries alone absorbed new labour in Australia at the rate of 50,000 workers per annum, each worker sustaining 5.2 other inhabitants. He concludes that, if this rate of expansion in manufacture could be maintained, manufacturing industries would enable Australia to absorb population increase at the rate of 300.000 p.a., or more than a quarter of a million immigrants. Though he is doubtful whether this rate can be maintained in future, he holds that a yearly expansion by only 4.2 per cent would absorb 21,000 workers now and about 30,000 workers after ten years, corresponding to an absorptive capacity of from 70,000 to 130,000 immigrants p.a., provided that costs are controlled and an adequate tariff policy is pursued.

Impressed by the fact that secondary and tertiary production tend to cluster around the centres of densest population, Coombs arrives at quite different conclusions. He submits that it might be advantageous to Australia and to the rest of the world if there were a reversal of the stream of migration and a net balance of people returned to Europe.[3]

---

[1] S. M. Wadham, *The Future of Immigration*, p. 162. The validity of this argument seems to be little affected by the development during the war years when the export demand for Australia's primary production exceeded the supply. Conditions are likely to remain favourable during the period of reconstruction owing to the back-log of accumulated demand, the exhaustion of stocks, and the breakdown of agricultural production in Europe. But a long-term migration policy cannot be based on such temporary factors.

[2] L. Withall, *ibid.*, p. 208.

[3] Coombs in *The Future of Immigration*, cf. Chapter VII, 5.

The problem of providing the necessary capital is of vital importance for the absorption of immigrants both in primary and secondary production. Eggleston and Parker[1] estimate the average cost of equipping each breadwinner with housing, services and a proportionate part of farm and factory equipment to support him in a balanced community as high as at least £1,000 for each additional inhabitant. There are three possible sources for the provision of this capital:

(1) The immigrants may bring it with them.
(2) The capital may be borrowed abroad.
(3) Sufficient capital may be available out of savings.

But the number of suitable capitalist immigrants is limited, so that the community is little affected by their admission. Large external loans may have unfavourable effects within a free system, and it is maintained that Australia has experienced their disadvantages in the past.[2]

Out of the available savings provision has to be made for the natural increase of the population, which requires about £50 millions, if we adopt the £1,000 per head estimate mentioned above, and the excess of savings over this figure plus the amount acquired by external borrowing could be used for financing migration. This argument leads Eggleston and Parker to the conclusion that the maximum absorptive capacity of Australia is not likely to exceed 40-50,000 immigrants p.a. (corresponding to an annual capital investment of £40-50 millions) for some time to come, unless at the expense of living standards. It is obvious that a country needs less capital for financing its immigration when its population is declining. No new capital equipment is required for settling the immigrants, who only make up for the loss caused by natural decrease. The authors of this estimate do not claim that it is valid under the economic conditions which prevailed in Australia before the war. They stress the necessity of taking into account the difficulties to be met with on the export market, and they hold that when export prices are low, unemployment becomes almost unavoidable, and that the only solution of the problem for a new country is *emigration*, as no alternative avenues of employment are available. The effect of unemployment on the absorptive capacity will be discussed more comprehensively below.

[1] F. W. Eggleston and G. Parker, *The Growth of Australian Population.*
[2] Cf. Chapter VII, p. 423.

ii. *Necessity and Nature of an Actual Survey of Existing Possibilities*

We do not attempt to submit an estimate of our own or to weigh the relative merits of the many estimates which have been made. Most of them arrive at widely different results and appear inconsistent with one another because they value differently the various factors which determine the capacity of absorbing immigrants, and leave some of them explicitly or implicitly out of account. They are of theoretical interest in so far as they indicate the bearing of the various economic factors on the problem of absorptive capacity, but they are of little help if we want to know the actual number of immigrants whose admission is desirable in any definite year.

Three alternative methods suggest themselves:

(1) That the State, while adhering to the principle of free migration, should stop or restrict immigration as soon as the first symptoms of maladjustment are observed. Such a policy is unlikely to remove the disadvantages inherent in unselected free migration. Bottlenecks which make State interference necessary will under conditions of free migration upset the equilibrium long before the absorptive capacity has been reached.

(2) An immigration quota may be fixed every year by the trial and error method. General indices and such as are suggested by the methods previously described would be useful for finding this quota, which could be adjusted in accordance with the experience of preceding years. But all these adjustments also are based mainly on conjecture, as it will seldom be possible to establish an unequivocal causal nexus between immigration and the economic changes which have occurred. This method is, however, very useful if combined with (3).

(3) If a country has decided upon a positive immigration policy and is desirous to admit as many immigrants as it can absorb, no short-cut method for determining its absorptive capacity is likely to yield satisfactory results. In order to reduce the margin of error as much as possible a factual survey of existing opportunities is needed; a survey of course entirely different in scope and purpose from that of unexploited resources discussed in the previous section (page 110).

iii. *Principles to be Adopted for the Survey*

The necessity of such a survey is most plausible for countries which have to cope with unemployment. High unemployment figures are certainly no evidence that a country is unable to absorb immigration. But unemployment suggests that certain categories of immigrants may not be absorbable or could be absorbed only by increasing native unemployment. The direct and indirect effect of immigration on unemployment will be discussed later (cf. Chapter VI); anticipating the conclusions from this discussion we may say that many types of immigrants create employment either directly or indirectly. The mere increase of consumption caused by the inflow of immigrants has a stimulating effect on the labour market, so that any immigrant contributes to relieve unemployment. But if the community has to bear the full cost of this consumption without obtaining any other advantages, it might find more efficient means of stimulating employment ·and might feel entitled to exclude as unabsorbable those prospective immigrants who have no chance of finding employment and can be supported only by public assistance. The same applies to an immigrant who can find employment only at the expense of a native who is equally well suited for the job in question. This, however, is not likely to happen very often. The native has an equal or better chance, and if an immigrant is preferred to him, he has failed in competition. [1]

It has been much disputed whether it is consistent with the principle of absorptive capacity to admit immigrants who find employment by under-cutting wages or even by working for a remuneration below the subsistance level of the native worker. The problem has become less topical, since most immigration countries have now, to a large extent, minimum wage-rates fixed by law or by collective bargaining. It can hardly be denied that the rapid development of production in the United States, on which her present high standard of living is based, could have been achieved only by the employment of huge masses of immigrants who were, as we have seen, paid at a much lower wage rate than the native workers. It might easily be concluded from this experience of the United States and from the result of similar practices in other countries that no objection can be raised against the admission of immigrants who can be absorbed only if they are prepared to work for a wage rate which is not attractive to the native workmen. The immigration policy of all countries with a high standard of living, however, aims at preventing any immigration which can be absorbed only if the immigrants remain satisfied for an indefinite time with a standard of living lower than that of the old stock. It is held that the economic

[1] Cf. Carr-Saunders in *Service in Life and Work*, Vol. 7, No. 28.

advantages which might be expected from this type of immigration—even when it is not harmful to native employment—are outweighed by disadvantages of a social nature. Yielding to these arguments, we must limit the absorptive capacity so as to cover only those immigrants who can be absorbed without discrimination against their standard of living; they can be considered as absorbed only if they can attain, after a period of transition, a standard similar to that of the natives.

An examination of the actual openings on the labour market during a period of general unemployment shows that such unemployment does not preclude scarcity of labour in certain branches of production. The unemployed are not a homogeneous reserve army from which each industry can draw men with the required qualities. Many of them are unemployable, or are specialized for a certain type of work. Most of them, especially in the case of ageing populations, are attached to their homes and cannot easily be removed to another part of the country. The immigrant is more mobile and in this respect more easily employable. In countries with high standards of living certain occupations are unpopular, so that even in times of depression vacancies exist in them. The United States and the British Empire, for example, could have absorbed great numbers of immigrant domestic servants during the depression, without their admission markedly reducing the level of remuneration for such services. It is the object of immigration control to ensure that the occupational composition of the immigration is such as to provide those types of labour which can be absorbed. A specified assessment of the demand for immigrant labour seems to be indispensable for a country that has to cope with the problem of large-scale unemployment.

At first sight, it seems that a wider view can be taken under conditions of fairly full employment. But it is easy to see that full employment cannot be taken as a criterion of the absorptive capacity of a country, if it is the outcome of State intervention and does not reflect a genuine demand for additional labour. Sir William Beveridge postulates that it must be the aim of a democratic employment policy that there should always be more vacant jobs than unemployed men. It is widely recognized that the State can create an effective demand for practically any supply of labour, if temporary unemployment during periods of readjustment is disregarded. The adoption of this policy implies that there would be vacancies for new arrivals even if their employment should tend to lower the average productivity per head of the total occupied population. Under such conditions a substantial inflow of immigrants could be absorbed relatively easily, but presumably at the expense of the standard of living in the receiving country.

Further investigation is necessary in order to ascertain that immigration does not lead to dislocations on the production side. If we hold that, at the present stage of economic development, the maintenance of equilibrium requires a planned co-ordination of the productive effort of the community, it is still more advisable to inquire whether the line of production intended by immigrants fits into the general scheme and whether the capital equipment for the new production can be provided without disturbing the equilibrium. Similarly there is the risk that too sudden an increase of consumption as a consequence of large-scale immigration may upset the whole price system of the community. A sudden increase of demand for houses and other consumers' goods which cannot at once be met by a corresponding expansion of production or of imports, may at first cause a boom, but may lead to a general rise in the cost of living and production, so that the boom is soon followed by a slump. The capacity of absorbing immigrants is therefore at any time limited to that volume of immigration whose demand for goods can be satisfied without upsetting the price system of the community. This limit can best be ascertained by an investigation into the relevant facts.

The self-adjusting mechanism of the *laissez-faire* system did not ensure that immigration always occurred in accordance with the absorptive capacity of the receiving country. It seems that cyclical fluctuations were caused or intensified in immigration countries during that period by admitting immigrants in excess of the country's absorptive capacity. But this excessive migration could not do much harm to the progress of rapid economic expansion in these countries. The volume of immigration, contracted during the depression and equilibrium, was usually re-established on a higher level than before. In the case of Australia, for example, immigration in excess of absorptive capacity had in the long run even a favourable effect. Australian immigration in the past has been characterized as having been accomplished "in the boa-constrictor habit of bolting her immigrants and then resting until they have been digested". Though this method caused unpleasant symptoms of indigestion, Australia got the immigrants whom she urgently needed. They were attracted in excessive numbers by the gold rush in the fifties, by the boom in the eighties and by the mineral finds at the turn of the century, whereas under normal conditions immigrants preferred the American continent, so that Australia in spite of many efforts had been unable to attract the steady flow of immigrants necessary for the development of her vast natural resources. Therefore it may have been wise to admit immigrants in excess of absorptive capacity when they were prepared to come.

Broadly speaking, it may be said that the adjustment of forthcoming immigration to the absorptive capacity of the receiving country is indispensable under present conditions, with the population trend stationary or declining and with the limitation of further development of natural resources by the contraction of the demand for primary goods; it was less urgent for the immigration countries of the nineteenth century with a population rapidly growing by natural increase and with practically unlimited opportunities of developing their natural resources. In the latter case, as we have seen, excessive immigration could be entertained without serious harm to economic progress. After a certain minimum density of settlement had been reached, immigration served mainly to speed up the development which might have been achieved at a slower rate with less immigration or through natural increase alone. Immigration below absorptive capacity was likely to retard economic development, but slow progress may have been preferable to a rapid change in countries with a relatively high standard of living.

Under present conditions the immigration countries cannot any longer rely on natural increase; if they need an increase of population for their development they must depend largely on migration. On the other hand, the immigration countries have become more susceptible to immigration above absorptive capacity as they have become susceptible to any disturbance of equilibrium, and as economic life has become more "bumpy" and insecure. As long as this demographic and economic trend continues, it is increasingly important for those countries which are likely to gain from immigration to secure that volume of immigration which corresponds as nearly as possible with their absorptive capacity, and hence to find a reliable method for determining this capacity.

iv. *Experience of Palestine*

Having stated the case for a regulation of immigration according to the absorptive capacity of the immigration country and outlined the criteria which have to be applied to determine this capacity, it remains to inquire how these principles are likely to work in practice. The immigration policy of one immigration country, Palestine, was governed by this principle during the period from 1922 to 1937. It has been abandoned mainly for political reasons, though this period of immigration at full absorptive capacity has transformed the whole of Palestine from an economically undeveloped "backward" country into the most prosperous part of the Near East.[1]

Palestine held a unique position among the countries of immigration. She was the only existing country whose Government was bound by its constitution, the Mandate, to pursue an active migration policy. As the National Home of the Jewish people Palestine has attracted Jewish emigrants (and capital) who on merely economic grounds might have gone elsewhere or might not have emigrated at all. We therefore cannot conclude from the fact that the principle of absorptive capacity has produced satisfactory economic results under the conditions peculiar to Palestine, that its application in other countries would be equally successful. But, as the preceding argument has shown the importance of the concept of absorptive capacity for any country of immigration, it seems pertinent to give an outline of the method which was applied in Palestine.

Under the Mandate it is the duty of the Administration "while ensuring that the rights and position of other sections of the population are not prejudiced" to facilitate Jewish immigration under suitable conditions.[2] Such control has been imposed by applying the regulative principle of economic absorptive capacity. This was laid down in the Statement of Policy of 1922[3] by Mr. Winston Churchill. Furthermore it was made clear in 1931 by the then Prime Minister, Mr. Ramsay MacDonald, that "the considerations relevant to the limits of absorptive capacity are purely economic considerations."

---

[1] Return to this principle was recommended by the *Anglo-American Committee on problems of European Jewry and Palestine*. "The well-being of both [Arabs and Jews], the economic situation of Palestine as a whole, the degree of execution of plans of further development, all have to be carefully considered in deciding the number of immigrants for any particular period" (Report April 1946, Cmd. 6808, p. 7).

[2] Mandate for Palestine, 1922, Article 6.

[3] The Churchill Memorandum of June 3, 1922, Br. White Paper, Cmd. No. 1700. It was stated that immigration "cannot be so great in volume as to exceed whatever may be the economic capacity of the country at the time to absorb new arrivals. It is essential to ensure that the immigrants should not be a burden upon the people of Palestine as a whole and that they should not deprive any section of the present population of their employment."

Immigration into Palestine has been regulated by Immigration Ordinance No. 38 of 1933. Three main classes of immigrants are distinguished:

(1) Persons of independent means.
(2) Dependants of permanent residents and of immigrants.
(3) Persons who have definite prospects of employment in Palestine.

As to category (1) it is presumed that any immigrant who has a capital of at least £1000 at his disposal can be absorbed. Such immigrants have an indefeasible right of entry, but evidence is required from them that they have this capital at their *free* disposal and that they have not merely obtained it temporarily in order to satisfy the immigration authorities. There is, however, nothing to ensure that the immigrant leaves his capital in the country after his admission. The large number of capitalist immigrants represents the most singular feature in the economy of Palestine. The vast amount of capital which has been invested by them does not require any remittance abroad for interest or sinking fund. We have seen that in the case of Australia such payments are considered as one of the criteria for determining the absorptive capacity of this country.

The second category, comprising mainly wives, parents over 55 and children under 18 of previously immigrated residents, is not directly subject to an examination as to whether their admission is compatible with the absorptive capacity of the country, but indirectly their number affects the number of immigrants which is admitted under the third category (Category C of the Immigration Ordinance).

The volume of this class of immigration is controlled by a Labour Schedule prepared every six months. It lays down the maximum number of persons by *sex, age, industries,* and *callings* which corresponds to the absorptive capacity of the country, and which will be admitted during the next six months. It consists of five parts:

A. Nominated experts and skilled workers.
B. Skilled workers not named.
C. Relatives of working age.
D. General labour including agricultural labour.
E. Departmental reserve.

The evidence of a definite prospect of employment is in the case of "nominated experts and skilled workers" provided by the prospective employer, who has to make an application and to guarantee that he is in a position to employ the immigrant in question at a stated salary for a period of at least twelve months.

In the case of workmen not specifically named, evidence is provided by the Jewish Agency, the representative of Jewish interests in Palestine.

This agency, in close collaboration with the Department of Migration of the Palestine Government, makes twice a year a survey of the economic situation of the country and of the prospects for Jewish labour and for non-Jewish labour so far as it is affected by the Jewish sector. The request of the Jewish Agency for the introduction of a certain number of labour immigrants within the next six months is based on the results of this survey, and is accompanied by a guarantee given by the Jewish Agency to the Government that the immigrants applied for will have employment for at least one year. But this guarantee has no great practical importance, as no control is exerted over the employment of the immigrants after their admission.

The following principles have been adopted by the Government as a basis for the determination of the absorptive capacity of Palestine in respect of Jewish labour:

(1) "The Labour Schedule is deemed to cover only demands for labourers who are likely to enter permanent employment. Demands for temporary or seasonal labour are disregarded, unless there are reasonable prospects of transferring this form of labour to reasonably permanent employment."

(2) "When a decision has to be taken as to whether a certain field of employment is of a permanent or temporary nature, the probable future absorptive capacity of the industry in question is taken into consideration. In other words, as far as possible labour requirements are considered, in the long run, in the light of permanent factors of development."

(3) "No demand for additional Jewish labour is accepted when the intention of the prospective employers is to displace Arab labour already employed." (Minor deviations from this rule have been permitted in a few cases.) [1]

The method applied in preparing this labour schedule is a rather complex one. For our present purpose we can omit all those details which are concerned only with conditions peculiar to Palestine, and limit our description to those elements of the procedure which could easily be adopted by other countries of immigration. It has been described as an inductive method. [2] Each occupation is surveyed separately and a census is taken of

---

[1] Cf. Palestine Royal Commission Report, July, 1937, Cmd. No. 5479.
[2] Cf. Minutes of this Report, § 978.

all vacancies likely to occur within the next six months. Individual applications for additional labour are examined, and are approved only if they are compatible with the prospects and financial standing of the applicant. The total application is composed of the approved individual figures of all the occupations. Allowances —usually deductions—are made in order to adapt these figures to the economic trend. For this purpose a number of indices are used which are supposed to reflect either the general economic trend or the prospects of particular branches of production. Such indices are:

The number of newly arrived capitalist immigrants; the movements of railway freights; consumption of electricity; imports of capital equipment, mainly machinery; the demand for building materials; the number of buildings under construction and of building permits issued; movements of prices for export goods; imports of consumption goods which can also be produced locally.

The maintenance of a certain reserve of unemployed is considered necessary in order to ensure stability in the labour market and a normal wage level and in order to prevent a sudden shift to jobs which can carry higher wages in the case of unexpected demand. An allowance for existing unemployment is therefore made only when it exceeds what is considered an adequate reserve. New supply of the labour market by natural increase or by immigrants not belonging to the Labour Schedule is generally not directly taken into account. As the process by which new persons enter the labour market is continuous, they are accounted for in the census either as employed or unemployed, so that no extra allowance is made for them, and correspondingly no allowance is made for those who are leaving the labour market because of old age, death, or on any other ground.

15 per cent is added to the figure arrived at by this method. This represents the probable demand for miscellaneous services such as domestic service, catering, etc., which are not included in the survey. The greatest pains are taken to assess the absorptive capacity of agriculture and industry as accurately as possible. Every plantation and most agricultural settlements are visited twice a year by an expert; their returns are checked and an estimate of their prospects and demand for labour is made on the spot. The industrial survey undertaken for the purpose of the labour schedule covers only 40 per cent of the whole industry.[1]

[1] Out of a total of about 6,000 enterprises existing in Palestine before the war, about 1,500 were industrial establishments; the rest were handicrafts employing less than five persons each. The share of the Jewish sector in the total was about 75 per cent.

The firms are so selected that they can be considered as a representative sample. The development of each of these firms since the last survey, its application for the next and for previous labour schedules are checked in the same way as in the agricultural sector; in addition all new establishments are visited. The returns from this investigation provide the main index for estimating the demand for industrial labour within the next six months.

As already mentioned, the whole survey was up to 1937 made by the Jewish Agency in co-operation with and under control of the Government, so that their estimates of the capacity of absorbing immigrant labour were based on the same data; nevertheless their estimates used to differ widely. On the average, since 1933, the number of certificates applied for has been double the number granted[1]; the same data were differently interpreted and the same indices differently weighed, but it is obvious that both estimates were to a certain extent biased. The Jewish Agency has maintained that the Government constantly underrated the absorptive capacity of the country; indeed a considerable volume of illegal Jewish and Arab immigration was easily absorbed during this period. On several occasions the influx of capital, due to the increase of capitalist immigration after 1933, created such a demand for labour that in spite of advances on the next schedule, which were allowed by the Government, a shortage of labour was felt, which had adverse effects on the price system and on the whole economic development of the country. On the other hand, in 1926 and 1927, when as a consequence of the currency restrictions in Eastern Europe capitalist immigration into Palestine suddenly declined, a depression occurred which brought about unemployment and an outward net balance of migration, which has been taken as evidence that previous immigration was above absorptive capacity. But as a whole Palestine has been spared major depressions and unemployment,[2] though her whole economic structure makes her much more susceptible to heavy fluctuations; she has—unlike other countries of immigration—few unutilized natural resources which lend themselves easily to exploitation. Her absorptive capacity is largely determined by the inflow of capital, by the quality of her immigrants, and by the world demand for her production.

Our description of the Palestine immigration regulations has

---

[1] Cf. *Great Britain and Palestine*, 1915–1939, The Royal Institute of Int. Affairs.
[2] Avderse economic conditions in 1936–1938 were the consequence of the Arab revolt.

revealed both the advantages and the shortcomings of the direct method of measuring a country's absorptive capacity. It is based on the real demand for immigrants, so that it becomes possible to distinguish between various categories of immigrants, and to find out how many of each category are likely to become absorbed and how their admission will affect the standard of living. It seems that the margin of error inherent in any estimate can be reduced by the direct approach much more than by any other method. A method which yields information as exact and detailed as possible is needed if the principle of absorptive capacity is to be adopted for practical purposes in order to determine what volume of immigration can be admitted within a given period.

v. *Objections to the Adoption of the Principle of Absorptive Capacity*

The many shortcomings of the method are easily seen. In Palestine the survey is undertaken by an agency which is highly interested in the promotion of immigration and has to deal in the Jewish sector with a native population which is also convinced of the desirability of large-scale immigration, so that all possible openings will be taken into account. It cannot be presumed that this will be the case with other countries, where immigration has often to meet with prejudice and resistance. A survey concerned with finding new openings for immigrants can therefore not always rely on the co-operation of the native population, and its success depends largely on the efficiency and initiative of the government department concerned. Moreover, it is questionable whether decision by officials is a suitable instrument for distinguishing between vague projects which have to be excluded from the estimate and practical propositions. It may be argued that the decision whether a new project justifies the admission of immigrants is better left to the entrepreneurs who take the risk of the new enterprise, and that officials are likely to take a too narrow view of the prospects, so that the volume of immigration will be fixed below capacity. It is obvious that in a system of free enterprise a new venture cannot be definite in all details. Even if its start is promising, it remains a matter of opinion whether it causes undesirable competition with existing production and whether it will eventually become a failure and merely increase the amount of idle capital equipment and the number of unemployed. The same difficulty arises in deciding whether the special knowledge or experience of an immigrant is useful to the country or whether the same work could be done by an unemployed resident.

If the admission of the immigrant is not followed by a control of his activities after entrance, it is possible that the whole scheme of the immigration authorities may become ineffective. In some countries of immigration openings for agricultural labourers have been created by the general tendency of the population to move from rural districts into large towns, attracted by the better payment for industrial work and by the amenities of town life, without being deterred by industrial unemployment. The same trend is evident with immigrants who have been allocated to agricultural work. Though they would not have been admitted as industrial workers, they often flow back to the towns, where they may not be wanted. Similar cases occur also in other categories of immigrants, e.g. domestic servants; when the self-interest of the immigrant is in disharmony with the intentions of the immigration authority, he is tempted to follow his own interest. The remedy against such "abuses" seems at first sight obvious: the establishment of immigrant control which makes change of residence or of occupation subject to a special permit. Such procedure would not meet with much objection within a largely planned community where the free play of individual self-interest is generally limited by State regulations, but its value is very questionable in an economic system otherwise free.[1] Under it the immigrant becomes a second-class resident, and this discrimination must have an unfavourable effect on his prospects and possibly also on his desire to become integrated with the rest of the population. He becomes less mobile, so that one asset of the immigrant, his greater mobility, is lost. If we conceive the immigrant—apart from temporary immigration—as a potential future citizen, the control can necessarily only be exerted for a limited transitional period and can be justified only during a period of heavy general unemployment.

All these objections may be irrefutable, but they are not so momentous as to invalidate our main argument. Similar disadvantages are connected with any State intervention, and as soon as we are convinced that a free economic system leads at the present state of production to undesirable results, we have to put up with certain disadvantages of planning, provided that its results are more satisfactory in general. In the case of migration we have tried to show that the restoration of free migration cannot be expected to solve the problems which have arisen in connection with demographic, economic and social developments since 1914,

[1] Such control is exerted in Australia on certain categories of immigrants.

that the usefulness of migration is limited by the absorptive capacity of a country, and that only under particular circumstances will free migration harmonize with this capacity. The issue is therefore a practical rather than an ideological one: to find a method which serves the social ends of intervention and preserves as much as possible the advantages of free migration. The method suggested above is far from being perfect. Much scope is still left to practical intuition and to trial and error; satisfactory results, therefore, depend largely on the efficiency and good will of the authorities, but we see no reason to assume that both will not be forthcoming. It is true that State intervention is at present largely influenced by vested interests and nationalistic ideas, but it is equally true that, so long as this attitude persists, the restoration of free migration is out of the question.

After discussing the limitations set to the volume of desirable migration by the carrying capacity and absorptive capacity of the immigration countries, it is appropriate to remember that neither the achievement of full carrying capacity nor that of full absorptive capacity is an end in itself; both concepts are relevant because they indicate that volume and composition of immigration which is consistent with the maintenance or the achievement of a certain standard of living. Their value is relative, and depends upon the standard of living which underlies the estimate. If it is the object of migration policy to raise the standard of living of the receiving country, it is our concern to find the volume of absorbable migration which is associated with a standard of living as high as possible; but if the regulation of migration is aimed at diminishing discrepancies between the standards of living in immigration and emigration countries, conditions in the emigration countries must be taken into account, and accordingly a lower standard of living will be taken as the basis for estimating the volume of immigration which can be absorbed.

Generally speaking, so long as we can distinguish between countries whose demographic situation is such that a population decrease by emigration is likely to raise their standards of living and those which are likely to profit by an increase in numbers through immigration, it is both in the general interest and in that of the receiving country that the latter should admit at least as many immigrants as are likely to raise its standard of living. The convenient simplification of distinguishing between immigration and emigration countries does not, as we have seen, cover the whole problem. Many countries have large-scale immigration and emigration at the same time. Such an exchange of population cannot be considered as wasteful misdirection due to the shortcomings of free migration. The factual survey of the absorptive capacity which we have outlined, indicates the nominated individuals and the categories of immigrants which can be absorbed, no matter whether their absorbability is a consequence of previous or of simultaneous emigration or of any other reason. In a democracy the State can plan immigration and can assist emigration, but it cannot—except in cases of emergency such as war—prevent its subjects from emigrating, so it may happen that even when migration is planned, immigration and emigration of the same categories will take place.

c. CAPACITY TO ASSIMILATE IMMIGRANTS

The whole principle of taking economic absorbability as the standard for desirable migration, however, needs re-examination in the light of considerations which are mainly non-economic. We have to take into account the policy of immigration countries to admit only immigrants who are likely to become assimilated to the old stock of the population and whose assimilation is deemed desirable. It is claimed that in order to ensure harmonious co-operation between the elements of the population, any immigration policy must ensure that unassimilated immigrants do not form too large a fraction of the whole. The recognition of this claim implies that the principle of economic absorptive capacity can be applied only when it does not interfere with the principle of assimilative capacity. The growing consciousness of national or racial difference between immigrants and the old stock of the population caused the problem of assimilation to become a main issue in the immigration policy of the inter-war period. It has a direct bearing on absorptive capacity in so far as it may be easy for a country to absorb immigrants of similar extraction, whereas those whose foreign origin is easily recognisable may have to meet with so much friction and so many obstacles that their absorption becomes virtually impossible. Though our inquiry is mainly concerned with the economic aspect of the problem, we cannot disregard the impact of national consciousness on the volume of migration. We can, however, give only a short outline of the various claims which have been made in this highly controversial matter, fully aware of the fact that the issues at stake can be treated satisfactorily only by a comprehensive investigation.[1]

i. *Process of Assimilation*

"Assimilation is the process by which individuals of different cultural heritages occupying a common territory achieve cultural solidarity, sufficient at least to sustain national existence."[2] Its aspects are twofold. Outwardly, it requires that the immigrants adopt the native language, customs, and so on; in short, that they become indistinguishable from the old stock. But this would be mere mimicry and not assimilation if it were not accompanied by a process of adopting the psychical characteristics of the native population.

Assimilation takes place gradually; the precise time it requires depends on various circumstances. If the initial differences are but little it will be comparatively short. It will be—other things being equal—much easier for a British immigrant to become assimilated in the United States, or for a Spanish immigrant to become assimilated in Argentina, than conversely. Generally speaking, the time required will be shorter with young persons than with elderly people, shorter with individuals than with families which hold together, and shorter with single families than in the case of the collective immigration of whole groups of families of the same origin; i.e. shorter in cases of infiltration than in cases of group settlement. Moreover, it is largely determined by the social relationship between natives and immigrants. A hostile attitude on the part of the natives will inevitably delay the process of assimilation or render it impossible. If the immigrant is debarred from social intercourse with the natives, he has fewer opportunities of becoming acquainted with their way of life and their cultural achievements, and he is compelled to confine his intercourse mainly to members of his own group. Any discrimination is apt to produce national and social self-consciousness on his part, so that he will become more reluctant to abandon his own cultural tradition. The same is likely to happen if the immigrants believe that their own culture is superior

---

[1] Duncan, *Immigration and Assimilation*; Huxley-Haddon-Carr-Saunders, *We Europeans*; Carr-Saunders, *The Population Problem*; Jennings, *The Biological Basis of Human Nature*; F. Boas, "Changes in the Bodily Form of Descendents of Immigrants", *Am. Anthropologist* XIV; T. R. Garth, *Race Psychology*; A. J. Toynbee, *A Study of History*, I, pp. 243 ff.

[2] R. E. Park, "Assimilation", in *Encyclopædia of the Social Sciences*.

to that of their new country; they are then less inclined to adopt its manners, dress and speech. · But this attitude cannot last long, provided no outside interference is forthcoming. Under the modern technique of production with its highly developed division of labour it is hardly possible for any minority to lead permanently a symbiotic life,' and to keep aloof from the social life of the rest of the population without the risk of serious economic disadvantages, so that this attitude can but delay the progress of assimilation. As we have seen in Chapter III, European migrants tend to prefer for immigration countries whose culture they deem superior or at least not inferior to their own; they will therefore generally have no reason to object to assimilation which has such great practical advantages for them.

Willingness to become integrated with the old stock, however, will be significantly hampered if the country of emigration tries to interfere in this respect. Before the war certain emigrant countries extended the scope of their aggressive nationalistic activities to their emigrants. They pursued a policy which was aimed at preventing the assimilation of these emigrants and at keeping alive their allegiance to their former "Vaterland". The organization of national schools and of other social and educational institutions, promises and threats, served to create a minority abroad which was loyal to their country of emigration, and in the case of conflict antagonistic to the country of immigration. It is obvious that no State can tolerate the existence of a potential "fifth column" without jeopardizing its own security and independence. With the defeat of the Axis powers these obstacles to assimilation have been greatly reduced. But non-aggressor countries also have an interest in promoting the goodwill of their former nationals and in preventing their full assimilation. In the economic field this goodwill may find its expression in money remittances and closer trade relations between the sending and the receiving country (see below, Chapter VII).

It is the combination of these various concurrent and counteracting forces and circumstances which determines the duration of the assimilation process in each individual case. Only under favourable circumstances will the first generation of immigrants succeed in becoming completely assimilated. Otherwise even the immigrant's children and grandchildren, though native born, will not always be able to adapt themselves to the social and cultural environments of the new country.

ii. *Differentials in the Assimilability of Different Ethnic Groups*

It is held, however, that certain types of immigrants are practically unassimilable, viz. those whose genetic constitution differs essentially from that of the native population. It is not too much to say that, under present conditions, the existence of easily distinguishable physical differences, due to a different genetic constitution, between natives and immigrants precludes complete assimilation for the obliteration of external marks of diversity, which is looked upon as the main requirement of assimilation, becomes in this case practically impossible. The members of the various ethnic groups of the Negro, Mongol and leucoderm type are inter-fertile, so that the problem could be solved in theory by constant intermarriage of the immigrants and their descendants with "pure" natives, over many generations. Intermarriages between these different types, however, have at present to meet with considerable resistance[1]; this way of assimilation is therefore in most countries of assimilation restricted to exceptional cases.

Mental differences between natives and immigrants, due to a different genetic constitution, can, of course, not be traced so easily. But it has been maintained that external assimilation in the case of immigrants with a physical genetic constitution similar to that of the natives merely conceals the existence of inherited mental characteristics which are undesired in and alien to the country of immigration. If this were so, complete assimilation could in this case also only be achieved through constant intermarriage, the implication being that the assimilation of large-scale immigration of racially different groups might eventually alter the genetic constitution of the native stock. Although the resistance to intermarriage is probably less intensive here than in the case of inherited physical differences, it would provide a strong case for the exclusion of those ethnic groups whose mental genetic endowment is considered by the immigration country as inferior to that of its own stock.

It appears, however, that the common presupposition that these mental differences are entirely or mainly of a permanent or genetic nature is unwarranted. "With the best will in the world it is in the present state of knowledge impossible to disentangle the genetic from the environmental factors in matters of 'racial

---

[1] Marriages between whites and Mongolians are prohibited in the U.S.A. by fourteen States, including those where Mongol immigrants are most numerous (Davie, *op. cit.*, p. 215). Intermarriage of Negroes with white people is forbidden by law in thirty States of the U.S.A.

traits', 'national character' and the like."[1] This statement does not entirely exclude the existence of innate, genetic differences between human groups in regard to intelligence, temperament and other psychological traits, but these differences are only matters of general averages and proportions of types. There will be in every ethnic group "a great quantitative range and a great qualitative diversity of mental characters, and different groups will very largely overlap with each other."[2] If we accept this result of scientific research, in spite of the innumerable attempts of nationalistic propaganda to provide evidence for the innate superiority or inferiority of certain groups, we can be satisfied that it is unwarranted to assume a priori that an immigrant or his offspring is unassimilable, or that his assimilation is undesirable, because he is a member of a different ethnic group; as mentioned above, the only possible exceptions are members of those groups who display inherited physical differences.

Granted that it is under present conditions the duty of a Government "to take such steps as experience may prove necessary, to ensure that such immigrants as are admitted become assimilated" it may be doubtful whether "special restrictions on the entry of members of certain groups because they become assimilated more slowly than others and the exclusion of other groups because they cannot become assimilated",[3] represents the most adequate immigration policy. Experience shows that natives have always objected to the immigration of foreigners of differing customs, speech and manners. "The new arrivals have always appeared stupid, unprogressive, and inclined toward pauperism and criminality. In time these immigrants became in turn the native citizens who look with disgust on still later arrivals."[4] In the history of U.S.A. immigration about a century ago the "wild" Irish and the "dumb" Dutch were the main object of antagonism, and their exclusion because of their inherent inferiority became a popular demand. Only a few decades later they were regarded as assimilated, and similar prejudices were directed against the immigrants from Eastern and South-Eastern Europe; these were characterized as inferior and unassimilable, and when they were practically excluded by the quota system, the same slur was put upon Mexican immigration. It appears that such claims are strongest when the volume of immigration is

[1] Huxley, *We Europeans*, p. 79 (Pelican Ed.).
[2] Huxley, *loc. cit.*
[3] Carr-Saunders, *World Population*, p. 219.
[4] Riegel, *Introduction into the Social Sciences*, Vol. II, p. 669.

greater than can easily be economically absorbed. Then a hostile attitude on the part of the natives makes the assimilation of the new immigrants impossible or at least very difficult, and it is then easy to prove that their groups ought to be excluded because they cannot become assimilated. It seems probable therefore that the problem of assimilation would not offer any insurmountable difficulties if future immigration were always adapted to the economic absorptive capacity of the country and if the immigrants were given a chance to become assimilated. Membership of a certain ethnic group is only one and probably not the most important criterion for determining the duration of the process of assimilation and its possibility and desirability. If it is possible to create an atmosphere of mutual respect between natives and immigrants, to encourage social intercourse between them, to refrain from discrimination and from enforcing assimilation, to eliminate by individual selection all those who are unfit to become assimilated, and finally to frustrate any attempt at interference by nationalist emigration countries. A harmonious co-operation between natives and immigrants will be possible, even if immigrants not yet fully assimilated form a comparatively large fraction of the population. When these principles are disregarded the assimilation of a comparatively small number of immigrants becomes problematic.

This argument, though it presumes the necessity of full assimilation, implies that our previous conclusion which suggested the absorptive capacity of a country as a suitable criterion of the volume of desirable immigration, has not been invalidated by the problem of assimilation It seems reasonable, however, that a receiving country, so long as the supply of immigrants is greater than that volume which corresponds to the absorptive capacity, should prefer those immigrants whose hereditary endowment is similar to that of its natives, but this preference should not exclude the admission of members of less similar groups if the method of individual selection indicates that they are better suited than prospective immigrants belonging to the privileged groups.

iii. *Necessity for Immigrants to Become Assimilated*

We began our discussion of assimilation by suggesting that harmonious co-operation between natives and immigrants requires that the immigrants become assimilated to the native population. We accepted the definition of assimilation as the process by which individuals of different cultural heritages occupying a common territory achieve cultural solidarity, sufficient at least to sustain national existence. This definition is vague in so far as it leaves entirely open what degree of cultural solidarity is necessary in order to sustain national existence. The interpretation which we used in our argument was the widest possible. We presumed that the ultimate end of assimilation was to make immigrants and natives indistinguishable from one another as different groups. We felt entitled to do this because the same assumption underlies all discussions of the assimilability of different groups of immigrants and also the conclusions drawn from these discussions. Since this wide interpretation is not implied in our definition, it remains to inquire whether any stage of assimilation short of full integration is likely to ensure national existence. The bearing of this question on the general line of our argument is obvious: if this margin is wide, if many immigrants who have adapted themselves in a broad sense to the way of life of the immigrant country, but are still easily recognizable as foreigners, can be considered as assimilated, the range of assimilable immigrants is greatly extended and a less strict selection or fewer safeguards are necessary than in the case when full homogeneity is required.

Our definition indicates a close relationship between the concepts of "assimilation" and "nation". It is not possible, however, to determine generally what amount of variety is compatible with national existence. The answer has differed in the various stages of the development of the nation-State, and differs for the various existing forms of nations. Nations enter into the European system at the end of the fifteenth century. Historically the State precedes the nation. Most nations were formed by a process of integration, more or less heterogeneous elements becoming united under a single government, usually a monarchy. Common history and tradition, common interests and the efforts of the Governments transformed mere political unity into an organism of the kind we call a nation. The self-consciousness of nations is a product only of the nineteenth century; it was mainly the impact of the French Revolution which brought about a conversion of this process, so that the dynastic idea lost its power to create nations. It is now the nation which makes the State. It seems that the growing prevalence of the national element in the nation-State has produced among nations a tendency to make their components as uniform as possible, so that they become more susceptible to the heterogeneity of immigrants. It has also led to a change of ideology. The principle on which the nation is now based is not mere "contiguity—the sweet ties of neighbourliness, strengthened by old and common tradition, which unite the racial blend that inhabits a given territory and make it a nation of the spirit"; the dominating principle becomes now "blood—or the idea of a nation as a group of kinsfolk united by an intimate consanguinity within their gates, but divided from the stranger without by an impassable barrier of difference."[1] Ernest Barker calls the former a reality and true nationalism, and the latter a simulacrum and false nationalism. In real life "false" nationalism has become a reality, it serves as an argument for the exclusion of immigrants of differing racial origin and for the idea that only immigrants of the same extraction as the native stock are assimilable.

The effect of this militant nationalism on the possibility of assimilation cannot be under-estimated. Individualism, tolerance and cosmopolitanism are incompatible with it. About twenty-four centuries ago Pericles praised the people of Athens: "In our private intercourse we are not suspicious of one another nor angry with our neighbour if he does what he likes." It is obvious that where such an attitude prevails, harmonious co-operation between diverse elements of a population is easily achieved and that the requirements of assimilation are satisfied if common interests and a common loyalty to the community can be established. Similarly, if the part attributed to the State is only a "negative" one, and if the links provided by national consciousness are considered as obstacles to the establishment of world economics and of one international culture—an opinion widely held in England about a century ago—the problem of assimilation becomes an issue of minor importance.

Another factor which affects the attitude towards assimilation has been already mentioned in another connection. The present form of high capitalistic production with its widely developed division of labour, favours and requires a more thorough assimilation than do more primitive forms of production. German peasants who settled in Russia, Transylvania, Pennsylvania,[2]

---

[1] E. Barker, *National Character and the Factors in its Formation*, p. 276.

[2] As early as 1751 Benjamin Franklin wrote: "Why should Pennsylvania, founded by England, become a colony of aliens who will shortly be so numerous as to germanize us instead of our anglifying them?" (Works of B.F., Vol. II, p. 233, repr. in Abbot, *Historical Aspects of Migration*. The Pennyslvania Dutch did not germanize the U.S., after more than 200 years in America they remain unassimilated, though belonging to those groups which are considered by present American legislation as easily assimilable.

Argentina and elsewhere formed practically self-contained communities and remained socially and geographically segregated. They had neither the wish nor the opportunity to become assimilated; they did not meet with any conspicuous resistance on the part of the natives and retained their language and customs for centuries.

In a period of transition to higher forms of capitalistic production immigrants may remain unassimilated without much harm to themselves or to the community so long as they perform a vital economic function and cannot be replaced by natives. The immigration of German Jews to Poland in the Middle Ages, of Spanish Jews to other Mediterranean countries after their expulsion in 1492, of Lombards to England and of Chinese and Indians into various countries at an early stage of capitalistic production are only a few instances of this kind of immigration without assimilation. It is possible only during periods of transition, and is likely to lead in the course of the development to friction and even to catastrophe in periods of depression as soon as the alien elements are replaceable by natives.

The consequences of unassimilated Chinese and Indian immigration into Malaya may be different though not less unpleasant. The rapid development of primary production in Malaya during the last few decades was due to mass immigration of Chinese and Indian labour resulting from British enterprise, capital and administration. "To the Tamil coolies and the Chinese Malaya was what America represented to immigrants from Eastern Europe; but unlike these immigrants they swamped, instead of being absorbed by, the original inhabitants."[1] The Malays, generally conservative and unprogressive, cannot compete with the newcomers, and in contrast to them, have derived little benefit from the opening up of their country. Out-numbered by Chinese and Indians they have been transformed from poor men in a poor country to poor men in a rich country and the prospect of overcoming existing friction between the national groups by means of assimilation seems to be very remote.

Having outlined the main factors which determine the degree of assimilation necessary to establish harmonious co-operation between natives and immigrants, it becomes evident that no generally valid standard can be evolved for this. It differs for each country according to its stage of economic, political and cultural development and the composition of its population. The

[1] A. Campbell, *It's Your Empire*, p. 194, London, 1945.

problem has different aspects in Australia, whose population is mainly of Anglo-Saxon origin, in the United States, whose population is composed of elements from practically all European nations, in France, with her declining population, in Switzerland, with her four strictly separated national elements; it is different in countries which have not yet abandoned the ideals of tolerance and the rights of man and those which have replaced them by the belief in the primacy of the racially determined nation-State. It appears, however, that during the inter-war period, immigration policy was largely influenced by this ideology, as well as by Governments which denounced it as "false" nationalism, and that economic considerations were held to be of secondary importance.

Before the outbreak of the First World War public opinion in the United States, in spite of protests against new immigration, firmly believed in the magic power of the American melting-pot. But during that war it became evident that some elements of the U.S. population were far from being amalgamated.[1] Large parts of it had not severed their links with the country of origin, they had not acquired the most fundamental sign of assimilation, common loyalty to their new country, but tried to influence American policy according to the interests of their former countries without regard to American traditions and interests. The U.S.A. recognized the danger to her national existence inherent in this lack of common loyalty. The melting-pot came into disfavour and was replaced by the housewife's soup kettle in which every available vegetable is placed. It is suggested that the final dish will not be good unless the various ingredients are right and are mixed in the proper proportion.[2] This new metaphor is used to indicate that the U.S.A. does not need complete homogeneity as achieved by the melting process, but that it is essential to her well-being that, apart from a general restriction on immigration, the share of any one nation in this restricted immigration must also be limited. The American quota system is the result of this policy. It has been characterized by Duncan as follows: "On the whole our methods of restriction seem to indicate that we accept the theory of Nordic superiority, that we use physical characteristics as a criterion for judging races, and that only the inferior representatives of racial groups

---

[1] Of the nearly 14 million persons of foreign birth in the U.S. at that time about 5 million could not read, write or speak the English language (Davie, *Immigration,* p. 370).

[2] Riegel, *loc. cit.*

desire to emigrate."[1] Our argument has tried to show that this system is from both the economic and sociological viewpoints inferior to other methods of regulating immigration.

The period of continually growing nationalism has produced a fundamental conflict of interest between the immigration and the emigration countries. Receiving countries require their immigrants to become fully assimilated, and tend to exclude all those whom they think unsuitable for this end: emigration countries endeavour to keep a hold on their emigrants and to check all tendencies towards assimilation. The Second World War is a dramatic climax in the history of sovereign nation-States. It is not improbable that it will represent the end of aggressive nationalism. What now seems utopian may at some time or other after the war become a reality: harmonious co-operation between individuals of different cultural heritages and different extraction, occupying one common territory.[2]

iv. *Naturalization*

Until his naturalization the legal status of the immigrant is definitely inferior to that of the native. As an alien he may be subject to expulsion or be restricted in the choice of his residence or employment; he may not be eligible for social insurance or public assistance benefits; he may be excluded from subsidized housing schemes or from schemes for reduced fees for' the education of his children. Most new countries, it is true, refrain from such discrimination, which presents a powerful obstacle to assimilation; and for all practical purposes their aliens are protected by the law as fully as their citizens. But without full civic rights their share in the public life of their country of adoption must remain limited. If they have a fair chance of becoming naturalized in due course, they can, as future citizens, after their admission identify themselves with the new country and are encouraged to give up their former nationality, "It is in our view," says the author of a British Government report, "of great importance that the migrant should from the earliest possible moment after his arrival in his new country, regard himself as a citizen of that country, with all the rights and obliga-

---

[1] Duncan, *Immigration and Assimilation*, p. 495.
[2] This may take the form of "cultural pluralism". The simile used is the orchestra in which the cultural inheritance of each nation has to play an essential part.

tions of such citizens. It is equally desirable that the Government and people of that country should regard the migrant from the first, in practice if not in law, as a full citizen of that country, dependent upon and responsible to his new Government and his new fellow-citizens alone for the rights and obligations of a citizen and a neighbour."[1]

This recommendation implies: (i) that in principle any alien admitted as a permanent immigrant—in contrast to seasonal workers, students, etc.—should be eligible for naturalization; (ii) that rights of citizenship should be granted as early as possible. The significance of these implications depends partly upon the concept of assimilation and assimilability adopted by the receiving country, partly on the extent to which naturalization is used as a means of accelerating the process of assimilation and economic absorption. A relatively short period of residence— say three years—an elementary knowledge of the language and the institutions of the new country and the absence of a criminal record may be regarded as minimum requirements, if it is anticipated that the applicant will become gradually integrated in the nation after he has been granted equal legal status.

3. FACTORS DETERMINING THE VOLUME OF EMIGRATION DESIRABLE

Our discussion of the limits set to the usefulness of migration has so far been concerned only with conditions in immigration countries, with the limits set by the absorptive and the assimilative capacity of the immigration country. When we dealt with the economics of declining populations it became apparent that similar problems exist for countries of emigration. Harmony between the economic self-interest of the emigrant and that of the country of emigration can be assumed only so long as the decrease in numbers caused by emigration has a favourable effect on the standard of living in the emigration country. This assumption is not justified in the case of emigration from countries whose standard of living is low or is falling owing to the adverse effects of population decline, brought about through either natural decrease or emigration. Moreover, too large a volume of emigration at a time is likely to lead to economic disequilibrium

---

[1] Report of the Inter-Departmental Committee on Migration Policy, Cmd 4689, 1935, p. 20.

in the emigration country, comparable with the disturbances caused by too rapid immigration. Capital equipment and durable consumption goods sold by immigrants will affect the price level and the production of these goods, and a sudden contraction of the demand for consumption goods may lead to a general depression in the emigration country; so, broadly speaking, emigration cannot be expected to bring relief from existing unemployment, but may under certain circumstances, as previously seen, even produce more. All this applies mainly to industrialized countries, while densely populated agricultural countries whose production is largely based on subsistence farming are more likely to profit from large-scale emigration.

A. SELECTIVE EFFECT OF FREE EMIGRATION

When analysing the concept of absorptive capacity of a country we saw that it was necessary to distinguish between different classes with different absorbability. A similar distinction has to be made in the case of emigration. It is obvious that the emigration of the most valuable elements of a population is against the interests of the community—though it may improve to a certain extent the prospects of those who remain behind— even if on general grounds a decrease of the population seems desirable. These instances indicate that there is from the mere economic point of view of emigration countries a good case for the regulation of emigration; but the issues suggested by these considerations have become evident in the past only to a small extent. In the past free emigration generally worked satisfactorily; at least no major economic disturbances can be attributed to too high a rate of emigration; obviously in real life free emigration has never reached the theoretical limit to its usefulness. Indeed in modern times the rate of emigration has never caught up with the rate of natural increase in the emigration country. All emigration countries, except Italy and Ireland, continued to expand in numbers in spite of large-scale emigration, so that the drawbacks of a declining population could not be experienced. What probably happened was that emigration slowed down an otherwise too rapid rate of population growth, thereby assisting the economic development of the emigration countries, all the more since we can presume that these countries were over-populated in the sense already outlined, that in the given state of technical knowledge, with the given amount of capital equipment and natural resources, a smaller supply of labour would have yielded a higher real income per head. Compared with these advantages, the disadvantage inherent in any free emigration, the possible loss of the most active elements of the population, did not weigh very heavily, as on the other hand the immigration countries could be used as a dumping ground for the least desired elements.

B. EFFECTS OF LARGE-SCALE EMIGRATION

i. *In Ireland*

In the case of Italy emigration exceeded natural increase in 1905–1907 and in 1913, but the volume of emigration has not in the long run been sufficient to keep the population stationary.[1] This is not true for the population trend of Ireland. During the period of large-scale Irish emigration from 1841 to 1854 the Irish population decreased by 19.9 per cent, from 8,175,000 to 6,522,000. Other factors besides emigration may have contributed to bring about this extraordinary decline; with a smaller volume of emigration, starvation and postponement of marriage would perhaps have produced a similar effect on Irish population growth during that period, but it goes without saying that mass emigration was a less painful and probably more efficient means of adjustment. Ireland did not experience the disadvantages of a declining population outlined in the previous chapter; the general result of the heavy losses in numbers was on the contrary a considerable improvement in the well-being of the population,[2] and even a still larger rate of emigration would probably not have had adverse effects on the welfare of the country. The results of Irish emigration during that period— the only migratory movement in modern history which comprises a considerable proportion of a country's total population and which was accompanied by a definitive population decline— do not, therefore, support our argument that emigration may cease to be useful to the emigration country if it leads to a negative growth of population. In the particular case of Ireland the advantages of emigration were so overwhelming that its possible disadvantages were of no importance. A merely agricultural country with an extremely low standard of living, little division

[1] Cf. Carr-Saunders, *World Population*, p. 200.
[2] Cf. D. A. E. Harkness, "Irish Emigration", in *International Migrations*, Vol. II, p. 276.

of labour, unable to withstand the competition of agricultural producers overseas on the export market after England's adoption of free trade, prevented from transferring to more capitalistic methods of production by lack of capital and other obstacles, continually threatened by famine, Ireland showed the typical characteristics of an over-populated country, whose standard of living is largely determined by the density of its population and where the concept of optimum population is not invalidated by the counteracting effects of rapid population changes. In the case of Ireland, if we take her economic structure under the given circumstances as unalterable, the theory of optimum population could be applied without the qualifications which we found it necessary to make for countries on—or moving towards—a higher level of capitalistic production. For Ireland the only limit to the usefulness of emigration was the optimum point of population, and there is no reason to assume that free migration could have ignored this mark.

The decline of population has continued in Ireland, though at a slower rate—to-day Eire and Northern Ireland combined have a population of about 4,250,000. The volume of oversea emigration has gradually contracted, partly as a consequence of the change in Eire's political status and of less favourable conditions abroad, partly because the population pressure has been greatly relieved by the fall in numbers. The net balance of Ireland's intercontinental migration was about zero for the last two pre-war years, owing to some re-migration from overseas.[1]

ii. In Italy

Italy's experience with large-scale agricultural emigration seems to have been less favourable. Where the local diminution in the supply of agricultural labour was only slight, as for instance in Tuscany, emigration has probably brought relief. But, according to R. F. Foerster,[2] large-scale emigration in many districts of the South has produced effects which have been officially compared with those of a pestilence. Whole villages decayed and were practically abandoned. The supply of labour consisted mainly of the aged, the women and the children;

[1] Cf. I.L.O. *Year Book of Labour Statistics.* Emigration from Eire to England still continues. The annual net emigration from Eire to Great Britain is estimated as between 18,000 and 19,000 for the five pre-war years. Whether it has under present economic conditions a favourable effect on Eire's standard of living remains doubtful, though money remittances from immigrants in Britain and the U.S. have been a great help.

[2] R. F. Foerster, *The Italian Emigration of our Times*, p. 449.

wage-rates became higher. Land—and not only marginal land —had to be abandoned for lack of labourers; in other regions the cultivation became less intensive, pasture succeeded tillage, and the cultivation of grapes and vegetables markedly contracted. This situation became critical mainly for the class of small proprietors which represents the mass of the landed bourgeoisie; many of them could not afford to pay the higher wage rates, or could not resort to the use of machinery to the same extent as the proprietors of the medium or large estates. When the yield from a less intensive cultivation became too small, the owners had to sell or abandon their lands and take up some other occupation. Land values fell, but this tendency was counteracted in many districts by land purchases of emigrants either as investment during their absence or upon their return.

Foerster finds that money wages have risen in all the regions from which emigration has taken place. Employment, however, has in some places become less steady; for this reason, and mainly because of the rise in prices, real incomes have markedly risen only in some districts (Apulia and the Abruzzi). "Hence, generally speaking, the labourer who has stayed at home has benefited only slightly in an economic way by emigration."[1]

All countries but Ireland had during the period of heavy emigration a high rate of natural increase, and a still larger volume of emigration than was actually forthcoming would have been necessary in order to bring about a reversal of the population trend. Since the rate of natural increase has fallen so markedly, and in most countries of emigration has already come near to being stationary, a relatively small volume of emigration is in future likely to outstrip natural increase, and a revival of migration would probably reveal the limitations of the usefulness of emigration to the emigration country, as their economic structure is entirely different from that of Ireland a century ago.

iii. In the Depressed Areas of Great Britain

A study of the population movements in the depressed areas of Great Britain before the war gives us a fairly correct idea of the nature of these limitations for highly industrialized countries.[2] Those areas were considered as "depressed" which were particularly hard hit by the structural changes which occurred after

---

[1] *Ibid.*, p. 454.
[2] These areas regained their former prosperity during the war and are now known as "development areas".

the First World War. Certain districts associated with the staple industries (cotton and coal) notably the North-East coast, South-West Scotland, parts of Lancashire and Cumberland were soon after the war confronted with a marked fall in the demand for their products, with the result that heavy unemployment and a drop in wages brought the standard of living in these areas near to subsistence level, while the population in the South, where newer, growing industries are largely located, enjoyed a relatively high degree of prosperity. Internal migration from the depressed areas to the prosperous South seemed the obvious means of adjustment. From the viewpoint of the population in these districts the economic consequences of this drift to the South are not very different from those of genuine emigration.[1]

Indeed a constant flow of labour to the regions with better opportunities took place, but the mobility of labour away from these "special" areas was far from perfect, and spontaneous emigration did not bring much relief. Government intervention became necessary. This had two main purposes: the encouragement of new industrial development, and industrial transference, i.e. assisted internal emigration. Spontaneous and assisted emigration taken together have brought about a definitive decline of population in some of these areas. The census region Wales I, for example, in the intercensal period 1921–1931 lost 242,000 people or 12.3 per cent of its former population; from 1921 to 1935 some 47,000 people (on balance) left the Rhondda U.D., a number equal to 28 per cent of her total population. Owing to high birth-rates in most of the distressed areas, the absolute losses were much lower than is indicated by these figures. Four counties in South Wales, for example, lost between 1921 and 1936 over 17 per cent of their population through emigration, while the net fall in population was only 6 per cent.[2] But the heavy emigration has brought about significant changes of age-composition; the older age structure of the population must inevitably lead in future to lower birth- and higher death-rates, and hence to lower natural increase.

There can be no doubt that spontaneous emigration and the transference schemes of the Government considerably improved

---

[1] They are only less serious; re-emigration, for example, takes place at relatively small costs as soon as conditions have improved, the transfer of money both ways is unrestricted and cannot affect the stability of the currency, etc.

[2] With the exception of Wales all other regions of emigration showed slight increases in the absolute size of their populations during the intercensal decade 1921–1931.

the standard of living of the *emigrants*. The percentage of those who re-migrated because they were unsuccessful in finding employment after their emigration is relatively small. The great majority became settled in the London area and in the Midlands, though often at wage rates below the local level. But this emigration both in respect to its volume and to its composition seems to have had an adverse effect on the population remaining in the distressed areas. We have already mentioned the changes in the age composition of the population. In the case of South Wales 66 per cent of the net outward balance of migration 1921–1931 was under thirty, and 87 per cent under forty-five years of age.[1] Thus the depressed areas are left with a population heavily weighted by the older and to a certain extent the younger generations of non-working age. "With two-thirds of the migrants between the ages of fifteen and forty-four years, the areas are left with an increasing proportion of persons above and below working ages, and with this increase in the numbers of dependants per worker it is obvious that the standard of living in these areas must fall, so that the effect of migration is ultimately to *create further conditions of depression*."[2] But irrespective of age, emigration also lowered the qualitative average of the population left behind. The workers with most initiative and adaptability were most ready to move, and had the best prospects of finding employment elsewhere.[3] From the transference and retraining schemes of the Government all those were excluded who were not up to the average standard of efficiency; moreover, a large percentage of those who returned had been unable to find or keep employment, being less suitable than their competitors.[4]

A further distinction must be drawn between the emigration of skilled and potentially skilled workers and that of the unskilled. The emigration of unemployed unskilled workers is generally unobjectionable and beneficial from the viewpoint of the community and of the entrepreneurs, if the pool of surplus labour is stagnant and larger than is necessary to provide an adequate labour supply for future industrial development on which the recovery of the areas depends. But "the denudation of these

---

[1] Cf. A. D. K. Owen, "The Social Consequences of Industrial Transference" in *The Sociological Review*, Oct., 1937.

[2] S. R. Dennison, *The Location of Industry and the Depressed Areas*, p. 191.

[3] This argument is not invalidated by the fact that a certain number of the most efficient and socially most valuable workers also have preferred unemployment to emigration, because they were attached to their community, either by owning their houses or by their activities for community welfare.

[4] Cf. *Men Without Work*, pp. 77–82.

areas of skilled workers or of the most promising boys and girls available for entry into industry may actually increase unemployment by impeding the development of new industries and in time by decreasing existing industries still further."[1] In the case of the depressed areas it has become evident that large-scale emigration has prejudiced the prospects of economic recovery; this applies to spontaneous emigration as well as to the effects of Government intervention in this respect. It is therefore held that a policy of encouraging emigration and a policy of reconstruction by new industrial development or the adaptation of existing industry to the structural changes are incompatible with each other; that a community which loses rapidly in numbers through emigration cannot recover from depression; that the loss of population has a cumulative effect on the fall of the standard of living and prevents any constructive readjustment. These policies being incompatible with each other, it has been suggested that the only consistent alternative to reconstruction is the evacuation of these areas.

A more practical proposition is submitted by Professor Dennison. Any policy should be based on the discrimination between different types of areas, and also between different classes of unemployed in each area. There are areas which can be classed as hopelessly derelict, whose population-carrying capacity has become negligible because the natural resources on which their existence was based have become exhausted or valueless owing to the discovery of more suitable raw materials, and because they are geographically isolated or for other reasons unsuitable for the location of expanding industries. Evacuation and perhaps the transplantation of whole communities to better locations within the British Empire seems in this case the appropriate policy.

Complete evacuations are not unusual in the history of internal migration; one example is provided by deserted towns in U.S.A. mining districts. But it is obvious that difficulties increase with the size of the population concerned, with the proportion of unemployables it contains, and with the amount of capital invested in immobile durable consumption goods, apart from the question whether the economic advantages of evacuation would be sufficient to outweigh the amount of individual misery which would be created by such compulsory uprooting.

Professor Dennison believes that these difficulties could be

[1] Owen, *loc. cit.*

met by a compromise: The unemployed population of these derelict areas should be divided into those who have and those who have not potentially high employment value. The emigration of the former category should be encouraged and assisted; the latter class should remain in the distressed areas and should be assisted by "palliatives", by measures which are designed not to solve the problem, but simply to alleviate its symptoms. Such palliatives comprise schemes for land settlement and subsistence production.

For the areas which are depressed but not derelict a policy of reconstruction should be pursued by the encouragement of industrial development. Such a policy implies that emigration should comprise only those categories which are of relatively low employment value for the area, and a pool of unemployed should be left from which demand for labour could be satisfied in the course of future industrial development. Finally, in the case of some areas, it may be difficult to decide whether they must be considered as definitely derelict or whether there are prospects of recovery. Here a combination of the two policies may be unavoidable. But discrimination should then take place; the emigration of particular types of people should be encouraged, while the retention of other types is essential for the future of the district.

We have discussed the emigration policy of the distressed areas at some length, though it is largely a problem of internal migration,[1] while our main object is an inquiry into the mechanism of external migration. We have done so because it offers us an opportunity to study the economic effects of heavy emigration under conditions of modern capitalistic production and of population decline. As mentioned above, external migration had in the past, apart from the particular case of Ireland, no conspicuous effect on the growth of the population of the country of emigration, and when the emigration countries became more susceptible to losses through emigration owing to their reduced rate of natural increase, conditions in the immigration countries had made large-scale emigration impossible. But it is probable that such emigration would have occurred and may occur in the future in spite of the changed trend of population, provided that emigration is free and that the immigration countries are open to either free or regulated large-scale immigration.

---

[1] The percentage of emigrants from the depressed areas who left for overseas is negligible, mainly owing to the lack of opportunities in the countries of immigration during this period.

The discussion of certain aspects of internal migration seems relevant to our subject for yet another reason. The distinction between external and internal migration depends largely on the existence of sovereign States. In "a world where the relations between nations can be transformed in a given period of time, as the relations between England, Scotland and Wales have been transformed,'[1] i.e. if the United Nations were to set up a world organization involving a drastic restriction of State sovereignity, the distinction between *external* and *internal* migration would tend to lose its significance. An international authority would then have to cope with problems similar to, but by no means identical with those of Britain's distressed areas before the war.

c. CONCLUSIONS

The conclusions to be drawn from the experience of the depressed areas for the emigration policy of sovereign States are evident. Excluding the case of evacuation, it appears that the usefulness of emigration for the rest of the population under present economic and demographic conditions is limited; that mere economic considerations would justify—from the viewpoint of the State—quantitative and qualitative restriction of emigration. Certain categories of potential emigrants of high employment value should be excluded from emigration, and the total volume of emigration should not be so large as to bring about a population decline unless the adverse effects of such a decline can be met by the measures mentioned in the previous chapter, so that the possible advantages of smaller numbers outweigh the disadvantages of a numerical decline. Such a policy implies interference with the free mobility of the individual, exerted by his own country, which in a democracy is tolerable only under war conditions.[2] If we take for granted the right of the individual to emigrate, the experience of the distressed areas suggests what limitations are set to a policy of encouraging emigration.

4. METHODS OF SETTLEMENT

Having discussed the adverse consequences of excessive emigration, we return to the immigration countries. In Section 2

[1] Mr. Anthony Eden in the House of Commons, November 22nd, 1945.
[2] This does not exclude taxes on the transfer of property, provided they are not prohibitive

of this chapter we were concerned with problems of excessive immigration, in particular with the need for adjusting the volume of immigration to the receiving country's capacity to absorb and assimilate its immigrants. This capacity, it was pointed out, is determined in part by the way in which the new arrivals are settled. We have now to consider the relative merits of alternative methods of settlement.

A distinction must be made between settlement by infiltration and group settlement. Both agricultural and industrial immigration may take either of these forms. Infiltration has been defined as "the settlement, whether on the land or otherwise, of single individuals or families in existing communities as and where they may find room for themselves or room may be found for them."[1] Group settlement means the organized settlement of whole groups of immigrants in more or less segregated and self-contained communities. Such settlements are usually based on agricultural production; they are often concerned with the opening up of hitherto uncultivated land. A third form, self-contained and segregated individual settlement, is of merely historical interest.

A. INFILTRATION

It has been estimated that in the past infiltration has accounted for from 96 to 99 per cent of the total annual volume of migration.[2] It has been thus predominant mainly because it involves less risk, less planning, and less cost than group settlement. So long as the numbers concerned are relatively small it is not likely to produce friction or dislocation. This applies in particular to various forms of nominated immigration. Australia and New Zealand, for instance, received over a period of years only "nominated" immigrants. These are admitted on application by a friend or relative in the receiving country, who undertakes to look after his nominee, to provide employment for him, and if necessary to support him.

In Brazil the "letter of invitation" (*carta da chamada*) serves a similar purpose. It may be issued by relatives already settled in the country, or for agricultural work by the government of one of the Brazilian States. An agricultural company or an individual landowner is also entitled to issue such letters of

[1] Report of the Inter-Departmental Committee on Migration Policy, 1934, Cmd. 4689, p. 26.
[2] *Ibid.*, p. 27.

invitation,[1] but the worker must then hold a contract of employment covering a minimum period of three years in the first case and one year in the second. In the U.S.A. the applicant, except in special cases, has to hold sworn affidavits from friends or relatives already resident there.

Broadly speaking, immigration by nomination may be regarded as a fairly efficient means of avoiding the friction which might be produced by the infiltration of an equal number of non-nominated immigrants. Moreover the newcomer is greatly assisted by the personal ties with his neighbours or employers in adapting himself to the new way of life. But mass immigration as envisaged by many new countries cannot be achieved by this system alone. Its restrictive effect is easily seen. Would-be immigrants who may be well suited in other respects have to be rejected if they have no friends or relatives to nominate them, and residents in the new country willing to sponsor and provide work for immigrants may not know of any suitable candidate.

Infiltration is not confined to nominated immigrants. Its shortcomings become evident if it is regarded as a means of absorbing large-scale immigration in sparsely populated countries. Four main factors must be taken into account:

1. Immigrants tend to flow firstly into the large cities, secondarily into settled rural areas. The "empty spaces" would remain empty and the maldistribution of population characteristic of most new countries would be accentuated.

2. The absorptive capacity of the areas preferred by immigrants is relatively small. Mass immigration by infiltration is therefore conductive to the formation of bottlenecks. The local rate of economic expansion tends to be outpaced by the rate of immigration, with all the adverse consequences described in section 2.

3. The previous statement that immigration by infiltration requires little public expenditure needs qualification if large numbers are involved. A considerable amount of private and public investment is required to provide the newcomers with shelter and work in order to ensure their smooth absorption. To avoid slum conditions new streets or suburbs will have to be built; existing public utilities will have to be greatly extended at costs which may be higher than the initial costs of a new settlement in a sparsely populated development area.

4. Immigration by infiltration may lead to unorganized urban settlements of national groups because of the tendency of immigrants to take up residence where other members of their national group are already living. It is convenient to discuss the significance of this tendency under the next heading.

B. GROUP SETTLEMENT

An immigration policy which aims at a well-balanced population distribution, at making use of unexploited resources, and

---

[1] "Immigration and Settlement in Brazil, Argentina and Uruguay," *International Labour Review*, Vol. XXXV, No. 2, p. 219 (Feb., 1937) (F. Maurette and E. Siewers).

at opening-up undeveloped or under-developed areas cannot rely on infiltration as the only method of settlement. Under such conditions there is a wide scope for the group settlement of immigrants in both rural and urban communities. The opening-up of the land in America during the frontier period took place in an entirely different way. Broadly speaking, four stages of development can be distinguished. The professional trapper and Indian trader came first. These were followed by the "true frontiersman". All the equipment he needed was an axe, a rifle, a knife and a frying pan. He built a cabin near the river and cleared an acre or so of land to raise some Indian corn for himself and his horse, but lived mainly on deer and the fruits of the forest. He moved on when the "pioneer farmer" arrived. The latter brought a family, more tools and some cows and pigs, brought ten or fifteen acres under cultivation, planted wheat and oats and added a vegetable and fruit garden to his farm. He had to sell some of his produce in the nearest market in order to buy his land and pay taxes due to the government. When not favoured by good harvests his obligations exceeded his returns, and he often had to sell or to abandon his farm. He, in his turn, was succeeded by the "permanent farmer" who had capital enough to pay cash for his land and for improvements and who could extend his holding. His success depended largely on an improvement in marketing conditions due to the development of urban settlements.

If this interpretation is correct,[1] the opening-up of the North American continent, at least in its first stages, was largely due to individual enterprise, organized group settlement seeming to have been of little importance. The contribution of immigrants appears to have been relatively small. It was an American population reinforced by immigrants from abroad, as W. W. Trimble has put it, that opened the mines, subdued the forests and covered the prairies. The newcomers did not possess the experience and technique without which pioneer farming was bound to fail. "It was when the pioneer farmers departed that the immigrant farmers made their appearance. . . . And while the immigrants were moving in, the Americans were moving out . . . not all of them, but enough to give the invaders an opening wedge which they spread quietly and steadily in subsequent decades."[2] Normally the immigrant farmer bought a

[1] *Ibid.*
[2] M. L. Hansen, *The Immigrant in American History*, 1940, p. 67.

farm that was already cleared, If he came with capital he could do so soon after his arrival. Otherwise he and his family had to work in the towns or as farmhands, railway or road builders until they could buy a farm out of their savings. The Homestead Act of 1862 provided a powerful incentive for the immigrant to try his hand as pioneer settler. Under this Act he could secure a deed to a hundred and sixty acre tract of his own choice free of charge by cultivating at least part of it for a period of five years. Many immigrants hastened to make use of this offer without having the experience and capital—estimated at about $1000— necessary to make the homestead a success. Those who failed went back as wage-earners to the industrial cities or older agricultural communities; others took up employment for several months every year near their homsestead. Their savings provided them with the funds on which their survival as homesteaders depended. But it soon became apparent that the immigrant had a much better chance of success if he bought a farm or developed land in the older states on terms which were relatively favourable during this period of free land. By 1890 the public lands which were given away free or for a nominal fee were practically all gone; all land suitable for settlement and other natural resources had passed into private hands.

Though free land proved a gift of doubtful value for the immigrant, the statement seems to be true that "the passing of the frontier marked the closing of an epoch and the removing of the main drawing card to N.W. Europeans".[1] With the growing scarcity of fertile land, land prices rose, and less fertile land was taken under cultivation, so that new settlement meant diminishing returns. New capital intensive agricultural methods were developed and it was no longer thought feasible to put settlers with modest means on the land: American immigration became largely city-bound.

It is obvious that an enormous wastage of human effort and natural resources was implied in this method—or rather lack of method—of peopling a continent. In a modern, progressive world man and natural resources have become more valuable

---

[1] The forces which led to the opening-up of the North American Continent have not yet been fully explored. Undoubtedly the vast opportunities of the uncolonized regions exerted a powerful pull on the American, brought up in the pioneer traditions of his forefathers. But the literature on this subject indicates that push motives were by no means absent. Cf. Frederick J. Turner, *The Frontier in American History* (1920); W. J. Trimble, "The Influence of the Passing Lands", *Atlantic Monthly*, June, 1914; M. W. Hansen, *The Immigrant in American History*, 1940; R. C. M. Overton, *The Growth of the American Economy*, 1944.

and the opening-up of new sparsely populated regions depends on a common, thoroughly organized effort on the part of the immigrants and the native population.[1]

The difficulties likely to arise from the large-scale settlement of immigrants may be grouped under three heads:

(1) the formation of unassimilated minorities;
(2) costs;
(3) lack of suitable immigrants.

(1) The group settlement of immigrants normally implies that the newcomers have little contact with the native population. It was argued in Section 2 that the process of absorption and assimilation was greatly impeded by the tendency of immigrants to congregate in the great cities near their port of arrival and to live there as closed national groups. We saw that the settlement of groups of immigrants on the land in isolation from the natives also tended to delay their assimilation. But it does not necessarily follow from this that the newcomer's integration would be easier if immediately after his arrival he gave up any association with other immigrants of the same nationality. In the case of unorganized mass immigration adjustment normally occurs in two stages: "In the first stage of its stay in the foreign country, the immigrant group tends to adjust itself to the new situation as a closed single unit. Later some of its members prefer to make their own adjustment. We speak of collective adjustment as long as the group holds together in some way or other. As long as collective adjustment prevails, the single member of the group does not act according to his immediate personal interests but as a member of the whole social body. It is mainly his feeling of weakness and isolation in hostile surroundings which makes him subject his personal wishes to the requirements of the group. At this stage, therefore, mutual help and spontaneous co-operation is the rule, and each man uses his talents in the interests of the group. In addition, we find the whole group identifying themselves with the single member should he be attacked from without."[2]

Clearly, the extent to which the immigrant needs the help of his group to adjust himself to the new situation largely depends on the attitude of the native population. If they are co-operative the new environments may appear to him strange and difficult to cope with, but perhaps less hostile than those in his old country.

[1] J. Davie, *Immigration*, p. 181.
[2] K. Mannheim, *Diagnosis of Our Time*, p. 80.

But, even under such favourable circumstances intercourse with other immigrants of his own nationality, their experience and advice, will greatly assist him in overcoming material and psychological problems of adjustment.

The process of adjustment in two stages typical of the urban mass immigration before the 1914 war did not work very well. In many cases the second stage, individual adjustment, was never reached, or not until the second or third generation. Without a steady inflow of new immigrants the group is bound to stagnate, since its most vigorous elements are the first to leave. Moreover, even successful individual adjustment is painful and costly. It means giving up old associations and a second change of social environment. Conflicts can be greatly reduced with organized group settlement. It can be organized in such a way that both factors of adjustment, assistance from the old group and friendly contact with the native population, operate simultaneously.

How can this be done? Obviously it is not possible to suggest a formula of general validity. Too much depends upon particular circumstances, the location of the new settlement, the amount of capital available, the numbers involved, and not least the cultural background of natives and immigrants. However, it seems that prospects of success are fairly good in most cases, and that the optimistic view with regard to Brazil, quoted below, reflects the situation in many other immigration countries.

"The danger that assimilation will take place too slowly is really non-existent when a group of foreign immigrants are settled in a social environment which is already formed and find themselves side by side with a population of the country's own nationality or even with communities of aliens of other nationalities. Far from delaying assimilation, the settlement of groups of immigrants belonging to the same nationality—provided, of course, that it does not take place on too large a scale—is, in the opinion of the writers of this report, more likely to promote it, for besides the question of linguistic and social assimilation there is also that of adaptation to new living conditions, a process which is sometimes very difficult and is in any case more urgent. During this period of adaptation mutual aid, both material and moral, and a team spirit will develop more easily among settlers of the same origin. Constant contact with the social environment, particularly in the case of so friendly and cordial a people as the Brazilians, will then of itself bring about that assimilation which, if the settlers failed to adapt themselves to their new living conditions and to succeed in their new life, might very well never take place at all, or at best only at a lower social level, where the immigrant would indeed merge into the national population of the new country, but at the price of forfeiting the best of their own native qualities."[1]

Even in the favourable conditions which the authors of this Report presume, friendly and close contact with native groups and assimilation of their cultural background cannot be expected to develop automatically. It can be encouraged by various means, such as:

The teaching of the native language should be compulsory. Suitable teachers should be provided by the educational authorities of the receiving country, but there is no reason for excluding the use of the language of the sending countries in schools.[2]

It might be desirable to set up mixed settlements with a majority of immigrants of the same nationality and a minority of experienced native settlers and immigrants of other nationalities. In any case expert advice from qualified natives must be available for a number of years.

The new settlers should be encouraged to form co-operatives, e.g. for the purchase of raw materials and capital equipment and for the marketing of their production. These co-operatives could become affiliated to existing national organizations of the new country. The same applies to Trade Unions, sports clubs and to the organization of welfare and leisure activities in general.

The opening-up of new areas should not be done piecemeal, for this would leave the settlements in isolation during the first critical years of development, but according to a plan covering a whole region. If the available man power and capital is not sufficient for the development of several regions at the same time, efforts should rather be concentrated on one particular region, than small-scale development started in different regions.

c. Costs

During the inter-war period a number of development schemes had to be discontinued mainly because their costs were prohibitive. This is illustrated by the history of the Migration and Settlement Agreement of 1925 between the British Government and the Commonwealth of Australia. The agreement aimed at the satisfactory settlement in Australia of 450,000 persons from the U.K. within ten years. The Commonwealth undertook to raise loans up to £34,000,000 to be used for "the acquisition,

---

[1] Maurette and Siewers, *op. cit.*

[2] A Brazilian Legislative Decree of Aug., 1939, aims at speeding up the assimilation of the descendants of aliens by education and the compulsory use of the national language and their incorporation in patriotic associations and organizations for pre-Military training (*I.L.O. Yearbook*, 1933–40, p. 24). It seems doubtful whether assimilation can be speeded up by totalitarian methods.

resumption and clearing of land suitable for farms; advances to farmers for the erection of cottages for employees; farm settlement; afforestation; construction of certain public works, e.g. railways, roads, bridges, irrigation and hydro-electric works and similar enterprises tending to assist development in rural areas." Britain agreed to make a payment of £150,000 for every £750,000 loan raised by the Australian Government subject to the provision that, for every contribution of £150,000, ten thousand assisted migrants should be satisfactorily settled within 10 years. The most ambitious project approved under this agreement was the Western Australian Group Settlement Scheme which aimed at the settlement of 75,000 persons. The scheme had to be suspended since the cost was far greater than was expected. The indebtedness of the settlers to the State had to be reduced to an average of £1,000 per holding. Only holdings for about 1700 families or 7500 persons could be created, of which 1,000 were occupied by migrant settlers and their families. At the end of the first three years only two-thirds of the original settlers remained on their holdings. They are now carrying on with good prospects of success. Similar experiences have been registered in other parts of Australia and in Canada.

Failure was often due to factors which could have been easily avoided, such as selection of unsuitable sites, insufficient preparatory work, inefficient administration, and mistakes in the selections of the settlers.

The failures explain the negative attitude of the British Overseas Settlement Board to large-scale land settlement schemes. In their Report of May 1938 they reach the following conclusions: "We see no reason to suppose that conditions will be more favourable in the future than they have been in the past for large-scale land-settlement schemes, and apart from the fact that the number of people who can be settled under such schemes is entirely disproportionate to the expenditure involved, the risks of failure are so great and the consequences of such failures would be so serious, that we cannot recommend that the U.K. Government should participate in schemes of this nature save in very exceptional circumstances. . . ."[1]

The Dominions were in full agreement with this view. The small number of selected (mainly British) immigrants which they admitted could be much more easily absorbed by the process of infiltration. Since the war, however, the problem of peopling

[1] Cmd. 5766, p. 28.

the Commonwealth has become a national issue, and ambitious schemes are being considered with a view to attaining a rapid population increase by immigration.[1]

In this setting the question whether costs are prohibitive or not cannot be decided by applying commercial standards. Group settlement on the land combined with industrial development may in the long run prove a sound social investment. The pre-war economic structure of the Dominions with their surplus of agricultural production and rural population would hardly have justified any expansion of the agricultural sector.

There are two ways of combining agricultural with industrial development. Broadly speaking, schemes may aim at attaining the desirable ratio between primary and secondary production either in each settlement or within each development region. The former policy would give rise to mixed communities, the latter to separate industrial and rural settlements. In the past, group settlement of immigrants has been confined mainly to settlement on the land. Urban group settlement of immigrants has yet to reach the experimental stage. Tentatively it may be suggested that separate communities are preferable with schemes on a very large scale backed by ample financial resources.

With regard to Empire migration it has been sometimes suggested that urban immigrant settlement could be made a success if whole industrial communities were transferred from Britain to sparsely populated parts of the Empire. "Take the devastated areas South of the Thames, take Hull, take many other cities. Is it to be assumed that the industries which existed in those places before are going to justify their moving back to those centres of population? Are they going to be dispersed in the United Kingdom or are they going to be moved partly overseas?" asked Lord Barnby in the House of Lords on Empire Day 1943. His appeal and other schemes on similar lines met with little response either in sending or receiving countries;[2] they would contribute to the solution of the financial problem, but have little else to recommend them.

The preceding argument raises an issue which is relevant to immigration by group settlement in general: the relative shares in the cost of settlement of the individual immigrant, of private enterprise, and of public investment.

---

[1] For particulars see P E P Broadsheet No. 226, *People for the Commonwealth*, Oct., 1944.
[2] Cmd. 4689, p. 32.

i. *Individual Settlement*

Clearly immigrant farmers with independent means are from the financial point of view the most desirable settlers. Since they can usually pay off the market price of their holdings in a relatively short time, they can be settled either individually or in groups in areas already opened-up. The disadvantage of the higher prices of land is outweighed by the advantages of better marketing opportunities and better access to public services, cultural institutions, shopping centres, etc. It is of great importance that the settler in under- or undeveloped regions should also have some financial stake in the venture. If he starts with no capital of his own, interest and amortisation may exceed his returns, especially during the first years. Moreover without capital investment of his own, he may be tempted to walk off if the results of his work do not fully come up to his expectations.[1]

Unfortunately would-be immigrants of the first type are scarce, and relatively few of the second type are prepared to undergo the hardship and risk associated with pioneer settlement. The two ways then open will be discussed presently.

ii. *Private Enterprise*

Private settlement companies have played an important part in the opening-up of new land. "In some countries, practically no official organization exists, while in others, although they exist, they frequently have very limited financial resources and a very small field of action."[2] The Conference of Experts on migration for settlement convened by the I.L.O. in 1938 made it abundantly clear that it is undesirable to leave the organization of migration for settlement to commercial and speculative undertakings. They are ill-suited for this task in various respects. Often they are unable to provide the efficient organization and the considerable amount of capital indispensable for modern land development. Waste State land may be available at a nominal price, but in most new countries practically all fertile and well-located land is in private ownership. What is left is either submarginal or far from communications. In either case success depends largely on heavy capital expenditure and State assistance.

---

[1] This argument was taken into account in E. J. Wakefield's settlement schemes. Cf. Wakefield, *The Art of Colonization* (1849).

[2] "The Organisation of Migration for Settlement," Report of the International Conference on Migration for Settlement, Geneva, 1938, *I.L.O. Review*, May, 1938,

There are still vast reserves of privately-owned land extensively cultivated or not cultivated at all in under-developed regions which should offer much better opportunities for settlement than most of the State land, provided that the would-be settler could buy his holding at a fair price and on reasonable terms. If such land is bought, broken up, and resold on the instalment plan by purely commercial companies, the immigrant settler runs the risk of forfeiting his holding if he is unable to pay the instalments, which may be much higher than the return he can expect from his work. The company stands to gain from his failure, for it can resell the holding with all the improvements made by the first occupier to another applicant. "The settler requires very easy conditions of reimbursement, involving long-term credit operations far exceeding the capacity of a private settlement organization."[1] Land-owning railway companies in North and South America are in a position to offer holdings on more favourable terms than other private companies, since part of their profit comes from an increase in their own traffic brought by the new settlers. The land still under their control, however, is not very extensive.

The granting of settlement concessions to private companies has often proved a failure from the point of view both of the community and of the settlers concerned. "It has brought into suspicion a system which if cautiously practised may nevertheless be beneficial to all concerned; that suspicion now hampers even those private organizations whose purpose is solely or mainly social."[2] In Argentina and Chile official land has therefore for many years been used only for official settlement schemes.

In a number of new countries settlement transactions of private companies are subject to State supervision with a view to protecting the settler from exploitation. Such measures do not solve the problem. They tend to lead to a contraction in the operations of commercial undertakings, because prospective returns cease to be attractive to private enterprise.

iii. *Public Investment*

The preceding argument leads to the conclusion that in order to make immigration for settlement a success public authorities in the receiving countries must take an active part in its organization.

[1] *Op. cit.*, p. 370.
[2] Maurette and Siewers, *op. cit.*, p. 49.

The following recommendations were adopted by the I.L.O. Conference already mentioned:[1]

(1) The Conference suggests that it would be desirable to consider the development and, in immigration countries in which they do not already exist, the creation, of official technical, financial and other organizations responsible for immigration and settlement.

(2) If occasion arises, private organizations should also be developed and encouraged, if they furnish a guarantee, either through their rules or through the participation in them of the State or of public financial institutions or through the control exercised over them by the authorities, that the settlers' interests will not be sacrificed to commercial ends.

It is obvious that receiving countries will be prepared to allocate public funds to the promotion of settlement schemes for immigrants only if they can expect some return from this expenditure. Their criterion is not necessarily the prospective yield in the commercial sense; social, economic and demographic considerations which have been discussed in Chapter IV may justify the subsidization of settlement schemes for immigrants.

The success of large-scale immigration whether for settlement or otherwise depends however to a large extent on capital imports. The close correlation between immigration and foreign investment will be dealt with in Chapter VI. In the present context the question arises whether sending countries should participate in organizing the immigration of their own nationals. The active interest which Great Britain took during the inter-war period in the settlement schemes for British immigrants in the Dominions has been outlined on pp. 157–159. But the promotion of such schemes was regarded as an essential part of Britain's Empire policy, and financial assistance was confined to Empire migration. The scope for co-operation between sending and receiving countries is less wide in the absence of special incentives such as the Empire idea. The direct participation of the sending country in the financing of a particular development scheme will normally be impracticable.[2] Even so the sending country can greatly contribute to the financial success of such schemes. It can assist the receiving country in selecting suitable settlers. It can assist the would-be settler in the liquidation and transfer of his property. Co-operation of this kind was the object of some of the bilateral agreements referred to on page 58.

Obviously the financial assistance of approved settlement

---

[1] I.L.O., *Technical and Financial International Co-operation with regard to Migration for Settlement*, p. 142.

[2] The arrangement made before the war between a Paraguayan company and a settlement undertaking controlled by three Polish State banks is such an attempt.

schemes would offer a wide field for the activities of an international migration agency.

D. LACK OF SUITABLE IMMIGRANTS

The following qualifications apart from good character and health are required from the ideal applicant for land settlement schemes:

(1) He must be easily assimilable;
(2) He must have some capital;
(3) He must have some experience in farming.

Unfortunately all three do not very often go together. Immigrants from Great Britain and North-Western Europe, preferred in the U.S. and in the Dominions, are relatively scarce, and most of them lack farming experience and are ill-adapted to agricultural life. Suitable farm workers can easily be recruited from non-preferred countries, but most of them have not even their passage-money. They would therefore have nothing but their work to contribute to the initial costs of the settlement. Moreover farming experience gained in the old country is only of limited use under the entirely different conditions overseas.

(1) The problem of assimilability has been discussed on pages 135–141 and various means of speeding up assimilation have been suggested on pages 155–157. If our argument is right, the group settlement of unassimilated immigrants does not offer insuperable difficulties.

(2) The settler without any means has little prospect of success. Only under exceptional circumstances he will be able to finance his venture through outside agencies. If the receiving country were prepared to provide sites, capital equipment, etc., for settlers with no means of their own, it would have to give preferences to native applicants.

Opinion is divided whether immigrants with very little means should be encouraged to take up farming in group settlements on a subsistence basis, that is to say, farming that cannot be expected to yield more than the satisfaction of the most elementary needs. Submarginal soil, insufficient capital equipment, and isolated location with no opportunities for marketing the product are factors likely to produce conditions of subsistence farming. There is little doubt that millions could be settled under such primitive conditions at relatively little cost. Before the war it could be said that it was almost impossible to find in the emigration countries of Europe would-be settlers prepared to ask no more than the bare necessities of life at an extremely low standard. It is too early to say whether the same argument applies to post-war Europe with millions of uprooted persons and the prospect of starvation in many regions. But the receiving country also, even if sparsely populated, has reason to object to immigration for subsistence settlement. As the I.L.O. Report mentioned above puts it: Immigration established in such primitive conditions "would contribute nothing to the economic prosperity of the country—on the contrary, it would act as a dead weight hampering the social progress which every organized community must promote. In other words, in order that settlement may not be foredoomed to failure, there must be a chance, however small, of selling part of the produce of the land, and so by exchange of obtaining the goods and services essential to a civilized life. This is in practice the limit to the immigration of settlers in a country otherwise blessed with unlimited natural wealth."[1]

Under certain conditions pioneer settlement in undeveloped regions may offer a fair chance of future prosperity. If efficiently managed it tends to pass gradually out of the subsistence stage. Once the virgin soil is brought under cultivation and crops can be produced, the standard of living can be raised by a more developed division of labour. Economic progress in the receiving country is likely to lead to further development of the new region, and in particular improved means of transport may enable the settlement to find a market for its surplus products. Preconditions of success are that the population of the new community be large enough to make specialization profitable and that close co-operation between its members be ensured.

There are however other and perhaps more promising ways of settling the would-be immigrant of rural origin who has not sufficient means of his own. They tend to reduce the risk and the hardship which the pioneer settler has to face. The underlying idea is to find openings for the newcomer where he may get experience and can earn the money which he needs for taking up farming under less primitive conditions. Such openings are, of course, rare so long as ample supply of agricultural labour keeps wages at a very low level. But farm workers are likely to become scarce with further progress in the industrialization of new countries. Immigrants without capital could join group settlement schemes as labourers with a view to becoming members

[1] Maurette and Siewers, op. cit., p. 223.

at a later stage. They would be needed for road building and irrigation work; under the guidance of experts and provided with adequate capital equipment they would have to do the preliminary clearing, the preparation of the land, and the erection of buildings not only for their prospective holdings but also for other holdings, to be handed over to other members prepared to pay for the pioneer work.

(3) The suggestion has been made of establishing in the new countries special farms for selecting and training intending settlers.[1] During the period of training the applicants would cultivate the farm under skilled supervision and receive a share of the produce of their labour which should cover a substantial part of the initial capital expenditure necessary for taking up land and starting farming on their own account. After the end of the training period they would also be eligible for loans on favourable terms. The main objections to this plan are that such training farms would hardly be self-supporting, and that a long period of training and uncertainty about their future prospects would not appeal to many intending farmers. They would probably prefer to start work on their holdings as soon as possible under expert supervision. The obvious disadvantage of the latter method is the difficulty of eliminating unsuitable applicants, which tends to raise the percentage of failures and may endanger the success of the whole settlement.

The need for training is, of course, more urgent in the case of intending settlers without previous agricultural experience or experience in farm management. Reports from Jewish Settlements in Palestine indicate that under certain favourable conditions immigrants with an entirely urban background could be turned into successful settlers if they could draw upon expert supervision. But undoubtedly the risk of failure is very high. On the other hand there is reason to believe that immigrants from urban districts after a thorough agricultural training can be successfully settled on the land.

5. THE SCOPE FOR INTERNATIONAL PLANNING

Our inquiry into the usefulness of migration to the immigration and emigration countries sought to show that to a large

[1] For Canada, cf. Cmd. 4689, p. 30; for Venezuela: "The Organisation of Immigration and Land Settlement in Venezuela," Dr. Enrique *Siewers, I.L.O. Review*, July, 1939, p. 41.

extent general interest, the interest of the migrants and that of
the two countries directly concerned were in harmony under the
economic conditions which prevailed up to the First World War,
and that therefore free migration within a *laissez-faire* system was
an outstanding factor in economic progress during that period,
though even then regulated migration might have produced still
better results. We found that since then things have changed,
and that harmony of interests can be presumed for only a small
part of the migratory movements which would take place were
free migration to be resumed. It is certainly true that political
considerations, and the rise of economic and political nationalism
are largely responsible for the contraction of international
migration (and trade), and prevented any adjustment of the disparities between the standards of living in immigration and
emigration countries, but it was apparent that the self-adjusting
mechanism of the free system is likely to work less satisfactorily
with the reversal of the population trend, with fewer unused
natural resources in the immigration countries, and with the
adoption of more capitalistic methods of production.

At the beginning of this chapter we pointed out in general
terms the advantages of regulated as compared with free migration. We can now arrive at more precise statements. In discussing
the absorptive capacity of immigration countries we found that
one factor on which it depends is the standard of living which is
taken as the basis for the estimate. The absorptive capacity may be
relatively small, if it is determined by the immigration countries
with high standards of living in such a way as to cover only such
immigration as can be absorbed without a reduction of their
present high standard. We argued that this can be presumed
in the case of independent States, but that it would be desirable
from the general viewpoint and from that of the prospective
migrants to smooth out the wide divergencies between the
standards of living in immigration and emigration countries
even if that should involve a reduction of the standard of living
in the former. A similar consideration might apply to the regulation of emigration. It follows that the volume of migration
resulting from this kind of regulation by sovereign States cannot
be considered as an optimum. It might therefore be suggested
by advocates of the free system that free migration may after all—
in spite of its shortcomings—be preferable to regulated migration.
If in the light of this objection we examine the prospects and
relative merits of the four migration policies conceivable within a

non-totalitarian society, we can see that our previous statement remains valid.

These four types of policy are:

    (1) Re-establishment of free migration.
    (2) Regulation independently by immigration and emigration countries.
    (3) Regulation of migration by bilateral treaties between individual countries of immigration and emigration.
    (4) Regulation by international planning.

1. RE-ESTABLISHMENT OF FREE MIGRATION

We have seen above that a country can absorb a much larger volume of regulated than of free migration, so that the re-establishment of free migration would with a relatively small volume of immigration lead to a fall in the standard of living of the receiving country and to economic and social dislocation. It is therefore doubtful whether it could be restored without applying compulsion to the States concerned. Such compulsion presupposes the existence of an international executive. But if an international executive existed, the last-mentioned policy (4) seems the best solution of the problem.

The acceptance of the principle of free migration would also exclude a policy of assisted immigration or emigration. If an immigration country attempts to get hold of the most valuable elements of another country by promising them special privileges and by financing their costs of transport, the home country of the prospective emigrants may, instead of outbidding the competitive country, feel justified in raising objections to their departure or to subject it to the payment of special taxes; if, for example, they are just entering working age, the State could reclaim the amount spent on their education, etc. Similar arguments might be used of emigration implying the transfer of property. On the other hand, if the emigration country pays the emigrant in order to get rid of him, the immigration country should be entitled to examine whether he represents a useful increment to its stock. Both assisted immigration and assisted emigration are incompatible with free migration when the axiom of harmony of interests is no longer valid. It is true, however, that State assistance in some form or another accounted in the past for a certain percentage of migration, and it may be still more needed in future in order to bring about the necessary adjustments in the geographical distribution of populations.

Finally, so long as immigration can be used by other countries to gain political influence through their emigrants in the country of immigration, free migration cannot be considered a practical system.

2. INDEPENDENT REGULATION BY THE IMMIGRATION AND EMIGRATION COUNTRIES

The principles which should govern these regulations have already been outlined. In this case assisted migration cannot be objected to. As the States are autonomous in their migration policy, any State can take suitable preventive measures against the migration policy of another State which is opposed to its interests. Often, however, assistance will be in the interests of all concerned; the prospective migrant and both countries would be better off if migration, impossible because the migrant cannot afford the costs of transport, could take place. As we have seen, if autonomous States would regulate migration on the lines of their own economic interests instead of being governed by nationalistic prejudices or the requirements of vested interests, a revival of migratory movements would be possible and would tend to bring some relief to present population pressure, but the volume of migration would be limited to such an amount as would not lower the standard of living in the countries concerned.

3. REGULATION OF MIGRATION BY BILATERAL TREATIES BETWEEN COUNTRIES OF IMMIGRATION AND OF EMIGRATION

Broadly speaking, co-operation between immigration and emigration countries will promote migration and have favourable effects. It depends largely, however, on the bargaining power of the country of emigration how effectively the interests of the emigrants can be safeguarded. As the bargaining power of the most over-populated countries is relatively low, the claims of such countries and of their prospective emigrants will be prejudiced to a certain extent in the negotiation of bilateral treaties.

4. REGULATION BY INTERNATIONAL PLANNING

Though it may be true that migration can never achieve more than a partial cure for maladjustment of population, it seems that a maximum effect in this respect could be produced by international planning; it is difficult to see how the divergent interests discussed in this chapter could be brought into harmony without permanent international co-operation.

It should however be realized that an international migration authority cannot have as its object to press upon the receiving countries an immigration policy against their own interests. Such a policy is bound to fail, so long as the scope of international co-operation is limited by the recognition of vested national interests. Immigrants who are unwanted cannot be easily absorbed, and immigrants who cannot be easily absorbed are unwanted. In either case the immigrants are likely to remain uprooted and to become a liability on the receiving country.

But there are less drastic and more efficient ways in which an international migration authority could promote economic welfare by planned migration. It could urge countries which would be better or as well off with a higher rate of population increase than they have at present to admit a corresponding number of immigrants. It could assist such countries to organize their immigration and to select suitable immigrants. It could sponsor or undertake surveys of the natural resources of under-developed countries. If such resources could not be properly developed because of lack of man-power and capital, earmarked loans should be granted to the receiving country.[1]

Clearly planned international migration is not the only means of international co-operation which could raise the all-round standard of living (cf. Chapter III). But this is no argument against its promotion on the lines suggested above.

[1] At its meeting in October, 1945, the Executive Committee of the Preparatory Committee of the United Nations recommended the establishment, under the Economic and Social Council, of a Demographic Commission whose terms would include "general population and migration questions" (see Information Paper No. 10, United Nations Information Organisation). Apparently the work of this commission will be confined to the study of these questions and to recommendations.

CHAPTER VI

THE EFFECT OF MIGRATION

The broad conclusions we arrived at in the two previous chapters as to the usefulness of migration for both the immigration and emigration countries need further elaboration in two respects:

(1) When discussing the optimum theory of population and the economics of population decline, we found that the purely numerical aspect of the migration problem is of primary importance from the economic viewpoint only under certain conditions. Broadly speaking it could be presumed that unrestricted and unselected immigration into sparsely populated countries with abundant natural resources was likely to yield increasing returns. The application of the law of diminishing returns was seen to be legitimate in the case of unrestricted and unselected emigration from densely populated agricultural areas at a low stage of capitalistic production. Though this law is essentially concerned with variations of homogeneous factors, the fact that migration consists in movements of non-homogeneous populations could in these cases be neglected, as the qualitative differences are of minor importance compared with the economic effect of the changes in population size. We have also seen, however, that the usefulness of migration to countries with highly developed capitalistic production and with a declining rate of population growth is largely determined by the *quality* of the additional population, and therefore that a crude extension of the law of diminishing returns would then be fallacious. But it has so far been assumed that migration would result in an increase or decrease in numbers of the populations concerned equal to the number of migrants. This assumption, though at first sight obvious, needs further investigation, as it covers only the short-run aspect and does not cover possible implications on the growth of the populations in both the countries concerned which might be caused by migratory movements.

(2) We have suggested that the usefulness of migration for the countries concerned depended upon its effect on their standard of living. The concept of the standard of living, as we have seen in Chapter III, becomes problematic when applied to countries

with an advanced division of labour, wide differences of real income among the population, and different economic interests in the various groups. Clearly the effect of migration on the standard of living of these groups is significantly different. Normally, immigration which implies an increased labour supply may be useful to entrepreneurs, landowners and trade, but may have adverse effects on the standard of living of the working class in so far as migrant competes with native labour; on the other hand immigration of capitalists and entrepreneurs may be beneficial to the native working class but detrimental to native entrepreneurs and capitalists. We must therefore extend our inquiry by examining the effects of migration on the various factors which determine the standard of living of a community as a whole and of the groups of which it consists.

1. THE EFFECT OF MIGRATION FROM THE DEMOGRAPHIC VIEWPOINT

A. THE QUANTITATIVE ASPECT

i. *Malthus' Theory*

Though common sense would suggest that immigration involves an increase of population in the country of immigration and a corresponding decrease in the country of emigration, closer investigation shows that a qualification of this simple proposition may be necessary with respect to the effect of migration on the growth of the native stock in the receiving country as well as on the growth of the population in the homeland. We have already mentioned Malthus' attitude towards this problem. Holding that population would continually exert pressure on subsistence, he consistently concluded that in the long run migration would leave unaffected the size of the population in both the countries concerned. Migration might be useful and proper from a general standpoint in so far as it results in a more general cultivation of the earth and a wider extension of civilization, but the country of emigration can at best expect some temporary relief from pressure on subsistence. The losses would almost immediately be made up by earlier marriages and increased fertility, so that pressure would be soon as great as before. The State therefore has no reason to prevent its subjects from emigrating; any fear of depopulation from emigration is unfounded, the more so as people feel attachment to their homes and are prepared to emigrate only if in extreme poverty, or for political reasons; it would be "cruelty and injustice" to detain them.[1] Immigrants into a sparsely populated country would rapidly increase owing to the lack of pressure and consequently of the positive checks, but any immigration into a country with no unpeopled lands would inevitably reduce the birth-rate of the native stock.

The rapid population increase which occurred after the beginning of the Industrial Revolution was accompanied by a steady rise in the general standard of living; more recently the net reproductive rates of sparsely populated countries with extremely high standards of living have fallen below unity. In both cases the pessimistic view to which Malthus' theory leads proved unwarranted.

ii. *Pearl's Theory*

Numerous attempts have been made to state a natural law of population growth which avoids the shortcomings of Malthus' theory. Among these the theories of Pearl and of Gini are of special interest in connection with the migration problem, as they explain the effect of migration on the growth of population differently. Raymond Pearl maintains that human populations in a geographical area follow the same characteristic cycle of growth which he had found in laboratory experiments with lower living beings and which can be adequately described by a mathematical curve.[2] The basic postulate of this biological law is that increasing density of population is associated with adverse changes in birth-rates and death-rates, i.e. that the death-rate varies directly with the density of the population and the rate of reproduction inversely but according to the same law. The population grows at first slowly, but gains impetus as it grows, passing gradually into a state of rapid growth until a maximum of rapidity is reached; then it increases more and more slowly until finally there is no perceptible growth at all.[3] Pearl concluded from his statistical study of human population-growth

---

[1] Malthus, *An Essay on Population*, Vol 2, p. 36 (Everyman Ed.).

[2] The logistic curve which was first used by Verhulst in 1838 as an expression of the law of population growth. The equation of this curve is: $\frac{1}{y_0} = K + ab^x$. The three constants K, a, b can be calculated from the population size at different years. K represents the upper limit at which the population tends to become stationary.

[3] R. Pearl, "On the Rate of Growth of the Population of the U.S. since 1790 and its Mathematical Representation". *Proc. Nat. Acad. Sci.*, Vol. 6, No. 6, *Studies in Human Biology; The Biology of Population Growth*.

that this cycle is not sensibly influenced by the host of economic and social events which are supposed to affect it of logical necessity. Plotting the census counts of the U.S.A. population from 1790 to 1920, he found that the curve so obtained followed the logistic curve with remarkable precision. It shows no separate or disturbing effect from immigration in spite of the wide fluctuations of the volume of immigration over the period.[1] The sole effect of net immigration is—according to his interpretation—somewhat to steepen the general upward slope of the curve, i.e. the population may reach the later stages of the cycle more quickly than it would have done without immigration. He infers from this observation that Benjamin Franklin was right when he suggested that for the growth of populations migration was an unimportant factor as compared with natural increase.[2]

Pearl's argument becomes less convincing when reduced to its proper significance. The logistic equation is, as suggested by A. L. Bowley,[3] well adapted to represent rather roughly the recorded changes of population in selected countries; it expresses what may be regarded as a fundamental law of population, that is, that population cannot increase indefinitely in constant geometrical progression, but there is no reason *a priori* to suppose that the damping down of the increase is so regular or uniform that a mathematical function of the same form represents it in all times and in all places. That may be the case with breeding experiments of *drosophilae* in a laboratory, but its extension to human society and the exclusion of all kinds of social and economic influences seems entirely unwarranted, even if for certain periods and countries the agreement between recorded and calculated figures is remarkably close. This is undoubtedly the case with the U.S.A. population from 1790 to 1920, but even here differences between recorded and calculated[4] figures are for several periods not insignificant relatively to the immigration figures.

[1] Cf. Thompson & Whelpton, *Population Trends*, Table 85, p. 303.
[2] "The importation of foreigners into a country that has as many inhabitants as the present employment and provisions for subsistence will bear, will be in the end no increase of people—unless the newcomers have more industry and frugality than the natives, and then they will provide more subsistence and increase in the country but they will gradually eat the natives out. Nor is it necessary to bring in foreigners to fill up any occasional vacancy in a country. For such vacancy (if the laws are good) will soon be filled by natural generation." B. Franklin, *Observations concerning the increase of Mankind and the Peopling of Countries*, p. 51.
[3] "The Laws governing Population," Discussion in *Journ. Royal Stat. Soc.*, Jan., 1925 (Sowley).
[4] Moreover the calculated figures vary according to which of the various methods for the fitting of the curve is applied.

iii. Gini's Theory

Whereas Malthus and Pearl by somewhat different arguments come to the same conclusion that migration has no noteworthy effect on population, migration plays an important part in Corrado Gini's theory of population growth. He also tries to demonstrate the existence of a biological law governing the growth of populations which is generally applicable and is not affected by changing social and economic conditions. In his view every nation is subject to a cycle of growth similar to that of the individual. It is characterized by a rapid growth in the nation's youth, followed by a slower rate in the period of maturity. In the last stage of senescence numbers decline and the nation is doomed eventually to disappear, unless peaceful infiltration by immigrants from younger nations, or conquest by such nations, rejuvenates the senile stock and starts a new cycle of growth. Gini holds that this senescence of nations is an inevitable process. It becomes manifest by a numerical decline resulting from a decline in fertility beginning with the upper classes and spreading gradually over all classes, and it is accompanied by a biological degeneration in the hereditary qualities of individuals. This decline in fertility is only apparently determined by the effect of social and economic factors; the cycle of population growth is fundamentally a biological phenomenon. The old nations can escape extinction only by admitting members of younger nations whose integration may bring about the improvement in numbers and quality upon which survival depends. As in the light of this theory environmental factors have no marked direct influence on population growth or on the course of the cycle, we must expect that, contrary to Malthus' theory, emigration will result in a decrease in numbers which is not compensated by a correspondingly higher rate of increase of the rest of the population; it may even be that the nation loses by emigration the elements with the most reproductive vigour, so that emigration would possibly lead to a decrease in the rate of growth in the homeland.

Gini's theory is based mainly on historical evidence,[1] but his interpretation of the events is not entirely unbiased, and it is not difficult to find evidence from history which leads to quite different conclusions. As Thompson has convincingly argued,[2] population growth is determined by a great variety of circum-

---

[1] C. Gini, "The Cyclical Rise and Fall of Population," in *Lectures on the Harris Foundation*, 1929.
[2] W. S. Thompson, *Population Problems* p. 39.

stances, given by the variety of social environments in which people live and to a certain extent by physiological factors. "Hence it is a folly to search for a simple law of population growth; what should receive attention is rather the factors which determine its growth in a particular community at a particular time." Accepting this view, we can hardly expect any population theory to provide us with a ready-made answer as to the effect of migration on the growth of the populations concerned.

An investigation into the relevant facts seems to suggest that generally speaking, and in the long run, immigration tends to increase and emigration to decrease population. The extent of decrease or increase depends largely on circumstances, and any *a priori* assumption that losses and gains in numbers through migration will result in proportionate changes of growth by natural increase, or that migration does not affect the growth of the native populations at all, appears to be as unjustified as the generalizations derived from the various population theories already discussed. A study of the relevant statistics is undoubtedly very helpful in tracing the effect of migration on population growth, but it is obvious that statistical information concerning migration and changes of natural increase in the immigration and emigration countries during corresponding periods can provide conclusive evidence in this respect only if the causal nexus between migration and changes of natural increase can be established, if the possibility that the correlation has been caused by a third, independent factor can be dismissed. To decide whether this is the case, and what birth- and death-rates would have been apart from migration is, however, a matter of interpretation which cannot be dealt with entirely on the basis of statistical evidence.

iv. *Quantitative Effect in Countries of Emigration*

Large-scale emigration can affect the rate of natural increase of the remaining population in various ways. When emigration affords real relief from population pressure, it may be presumed that a stimulating effect on natural increase may soon be felt in three respects: (1) it may lead to earlier and more numerous marriages and in consequence to a relative rise of the birth-rate; (2) people may decide to have more children and may relax the practice of birth control; (3) the death-rate, especially that of infants, is likely to fall. On the other hand various factors are bound to exert an opposite effect. In periods of large-scale emigration the bulk of the emigrants consists of people in the reproductive age-groups which are associated with the highest birth-rates; the excess of men over women among the emigrants may lead to an unbalanced sex composition of the population in the homeland,[1] so that the birth-rate there is likely to become lower than it would have been if the emigrants had had the same age and sex composition as the whole population. The different age composition also tends to raise the death-rate of the home country, because the age-groups which mainly emigrate have the lowest death-rates. Finally, relief from population pressure and the resulting prosperity may under certain circumstances, contrary to the possibility mentioned above, lead to a fall of the birth-rate, as often occurs with countries or groups which are becoming more prosperous. The difference between the true rate of natural increase—i.e. the net annual fertility—and what this rate would have been if emigration had not taken place, would indicate the effect on natural increase of the changed sex and age distribution due to emigration, but such a computation would call for information about the sex and age composition of the emigrant population during the period concerned which is not available, and it would, of course, not take into account the effect of the various psychological factors. Though it is not possible exactly to determine the effect of emigration on the growth of the population in the home country, the available evidence indicates that we should not be justified in minimizing this effect in the past, and it seems plausible that the general population trend—as reflected by the fall of the net reproductive rates—the general rise in the standards of living, and the increased practice of birth-control tend to make population growth more susceptible to losses of population through emigration.

This statement, however, needs qualification. It applies to most European countries, i.e. to countries where fertility is already partly under control or can be brought under control relatively easily. It does not apply to the demographic situation in the Far East. It is doubtful whether a control over mortality resulting from higher standards of living in India and China is likely to lead to a fall in fertility or whether in accordance with Malthus' view any improvement in standards of living and vitality will be soon offset by rapid population increase producing once more symptoms of population pressure, extreme poverty and a rise in mortality. If the latter holds good, emigration can at best but

[1] Cf. below, pp. 181-182.

bring temporary relief to the sending countries, and it has been argued that the admission of Indian and Chinese emigrants to the new countries would contribute nothing to the solution of the Chinese and Indian population problem, while it might produce similar conditions in the receiving areas. This argument leads to the conclusion that discrimination against nationals of these countries is justified so long as fertility remains uncontrolled.

In any case the numbers involved are so large relatively to the maximum absorptive capacity of the new countries, that the effect of population losses by emigration on standards of living in the sending countries is bound to remain slight. Indeed, it is not so much emigration as industrialization and modernization of agricultural methods, from which the densely populated countries of Asia must expect relief from population pressure. [1]

In Europe the transition from primary to secondary production was associated with higher standards of living. Mortality responded almost at once to these changes, while fertility was little affected for some fifty years. The immediate and rapid fall in mortality combined with high fertility gave rise to the outburst of population during this period. A similar situation has to be faced in the near future in India and China. A downward movement of the death-rate in these heavily populated areas, unless accompanied without much delay by a parallel downward movement of the birth-rate could have catastrophic consequences. A sudden great surplus of births over deaths might very seriously retard and even wipe out the gains in standards of living which the people of these countries will hope to achieve by economic development. The pressure of population might express itself, internally, in civil strife and externally in international disputes and wars. [2] The essence of the matter is, as F. A. Notestein has put it, that the economic interest and humanitarian sympathies of modern nations have brought to these areas mainly those features of our culture which tend to reduce mortality, while their social and cultural pattern based on the large family system has remained practically untouched. Little progress in birth control can be expected in such environments.

The ultimate solution of the problem is to be found in the development of a society in which the individual's aspirations for himself and his family become incompatible with large numbers of children. A whole set of well-co-ordinated economic,

[1]These problems are dealt with in: B. Lasker, *Asia on the Move*, New York, 1945.
[2] E. Staley, *World Economic Development*, I.L.O. Montreal, 1942, p. 274.

political and social changes is required in order to attain this re-orientation of social values. These include the development of public health services, educational reforms, modernization of agricultural methods, industrialization and urbanization.[1] In this setting emigration can play a subsidiary but important part. It may provide the breathing space needed for the adjustment of fertility to the new low mortality rates. During this critical period population losses through emigration would tend to mitigate the effects of rapid natural increase. Moreover remittances from emigrants would help to prevent a new fall in standards of living during the transition. Returning temporary migrants would propagate in their homelands the new standards of value.

v. *Quantitative Effect of Immigration into the U.S.A. According to Walker's Theory*

From the days of Benjamin Franklin to the present the claim that *immigration* "instead of constituting a new reinforcement to the population simply resulted in a replacement of native by foreign elements",[2] has been used as an argument for prohibiting immigration. The main exponent of this view, Professor F. A. Walker, an official of the U.S. Census Bureau, claimed to have given empirical proof of its validity. He tried to show from census figures and immigration estimates that without any immigration after 1790, the native stock alone would have produced at least as large a population as the United States had after a century of heavy immigration. His arguments have been as often refuted as repeated. If we realize that the U.S.A.'s population amounted in 1790 to less than 4 millions, and that roughly 19 million immigrants entered the U.S. between 1820 and 1898 and about 36 million between 1820 and 1924, Walker's theory appears to lack any common sense; indeed it is in no way supported by sufficient factual evidence.

As the American standard of living had undoubtedly risen almost constantly during this period, Walker could not explain his theory by the Malthusian proposition that the growth of population is limited by the subsistence level. He maintained that the natives deliberately restricted their rate of increase in order to spare their offspring from contact and competition with

---

[1] F. W. Notestein, "Problems of Policy in Relation to Areas of Heavy Population Pressure" in: *Demographic Studies of Areas of Selected Rapid Growth*, Milbank Memorial Fund, pp. 135–158.

[2] F. A. Walker, "Restriction of Immigration," in *Atlantic Monthly*, 1896, p. 824. Cf. Thompson & Whelpton, *op. cit.*, p. 304.

immigrants. This suggestion seems to be borne out by facts only to the extent that certain kinds of unskilled work at very low wages were practically monopolized by immigrants, since natives did not consider these jobs desirable for themselves or their children. It is also probable that native birth-rates fell more rapidly in the states with heavy immigration than in other parts of the country. This observation points to certain indirect effects of immigration to be discussed below, but "the decline in the American birth-rate was not wholly or even chiefly due to the effect of immigration, for in the main it was due to the same causes which have led to a decline in other countries of European civilization."[1] It has been shown[2] that Walker's theory implies the assumption of an unrealistically high rate of natural increase for the native population where no immigration had occurred. Moreover, there is no evidence of a correlation between fluctuations in the volume of immigration and the fall of the American birth-rate. If we compare the decades 1820–1830 and 1840–1850, we find that immigration was more than eleven times as large in the latter period, but the birth-rate of women of child-bearing age declined by only 28 points as compared with 20 points in the former decade. From 1900 to 1910—the decade with the largest number of immigrants ever reached—the birth-rate of women of child-bearing age dropped only by 13 points, from 130 to 117, whereas during 1920–1930, with an immigration about half as large, the birth-rate dropped by 26 points from 113 to 87.[3]

Though the statistical argument of Walker and his supporters is admittedly weak, so that his extreme views have survived mainly in the realm of political propaganda, his theory has—as Willcox has suggested[4]—its value "as a challenge to the current belief that immigration regularly increased the population by an amount equal to its numbers". Such an assumption would be undoubtedly wrong, and it seems appropriate to examine in some detail the demographic and social structure of American immigration during various characteristic periods and to investigate to what extent structural changes of the immigrant population have affected the growth of America's population. We shall confine our attention to conditions in the U.S.A. because for this country more comprehensive statistical evidence is available

[1] Carr-Saunders, *World Population*, p. 205.
[2] Cf. Willcox in *International Migrations*, Vol. II, pp. 92–107; Thompson & Whelpton, *Population Trends in U.S.A.*, pp. 304–308.
[3] *Ibid.*, p. 309.
[4] Willcox, *op. cit.*, p. 103.

than for any other immigration country, and because roughly two-thirds of the total European overseas emigration during the period of free migration went to the United States.

Let us first consider the merely arithmetical aspect of the contribution of immigration to the growth of the U.S.A. white population, as compared with natural increase. According to the estimates of Thompson and Whelpton,[1] from 1800 to 1830 less than 5 per cent of the population growth arose from net immigration, and from 1830 to 1840 less than 15 per cent. In the decades from 1840 to 1910 immigration varied between 27 and 43 per cent, averaging about 33 per cent of the population growth; it fell to 17 per cent for the decade 1910–1920 owing to contraction during the war, and rose again to 21.6 per cent in spite of its much smaller volume as a consequence of the rapid decline of the U.S.A. birth-rate during that period, but the last decade brought a further decrease of immigration and for several years a negative balance of migration, so that the share of net and gross immigration has become insignificant in spite of the further fall in natural increase.[2]

vi. *Demographic Coefficients of U.S. Immigrants*

The addition to a population by immigration will in the long run remain proportionate to the number of immigrants only if the rate of natural increase of immigrant and of native population is the same. As already seen, under conditions of free migration a typical emigrant population differs from the population of the home country with respect to age and sex distribution. Similar differences exist between immigrants and the populations of the receiving countries, and it is our present object to inquire into the effect of these differences on the share of the immigrants in the natural increase of the whole population. Since natural increase indicates the excess of births over deaths during a given period, we are concerned with the effect of immigration on both the birth- and death-rates of the whole population. As only women of child-bearing age are able to exert an immediate and direct influence on the birth-rate, this category must be presumed to be most relevant with regard to the trend of the birth-rate of the receiving country; if females of child-bearing age are more numerous among the immigrant population than

---

[1] Thompson and Whelpton, *op. cit.*, p. 303.
[2] This trend is reflected in the fall of the percentage of foreign-born whites among the total population from 14.5 in 1910 to 8.7 in 1940.

among thè natives, it is likely that—*other things being equal*—immigrants will contribute more than their due proportion to natural increase. In the case of females below child-bearing age the time that must elapse until they are able to affect the birth-rate has to be taken into account. The influence of male immigration on the future birth-rate of the immigration country is, however, not negligible. If only females of child-bearing age should immigrate into a country having a considerable excess of females over males, it is possible that such an immigration would merely increase the number of spinsters and reduce the crude birth-rate and the net reproductive rate in spite of their own possible contribution. Therefore, if the sex composition is not fairly well balanced in the receiving country, male immigration may have as much bearing on future natural increase as female immigration.

In all new countries the sex ratio for the whole population is in favour of the males, so that at first sight, from the mere demographic viewpoint, in order to get a population with a well-balanced sex distribution, females not above child-bearing age seem the most desirable category of immigrants. This excess of the male population is due to the fact that free migration has always been preponderantly masculine. The sex ratio of the American white population varied from 103.2 in 1820 to 104 in 1880, 106.6 in 1910, 102.7 in 1930, and 100.1 in 1940.[1] This falling trend is due partly to changes in the volume and composition of immigration, partly to changes in the age distribution of the whole population and to differential mortality rates for males and females.

From 1820, when records began, to 1824, 296 male immigrants entered the United States for every hundred females. The sex ratio declined rapidly during the following decades, averaging about 150 from 1840 to the end of the century. The predominance of the new immigration brought a conspicuous change in the sex ratio, which rose to 228 for 1900–1904, to 230 for 1905–1909, and fell to 199 for 1910–1914. During the inter-war period the ratio markedly declined, and since 1930 male immigrants have been greatly outnumbered by females. The ratios are:

1925–29	1930–34	1935–39
122.1	82.4	78.5

This change in the sex ratio can be explained mainly as a

[1] The corresponding figures for England and Wales are 94.8 in 1880 and 91.8 in 1930; for Italy: 100.5 in 1880 and 95.7 in 1930.

7

result of the U.S.A. restrictions on immigration. Within the quotas allotted to every nation, preference was given to relatives of immigrants already in the country. As men had previously immigrated in greater numbers, it was mainly females who profited from this privilege.

Various other factors contributed, as for instance: the relatively large number of widows who joined their children in the U.S.A., and the relatively great absorptive capacity for female domestic servants during the period of heavy unemployment. Since the volume of immigration has become so greatly reduced, changes in the sex ratio of the immigrants are merely of theoretical interest and have no bearing on the sex composition of the total U.S. population.

The effect of the excess of male immigration has been compensated to a certain extent by emigration which, though so much smaller in volume, is still predominantly male. This is illustrated by the following figures:

	1910–14	1920–24	1925–29	1930–34	1935–39
Sex ratio for immigrants	199	132	122	82	79
Sex ratio for alien emigrants	417	324	251	182	161
Sex ratio for net immigration	157	91	81	− 21	27

It would be fallacious to suppose that a predominantly female immigration, which was the result of the American migration policy during the inter-war period, is desirable from the demographic point of view, since the American population had a surplus of males. The opposite is true; a policy of preferring male immigrants would be easier to justify. The reason is this: the predominance of males within the U.S. population is confined to the age-groups below twenty and to various age groups above thirty-four. In the age-groups which are by far the most important for reproduction and to which, as we shall see, most immigrants belong, there are fewer males than females.

Whereas immigration affects the trend of the birth-rate in the receiving country mainly by the number of immigrating females of child-bearing age and by their age distribution, the effect on the mortality rate is mainly determined by the age composition of the whole immigrant population. If immigration consists largely of age-groups with relatively low mortality rates, we can presume that their addition—other things being equal—will lower the mortality rate of the whole population. A comparison of the age composition of the American white population with that of the immigrants shows that the age-groups with the lowest mortality predominate in the immigrant population. Such a comparison can yield only approximate results, as immigration statistics before 1925 distinguish only between three broad age-groups which have several times been altered.

The following figures apply to the age composition of the U.S.A. population (percentages):—

Age				0–14	15–44	45 and over
1880	.	.		38.1	45.8	16
1920	.	.		31.8	47.3	20.8
1930	.	.		29.4	47.7	23.0
1940	.	.		25.0	48.3	26.7

The middle group (15–44) has remained relatively stable compared with the other two groups. It is much more strongly represented among the immigrant population, and it is associated with the lowest mortality rates.

Age composition of the U.S.A. immigrants (percentage)

Age				0–14	15–44	45 and over
1880–84	.	.		22.4	67.4	10.2
1890–94		.		15.1	77	7.9

Age				0–13	14–44	
1899–04	.	.		12.5	82	5.5
1905–09		.		11.9	83.4	4.7
1910–14		.		12.7	81.7	5.6

Age				0–15	16–44	
1920–24	.	.		18.6	72.2	9.2
1925–29		.		16.3	74.7	9
1930–31		.		17.1	72.1	10.8
1931–39		.		17.1	66.7	16.2
1940–42		.		14.1	61.7 (16–45)	24.2 (46 and over)

The large number of middle-aged persons among the immigrants is not only significant because of the effect on birth- and death-rates, but it tends also to decrease the proportion of idle dependents to productive workers. This aspect will be discussed later. A marked increase of the older age-groups at the expense of the middle group is noticeable after 1924, mainly as a consequence of the restrictive measures. These discriminated in practice against young people of working age by giving preference to relatives of earlier immigrants and by excluding other applicants without means or special qualifications. Since 1933 U.S.A. immigration has been largely recruited from refugees and from nationals of some of the neighbour states. Among the refugees were many elderly people who would not have emigrated but for persecution, and who were admitted to the U.S.A. on the strength of their special qualifications or their independent means.

It is obvious that the potential influence of immigration on the birth-rate of the new country is greater than that on the death-rate. An immigrant can contribute to the death-rate only once in a lifetime, but he or she, while of reproductive age, may several times affect the birth-rate of the receiving country. A study of the statistics of re-migrants from the U.S.A. even suggests that a considerable number of immigrants contribute only to the credit side of the account of natural increase, and prefer to die outside the country. The Chinese who for religious reasons feels bound to return to his home country before his death but leaves his offspring behind, is only one extreme instance which has become of little practical importance since the prohibition of Chinese immigration. But a similar tendency can be found with European re-migrants who, as we have seen, reduced net immigration during various heavy immigration periods to about two-thirds of gross immigration. The characteristic feature of this return movement is the large percentage of re-migrants belonging to the age groups of over forty-four.

U.S.A. Alien Re-migrants above 44 (in per cent of the total)
(in brackets the corresponding figure for immigrants)

1910–14	1920–24	1925–29	1930–34
11.1 (5.6)	14.8 (9.2)	22 (9)	24.6 (11.9)
1935	1936	1937	1938
28.5 (15.5)	30 (16.6)	32.9 (16.1)	33.8 (15.6)

Two categories of re-migrants account mainly for this discrepancy. (1) Immigrants who have been successful and have saved some money prefer to live in their former environment and hope by their return to profit from the lower cost of living in their home countries. (2) Immigrants who were less successful and at an advanced age have increasing difficulty in finding employment; they have nothing to lose, but may find some support or better prospects in their former home country.

The actual numbers of the immigrants, their sex ratio and their age distribution would determine the share of immigration in the growth of the total population if the same specific fertility and mortality rates applied to immigrant population and to native stock. But these rates differ for the foreign-born and for the native population. Foreign-born white women in 1920 and in 1929 in all age groups had considerably higher specific birth-rates than native white women. Specific death-rates were in all age-groups higher for foreign-born than for native-born whites. This is reflected in:

	Birth-Rates[1]		Standardized Birth- and Death-Rates Death-Rates[2]	
	1920	1929	1920–24	1925–29
Native-born whites .	96	77	10.7	10.3
Foreign-born whites .	135	91	12.8	11.3

An analysis of mortality in New York State[3] (1928–32) revealed the following differentials in standardized death-rates according to country of birth: native-born males 11.8; foreign-born males 12.9; Italians 10.4; Britains 11.5; Germans 12.6; Canadians 12.9; Irish 16.5 (highest mortality of all nationalities).

The differential birth- and death-rates are the result of a number of counteracting factors which need some discussion, as they have in more than one respect considerable bearing on the economics of migration.

The higher fertility of foreign-born women seems to suggest that immigrants from countries with high fertility rates continue to maintain these high rates after their immigration to countries with lower rates. This conclusion is to a certain extent supported by statistical evidence. San Francisco, Buffalo, Philadelphia, the cities most largely native, have a much smaller proportion of children than cities with a high proportion of foreign stock from the "new" immigration, such as New York, Chicago, Detroit. Generally speaking, wherever Poles, Italians, and other immigrants from South and East Europe predominate, a much higher ratio of children is found than in districts inhabited largely by natives and Northern and Western Europeans.[4] Other investigations indicate that whites of foreign or mixed parentage have on the average somewhat higher fertility rates than native whites of native parentage in the same localities.[5, 6] According to the

---

[1] Thompsen and Whelpton, *op. cit.*, p. 270. Computed by averaging specific rates and using as weights the age distribution of all women aged 15–44 in the 1930 Census. The differential would be smaller if the figures were corrected for cases of non-registration.

[2] *ibid.*, p. 246.

[3] Calabresi in *Human Biology*, 1945, p. 340.

[4] Cf. N. Carpenter, *Immigrants and their Children*; T. J. Woofter, *Races and Ethnic Groups in American Life*, p. 15.

[5] Lorrimer and Osborn, *Dynamics of Population*.

[6] In New York State (exclusive of New York City), for instance, the differential between the fertility of the foreign-born and native-born white women was 45 per cent in 1920 and only 8 per cent in 1934 (Clyde V. Kiser, *Recent Trends in Birth Rates*).

U.S. Census of 1930, the median size of urban families was 3.13 where the head was native white of native parentage, 3.19 for native whites of foreign parentage, and about 3.74 where the head of the family was foreign-born.

These differences in fertility are due not to any biological differences between native stock and the immigrants coming from countries with high fertility rates, but to social and economic causes, and that fertility rates are in the main determined by environmental factors. That this is so can be concluded from the rapid decline of fertility rates in European countries when standards of living rose, urbanization increased, and knowledge of contraceptive methods became more general; in this respect there is only a time-lag between the countries of old and new immigration. Until immigrants have adapted themselves to the new environment they tend to maintain their old standards, but gradually they adopt those prevailing in the new environment. The differentials between the fertility rates and family size of native whites of native and those of foreign parentage are therefore only small as compared with foreign-born whites, and the marked decrease of the differentials between foreign and native fertility indicates that even in the case of a resumption of large-scale immigration these differences would become smaller and much less important than they have been in the past.

The immigrants of the last fifty years or so have become to a large extent settled in environments which are associated with fertility rates below the average, and it is therefore to be expected that their proportionate contribution to the natural increase of the whole population will tend to become in the long run lower than the average.[1] The lowest fertility rates prevail generally in the large cities and the highest rates in rural districts, mainly among the farm population.[2] These differentials are more conspicuous and significant for the trend of population growth than those between native and foreign-born persons. As the overwhelming majority of all immigrants live in the large cities, they are subject to environmental influences which produce the lowest fertility rates. An indication of this urban character of immigration is given by comparing the distribution of the total population with that of the foreign-born whites. In 1930 56.2 per cent of

[1] It might be different if we could presume a constant flow of immigrants of a favourable age composition.
[2] This is indicated by the following Net Reproduction Rates for the White Population in the U.S.A., 1935–1940: Urban, 0.731; Rural-Non-farm, 1.146; Rural-farm, 1.572.

the total U.S.A. population lived in urban districts[1]; 15.6 per cent of these were foreign-born whites, while the rural population (43.8 per cent) contained but 4.9 per cent foreign-born whites. 80.3 per cent of all foreign-born whites lived in urban districts in 1930. The discrepancy becomes still greater if we compare the figures for the largest cities or for the immigration since 1914.

Within the urban population we can distinguish differential fertility rates for different social classes and occupations. The miners and unskilled labourers rank highest; they are followed by the semi-skilled, and they in turn by skilled workers and artisans. Much lower are the birth-rates among men in the white-collar jobs, particularly the highly educated or the most prosperous.

In the rural population the highest fertility rates are associated with farm labourers, followed by farm renters and by farm owners. These differentials are not very relevant for our purposes, owing to the small and rapidly declining number of immigrants among the rural population. In the period 1911–1914, 33.4 per cent of the immigrants with an occupation were farmers or farm labourers; this percentage fell to 12.1 in 1920–24, to 16.5 in 1925–1929, and to 6.9 in 1938. Moreover, most of them presumably became settled after their immigration in urban districts and occupations, so that their higher fertility standards could have had only a temporary effect. On the other hand the number of immigrants who switched over from urban to rural occupations can have been only negligible, moreover it is improbable that they adopted the higher fertility standards of their new occupations.

If we examine the trend of the occupational composition of the immigrant population, the rapid fall in occupations which are generally associated with high fertility rates is striking.

Occupational composition of white immigrants in per cent of immigrants with occupation

	1911–14	1925–29	1935–39
Professional	1.7	5.9	18.8
Skilled	20	30.8	27.8
Unskilled	74.7	55.6	28.9
Commercial	2	2.9	19.6
Miscellaneous	1.6	4.8	5.4

The changes in favour of the groups with low fertility rates reflect the selective effect of the restrictions and the growing share of refugee immigration.

[1] 56.5 per cent in 1940.

vii. *Lack of Evidence for Differentials in the Rate of Increase between Natives and Immigrants*

Regional and social differentials of fertility rates tend to narrow to the extent to which controlled is substituted for uncontrolled fertility. But the differentials remain and will continue to remain significant for some time to come. If it should become the object of immigration policy to halt the trend towards a declining population, it may become expedient to take into account the differential fertility of different groups of immigrants; but it would be fallacious to draw any definite conclusions from the high fertility rates of certain European nations or of the immigrant stock coming from these nations. These high rates are mainly a result of regional, social and occupational distribution and of lack of knowledge of birth-control methods; they are bound gradually to decrease with the further spread of birth-control and with the increase of immigrants in occupations with low fertility rates.

The differentials between specific death-rates of natives and foreign-born whites mentioned above can be similarly explained. Since the proportion of immigrants living in cities is larger than that of the native whites, the higher urban death-rates bear more heavily on them than on the natives. So long as the immigrants are largely employed in jobs associated with high death-rates, e.g. mining,[1] so long as it is mainly the least attractive and worst-paid jobs that are open to them and their living conditions are inferior to the native average, so long as their educational status is lower than that of the natives, their specific death-rates must be expected to be higher than those of the natives in general unless the adverse environmental effects are outweighed by differences in vitality, i.e. in the hereditary capacity for health and longevity. We found no evidence to support such an assumption, and we can safely conclude that differentials in mortality as well as in fertility rates are due to environment; they are mainly of a temporary nature, and tend to become smaller when the immigrants get the opportunity to adjust themselves to the environment of the new country. The rise of the standard of living for the lowest income classes and the improvement of social services tends to decrease these differentials in general. The selective effect of the immigration restrictions tends to increase the proportion of immigrants with relatively low specific

---

[1] Death-rates in districts with a predominantly immigrant mining population are not significantly different from those with a predominantly native one.

death-rates among the new arrivals, but changes in the age distribution, mainly due to these restrictions, make for higher crude death-rates among the latest immigrants.

We have tried to examine the various counteracting factors which in the long run determine the natural increase of the immigrant population. As these are subject to continual fluctuations for which no sufficient statistical evidence can be produced, no attempt has been made to weigh the relative importance of these factors and so to come to a definite, quantitative result.

But it is possible to get an idea of the numerical effect of a resumption of immigration on future population growth in the U.S.A. by incorporating into population estimates certain assumptions as to the volume of future immigration and the fertility and mortality of the immigrants and of their offspring. Thompson and Whelpton have calculated the future population size (a) with net immigration nil, (b) with a net immigration of a population of 500,000 foreign-born persons in each succeeding five-year period beginning in 1945. For the native population they assumed in both estimates a slight fall in fertility. The birth- and death-rates which they applied to an immigrant population of typical sex and age composition were those for the foreign-born white population; their American-born children, however, were assumed to be subject to the birth- and death-rates of the white population. According to estimate (a) the U.S. population would increase from 138.5 millions in 1945 to 161 millions in 1985, and then gradually fall to 159.4 millions in 2000. By estimate (b) the population in 1985 would amount to 166 millions. The peak would be reached ten years later with 167 millions and in 2000 the population would have fallen to 166.6 millions; that is to say, an annual net immigration of 100,000 persons or of 5½ millions within the next 55 years would lead to an addition of 7.2 million persons to the U.S. population at the end of this period.

Obviously the underlying assumptions are to some extent based on "intelligent guesses". It depends largely on the social and demographic composition of the future immigrant population whether they are likely to contribute more or less than the natives to the natural increase of the American population.

But our inquiry leads to the conclusion that the share of the immigrant population in the natural increase of the total population has in the past been greater than proportionate, that the

7*

differentials tend to decrease, and that the preponderance of urban immigration together with the rapid decline of fertility in the emmigration countries make it probable that the contribution of recent immigration to natural increase is less than proportionate.

This statement does not imply that immigration has in the past adversely affected the natural increase of the native stock, as Benjamin Franklin, Walker and his followers maintain. It seems likely, however, that some of the factors we have examined have had this effect, though in a more indirect way than Walker assumes. Large-scale immigration has been one of the main causes of the rapid urbanization and industrialization of the United States since the end of the nineteenth century. Urbanization and industrialization, as we have seen, bring about a rapid decline of birth-rates, and hence a certain causal relation is given between immigration and the decline in the fertility rates of the native population. Abundant supply of cheap immigrant labour in the American cities hastened this process (and had a large influence on the location of the new industries), which otherwise would probably have occurred at a much slower rate. The badly-paid occupations which are associated with high birth-rates became "immigrant jobs", leaving only comparatively few natives in these groups, while the natives advanced to a large extent to better-paid jobs associated with lower birth-rates. This indirect adverse effect of large-scale immigration on the rate of natural increase of the natives, which can be observed under the economic and demographic conditions which prevailed in the U.S.A. during the period of heavy immigration, cannot be taken as the effect of a generally valid law. Under different conditions, with the general level of birth-rates lower, birth control being practised by all strata of the population, the pushing up of natives to higher-paid jobs may have the opposite effect,[1] and may result in a rise of native fertility.

viii. *Rate of Natural Increase of Oriental Immigrants*

Our inquiry has so far been confined to movements of populations of European origin. The admission of Mongols or coloured persons is prohibited or greatly restricted in practically all immigrant-receiving countries of European civilization. Mass immigration of non-Europeans into the U.S.A. consisted mainly

[1] Cf. A. Myrdal, *Nation and Family*, 1941.

of Japanese and Chinese immigrants.[1] These movements, however, were stopped so early that the little statistical information available is not sufficient for us to draw conclusions as to the probable trend of Chinese and Japanese immigrant population, if a continuous flow of immigration had taken place.

The arguments for the exclusion of Mongol immigration in the U.S.A. and elsewhere are partly based on the assertion that the Mongolian peoples have rates of fertility so high that even the allotment of a small immigration quota would eventually result in an uncontrollable increase of these groups. Their "effective fertility" has remained relatively high, though it must have been adversely affected by the prohibition of immigration. The number of children under five years per 1000 women aged 20–44[2] amounted, according to the 1930 U.S. Census, to 1051 for Chinese and 824 for Japanese as compared with 481 for the white population. But there is some evidence that the trend of fertility of immigrants of Mongol origin is subject to the same environmental influences which we find operating with the immigrant population from European countries with high fertility rates. It is most likely that the second and subsequent generations of these immigrants, on coming into contact with the American way of living, tend to limit very decidedly the size of their families.[3]

B. QUALITATIVE ASPECT

The effect of immigration on the *quality* of the population of the receiving country is a still more controversial issue in the debates for and against large-scale immigration than the merely numerical aspect. In dealing with the assimilation problem we discussed how far existing differentials in the characteristics of members of different nations are due to the influence of environmental factors and how far to a different genetic constitution. This covers only one side of the quality problem. Even if it were granted in the immigration countries that the inhabitants of the various countries of emigration are in no way inferior to their own nationals in respect of their national characteristics, and that these differentials provide no argument against assimilation,

[1] It is only since 1930 that the U.S. Census has distinguished the Mexican stock in U.S.A. by "racial" components under the designations "white Mexicans" and "coloured Mexicans".

[2] This rate is supposed to measure "effective fertility"; according to Lorimer: "something between gross fertility and net reproduction".

[3] Cf. E. K. Strong, *Japanese in California*; and Penrose, *Population Problems*.

restrictionists could reply that the expected immigration did not represent a fair sample of the populations of the emigration countries, but rather a selection of their most inferior elements. On the other hand the advocates of large-scale immigration could reverse the argument: It may be true that certain nations must be considered as generally inferior in certain respects, but such inferiority does not apply to the same extent to the immigrants from these nations, since it is usually the best elements of a population which possess the initiative and energy required from an emigrant.

i. *Differentials between Natives and Various Groups of Immigrants in Intelligence*

It is easy to find evidence to support either of these opposing views. The social composition of the immigrant population is continually changing, and is so complex that any generalization must lead to unwarranted conclusions. From the very beginning of overseas migration, immigrants have represented a great variety of social types. Many of the early immigrants left their old countries because of their religious or political convictions, or because they were attracted by the independence and the wider scope for initiative and material success which life as pioneers in a new country offered to them. They included, undoubtedly, a large number with characteristics superior to those of the average member of the nations from which they came. The convicts, indentured servants, etc., who entered the country at the same time possibly included a relatively large number of the socially least desirable elements. It is probably true of any unselected immigration that the extreme cases, the most valuable and the definitely undesirable elements, are much more strongly represented among the immigrants than in the population of their native countries taken as a whole.

Among the many psychological traits which may be of importance in selecting immigrants, it is only intelligence for which techniques of measurement have reached a fairly advanced stage. But it is easy to see that other psychological traits, as reflected "temperament, character or personality", are at least as important criteria as intelligence for the selection of immigrants. Certain types of crime, for instance, require superior intelligence. Persistence, honesty, sociability and adaptability are qualities all-important for the success and the desirability of an immigrant.

As no general correlation can be assumed between the display of physical and mental characters, statements about mental differentials between various categories of immigrants are usually based either on personal impressions, which leave a wide scope to prejudice, on various statistics which are also subject to biased interpretation, or on the results of intelligence tests, which are open to criticism mainly as to the extent to which they exclude the effect of environmental factors. If we allow for all these objections, there still remains some evidence that people belonging to the lowest social strata are on the average less well endowed mentally than those from higher strata, and that cases of feeble-mindedness occur relatively often among the former. As the vast majority of the immigrants (under conditions of free migration) are recruited from the income classes at the lower end of the scale—though usually not from the very lowest class—unselected immigration may represent a sample which in respect to mental endowment is below the average, unless it be true that the immigrants have a higher mental standard than that general in the classes from which they come.

Under modern conditions no pioneer qualities are required of the typical immigrant. He is provided with affidavits and if necessary with his passage money by friends or relatives whom he is going to join. The formalities of obtaining passports and visas are dealt with by the steamship company or other agencies, so that the initiative required from him is often reduced to his signing on the dotted line. The chance factor of having friends or relatives abroad therefore plays a great part in the selection of modern migration. On the other hand this category of immigrants may be subject to a certain qualitative selection in so far as by preference those friends or relatives are encouraged to emigrate whose migration may be expected to become a success. According to the view of the U.S. Immigration Commission in 1911, immigration "represents the stronger and better elements of the particular class from which it is drawn".[1]

Many studies of the intelligence of immigrants and their children have been made in the U.S.A. by intelligence tests. The significance of these tests as a measurement of innate intelligence is limited. The ability they measure is to a certain extent developed ability; it is only partly determined by hereditary factors and partly by the opportunities of developing mental

---

[1] U.S. Immigration Commission, *Abstract of Report on Emigration Conditions in Europe*, p. 12, 1911.

endowment. The value of these tests therefore depends largely on the possibility of eliminating the effect of differences of environment on the results. This was obviously not the case with the intelligence tests given in the U.S. Army in 1917–1918 to drafted recruits who were first-generation immigrants. These indicate that the intelligence of immigrants from Northern Europe is considerably superior to that of those from the countries of new migration, but they do not allow for the fact that the former had come from more favourable home environments, providing them with better schooling and a better social inheritance, that they had on the average been much longer in the United States and had consequently a better chance of profiting from the opportunities there afforded for developing their intelligence than had the immigrants from Southern and South-Eastern Europe, who had mainly arrived during the years recently preceding the war.

The significance of the time factor becomes apparent if scores are calculated according to the length of residence in the new country. If the scale runs from 0 to 25 (lowest score denoting highest rank), the average of the White native-born is 13.77 as compared with 12.05 for all foreign-born. Those who have been in America from 0 to 5 years have an average score of 11.41, while those who have been there twenty years or more exceed the native-born with a score of 13.82.[1] But it cannot be claimed that this evidence fully invalidates the hypothesis of "Nordic" superiority, since the percentage of immigrants from northern and north-western Europe was highest among the groups with longest residence; it indicates only one of various alternative interpretations.[2]

Various tests given to school-children indicated but little difference in intelligence between those of native and those of foreign parents belonging to the old or new immigration. Other tests given to American-born school-children in four Massachusetts mill towns, representing a wide variety of ethnic groups, indicated a distinctly higher intelligence for the children of Swedes, Polish Jews and Englishmen than for those of American natives. The Russian Jews, Germans, Lithuanians and Irish were not significantly different from the American median, but the Canadians, Poles, Greeks, French-Canadians, Italians and

---

[1] C. C. Brigham, *A Study of American Intelligence*, Princeton Press, 1923.
[2] They are discussed by Clifford Kirkpatrick in *Intelligence and Immigration*, Mental Measurement Monographs, Series No. 2. Williams and Wilkins Company, Baltimore, 1926.

Portuguese scored significantly below the American level. Differences related to economic status and environment at home may have contributed to these results. A thorough analysis of the results of various large-scale intelligence tests[1] reveals the complexity of the problem. It shows that none of these tests provides any conclusive evidence that the differences in intelligence between various groups of immigrants and natives have a biological basis. "The problem of the relative capacity for intelligence of the various foreign stocks in this country (the U.S.) remains involved."[2]

ii. *Differentials in Criminality*

A similar interpretation should be applied to statistical comparisons of the criminality of native and foreign whites. The rate of crime commission according to such statistics[3] amounted to 517.5 per 100,000 for the foreign-born population and to only 404.1 for the native white population. But if due allowance is made for differences in sex, age, regional and social distribution, it appears that criminality among the foreign-born is much lower than among the natives. The National Commission on Law Observance and Enforcement found:[4]

(1) That in proportion to their respective numbers the foreign-born commit considerably fewer crimes than the native-born.

(2) That the foreign-born approach the record of the native whites most closely in the commission of crimes involving personal violence.

(3) That in crimes for gain (including robbery in which there is also personal violence or the threat of violence) the native whites greatly exceed the foreign-born.

(4) That in the commission of certain types of offence there is considerable variation among the different nationalities within the foreign-born group, but that the detailed data as yet available are insufficient, both as to quantity and accuracy, to warrant the formation of any final conclusion as to the comparative criminality of any particular groups.

(5) That there is insufficient information available to warrant any deductions as to criminal activity among the native-born of foreign parentage as compared with those of native parentage.[5]

---

[1] Cf. Lorimer and Osborn, *op. cit. passim.*

[2] F. Osborne, *Preface to Eugenics*, Harper & Brothers, 1940, p. 77.

[3] U.S. States Bureau of Census, *Report on Prisoners*, 1923.

[4] Report on *Crime and the Foreign Born*, publ. No. 10, p. 195.

[5] E. H. Stofflett in *A Study of National and Cultural Differences in Criminal Tendency*, Arch. of Psychology, has collected some evidence from which he concludes: There is a distinct tendency for the character of criminality of various national immigrant groups to change with the succeeding generation. The direction of the drift in character of criminality is away from the crimes of violence peculiar to the foreign-born of most national groups and towards predatory types of offence most common to the native whites of native parentage. There is no evidence of a tendency to any particular type of crime, which might be regarded as a trait of any national group, to persist through succeeding generations.

Though conclusive statistical evidence is lacking, the widely-held opinion that American-born children of immigrants contribute far more than their share to juvenile and adult delinquency is supported by circumstantial evidence. It is, however, easy to show that native American juveniles of the same economic and social classes as the children of immigrants become delinquent just as readily. "Deliquency among children of immigrants is simply a symptom of the disorganization that goes along with the breaking-up of the immigrant's traditional system without the possibility of adequate assimilation of his children to the new order."[1] It is held that too rapid and therefore superficial Americanization of immigrant children is conducive to the disintegration of family control and to juvenile delinquency.

Our inquiry into the qualitative aspect of the immigration problem has had a negative result in so far as we have found that the extensive investigations which have been made on this matter do not lend any support to the suggestion that large-scale and unselected immigration, such as occurred in the United States during the free immigration period, had any adverse effect on the qualitative composition of the population in the receiving country, and that no conclusive evidence has been found which would suggest significant qualitative differences of biological origin between immigrants coming from different nations or different social classes, in so far as qualities are concerned whose incidence can be measured by intelligence tests or statistical computations.

One positive point, though quantitatively of minor importance, may be noted: according to most immigration laws criminals and persons affected by mental disease are not admissible. Mental defectives, at least in the case of imbeciles and idiots, are easily to detect and consequently debar from admission. These defects seem therefore to be less widespread among foreign-born persons than among natives.[2] Cases of mental disorder or symptoms of potential mental disorder are more difficult to diagnose, but it has been possible to eliminate a certain percentage of mentally diseased would-be immigrants and so to reduce the rate of insanity for immigrants which might otherwise, for different reasons, have been unduly high.

---

[1] "Are our Criminals Foreigners?" Frederic M. Thrasher in *Our Racial and National Minorities*, Ed. J. S. Roncek, New York, 1939, p. 697, see also "Social Factors in Juvenile Delinquency," C. R. Shaw and H. D. McKay, in *Report on the Causes of Crime*, Vol. II, National Commission on Law Observance and Enforcements.

[2] No statistics are available for mental defects among natives of foreign parentage

The right of the receiving country to exclude criminals and mental defectives from admission is generally considered as compatible with the principle of free migration. This right may, however, be challenged by the countries of emigration if, possibly as the effect of the population trend, the demand for immigrants should become greater and if, as we have suggested, the present countries of emigration should find loss of population through emigration disadvantageous to their economic development. In this case it seems only fair and reasonable that the receiving country should not be allowed to select its immigrants by excluding the least desirable groups, leaving them as an economic burden on the country of emigration; it should rather be induced to take its share in these groups, even though doing so should imply a qualitative deterioration of its population.

2. THE ECONOMIC EFFECT

A. CRITERION FOR THE ECONOMIC EFFECT

Our previous statement that migration is desirable from the viewpoint of the countries concerned if it results in an improvement of the standards of living of those countries, needs further examination. The concept of standard of living is widely used in all discussions of population problems; a rise in the standard of living is often taken as identical with an increase in real income per head or in marginal productivity. These terms when applied to an analysis of the migration problem are supposed to indicate that the community concerned has become "better off". They have, however, even if non-economic factors are entirely disregarded, no generally accepted meaning, but have a great number of definitions which use a wide variety of criteria. The ultimate end of migratory movements remains therefore somewhat vague, if no precise meaning can be attributed to them.

Strictly speaking, the standard of living has no direct relation to real income; it is determined by that part of the national income which is spent on consumption and by the number of consumers. The standard of living as referring to a fairly homogeneous population has been defined as "the average amount of necessaries and luxuries enjoyed by the typical family in this group."[1] Definitions of this type express the idea which most

[1] Fairchild, *Outlines of Applied Sociology*. The merits of many other definitions are discussed in: H. E. Pipping, "The Concept of Standard of Life," in *Economic Essays in Honour of G. Cassel*.

frequently underlies the use of the term and which makes it statistically computable. Its shortcomings in respect to welfare economics consist mainly in the fact that it does not take into account the time factor. It is evident that our prospects for the future play a great part in our valuations and in our decision whether a particular change (for instance the admission of immigrants) has made us economically better off. "A standard is no standard unless it is extended over a certain period."[1] A group which enjoys boom conditions for a short period, owing to the inrush of a volume of immigration greater than it can absorb, but which is likely to suffer from the ensuing depression, cannot be considered to have improved its standard of living. Conversely, immigration may require for a certain time a reduction in the amount of necessaries and luxuries enjoyed by the group, but may result in a more than proportionate increase of enjoyment in the future; its present standard of consumption may have fallen, while its investments and prospects for future consumption have risen. This alternative between present and future consumption which, as we saw in Chapter III, the potential immigrant often has to meet, is also put before the countries of immigration. If an under-developed country wants to make use of its idle natural resources by admitting more immigrants, it is normally obliged to provide the additional capital equipment required. This may imply contraction of consumption in favour of investment at least until a yield from these investments is available (in the case of land settlement up to five years). The standard of living conceived as an index of present consumption may fall, prospective consumption for a long period may rise. On the other hand it may be obvious that immigration into a particular country has a beneficial effect on the country's standard of living for a fairly long period, but if it has, though sparsely populated, a high rate of natural increase, such an immigration may be detrimental to future generations by increasing the risk of overcrowding and population pressure at an uncertain time. This argument has often been used in the past to defend restrictions of immigration. It is clear that the rate of discount of future expectations and the time period which has to be taken into account for forming the relevant standard of living is quite arbitrary; that it is not possible to single out a particular period of time, say five years or one generation, as generally reasonable for the formation of the standard of living. It must rather be

[1] *Ibid.*

left to common sense to find the proper period in any particular case. If we grant this, the ultimate criterion of the usefulness of migration to the countries concerned: whether it makes them better off, becomes in such cases indeterminate.

A second difficulty arises when we apply the standard of living concept, which has—apart from the time factor—a definite meaning as reflecting the situation of a typical representative of a fairly homogeneous group, to the population of a whole country. The population of any country in an advanced stage of capitalist production is made up of many groups with different standards of living and with different vested interests, so that a change which is beneficial to some groups is likely to be detrimental to others. Landowners, entrepreneurs, traders and others may gain and unskilled workers lose from immigration and conversely from emigration. It is quite possible that in the long run, after necessary adjustments have been made, gains or losses may have the same direction for all classes of the population, though these will be affected to a different extent, but often the divergent interests of the groups will remain irreconcilable. To average net gains and net losses and by this method to arrive at a fictitious average standard of living does not seem a very satisfactory solution.[1] If migration results in a redistribution of incomes by increasing those of the highest income groups, and leaving a smaller relative share to the members of the lower income classes without increasing their absolute share, average real income and presumably average standard of living would rise, but the majority of the population would not be better off. Similarly, the average value may fall as a consequence of migration, but every member of the increased population may become better off. Since large-scale immigration adds in practice only to the population in the lower income classes, such a situation is not unlikely to occur, and immigration of this nature must be considered desirable. It is, however, controversial whether an immigration is desirable which has the effect of raising the standard of living of all the groups concerned, but creates a new group with a lower standard than that of any of the other groups. This new group is composed of immigrants whose standard of living relatively to that in the old country may also have improved. As already mentioned, such an extension at the lower end of the income distribution is widely considered as harmful and as incom-

[1] Similar objections may be raised against accepting the mean of the various standards of living as a suitable criterion.

patible with the idea of raising the standard of living of the population as a whole. These few examples tend to show that the standard of living concept does not provide an unequivocal criterion for the desirability of migration into a country with an economically heterogeneous population, since value judgments have to be used in order to weigh and balance the gains and losses accruing to different groups.

B. EFFECT ON WAGES

It seems therefore necessary to inquire in what way the various components of the economic system which serve the interests of different groups of the population are affected by various types of migration. We will begin with the impact of immigration on the wage-system in the receiving country. The typical case is that of the immigration of unskilled workers, or immigrants, who—no matter what their previous occupation—can find employment in the new country only as unskilled workers. Often they are single or, if married, have left their families in the old country. They have but very little means at their disposal, and must take any job at any wage. As they are generally used to a much lower standard of living than that of unskilled labour in the new country, they are in a position to undercut the prevailing rate of wages without hardship to themselves. As their bargaining power is only weak, it seems probable that large-scale immigration has at least primarily a markedly adverse effect on the wage-rates of all groups of native labour with which the immigrants are able to compete. This does not apply only to those industries and occupations which the immigrants actually enter, as there is within any one open market a tendency for the wage rate to be approximately the same in all industries. A fall in the wage rate due to large-scale immigration cannot be presumed in countries where labour is working under increasing returns, as has been the case with new countries in the first stages of their development. But this exceptional situation obviously does not apply to the United States during her mass immigration period before 1914, and it is also very doubtful whether under present conditions mass immigration, the supply of other factors remaining unchanged, could in any new country produce increasing returns for the labour factor.

If the quantity of any factor of production is increased, the reward per unit of this factor and of all other factors which are perfect substitutes will be diminished, and the rewards per unit to the co-operant factors increased. "The advent of Chinese immigrants in the retailing business *must* injure the British retail shopkeepers of New Zealand, and the steady flow of low-grade European immigrants *must* keep down the wages of unskilled workmen in the U.S."[1]

This simple proposition is the starting-point for Kleene's theory of wages.[2] Professor Kleene maintains that in the backward countries of Southern and Eastern Europe which are still in a precapitalistic stage of production, the Malthusian contention that natural wages tend to reach subsistence level still holds good. It is, he thinks, the supply of labour from these backward countries which also establishes the general rate of wages in the capitalist countries. The inflow of immigrants, so long as differentials in the standards of living between the capitalist and the backward countries are marked, makes the supply of labour in the former practically infinitely elastic. Immigration will therefore tend to bring the wage level of the United States near to that of the backward countries, allowing for a premium necessary to cover the expenses of migration and the deterrent effect of distance and unfamiliarity; the supply price for higher grades of labour, which is not immediately affected by immigration, is determined by the wages paid to the unskilled plus a premium in order to induce development out of the lower grade into the higher grade. It is to-day obvious that no satisfactory general theory of wages can be arrived at by singling out immigration as the factor which governs the wage level; the volume of world migration has so contracted that it can have no bearing on the general wage level.[3] But Kleene's argument seems less absurd if it is used only as an explanation of the wage rate for certain types of unskilled labour in the U.S. up to 1914. Then real wages for unskilled labour remained relatively constant,[4] whereas other incomes steadily increased. True, there always remained a wide margin between the U.S. wage level and that of the emigration countries with the lowest standards of living, which could be accounted for only by the assumption of a high premium. The arrival of more than one and a quarter million immigrants in prosperous years suggested

---

[1] A. C. Pigou, *The Economics of Welfare*, p. 660.
[2] G. A. Kleene, *Profits and Wages*, 1916.
[3] Kleene suggested as a possible alternative explanation the existence of precapitalistic sections with low standards of living within the capitalistic countries and internal migration from these sections.
[4] Cf. below, p. 205.

an almost infinite elasticity of supply. But in fact other forces tended to limit the supply of immigrants. The capacity of the steamship companies can be increased only with a considerable time lag; a small percentage only of would-be immigrants can afford the cost of emigration or have friends or relatives abroad who are prepared to advance the necessary amount; economic advantages alone are often not a sufficient incentive to emigration. On the other hand the increasing number of earlier emigrants may provide more opportunities for further immigration.

If we dismiss the assumption of an infinite elasticity of the supply of unskilled labour, we must also take into account changes in the demand for labour as determining the wage level. Moreover, a drop in the wage level for unskilled labour to the low standard of the backward countries (plus premium) is prevented by another counteracting force which renders the labour market with respect to immigrant labour more imperfect. So long as the inflow of immigrant workmen is comparatively small, the new supply, owing to its mobility, will be absorbed easily, without much friction or wage-cutting, in a new country. The immigrants will find employment mainly in those industries and occupations which have for the short period a relatively high elastic demand for unskilled labour. Unfamiliarity with language and methods of work in the new country will not seriously handicap their prospects; they will have ample opportunity of adapting themselves to the new conditions and will be able after a short period of transition to compete on equal terms with unskilled native labour. Things are different, however, when the supply of immigrant labour becomes so great that it brings about a marked fall in the wage rate for native workers. The attitude of the working class and of general opinion towards the immigrants becomes more hostile, prejudice against them grows; in order to find employment they are obliged to undercut the prevailing wage rate by a wider margin than would have been necessary without the discrimination against them; this undercutting is considered as a further proof of unfairness and increases the opposition to their employment. Eventually the opportunities open to them are limited to the most unpleasant jobs and to extra-marginal occupations where they have not to meet with native competition. Thus immigrant labour as a "non-competing group" becomes distinct from unskilled native labour and can no longer be considered as part of the (for all practical purposes) homogeneous factor of production, unskilled labour. In certain industries immigrant labour predominates; certain jobs become "immigrant" jobs. This development enhances the tendency of immigrants to concentrate in the big cities of the country, to occupy contiguous territory there and to form ethnic and national units, so that they have still fewer opportunities of adopting the language and customs of the new country and remain distinguished as one or more separate groups. Immigrant labour becomes predominant in various mining districts, in cotton mills, in the "sweated" clothing trade and in other marginal industries where working conditions are low. A similar development took place in France during the decade following the First World War, and in Britain, though here it was of relatively little importance, about the turn of the last century.

If we recognize immigrant labour under these particular conditions as a different factor of production, its wage rate cannot be directly associated with the wage rates for unskilled labour in general, but the relationship between them is mainly determined by the extent to which they are co-operative or rival. Native labour can be replaced by immigrant labour in various ways. The direct method of undercutting is not, of course, excluded by considering immigrant labour as a separate group inferior to native labour. It is only in so far as immigrant labour is used for the establishment of industries which at the native wage level are submarginal, that no native worker is replaced by an immigrant and that no competition between the two groups takes place, provided that the product of the new industry does not compete with and is not a substitute for products of native labour. In industries which formerly employed natives at wage rates corresponding to the relatively high standard of living of American unskilled workers, in mines, in cotton mills, in road and railway construction and maintenance, low immigrant wages become the standard rate, unless the native workmen succeed by organized resistance in keeping out the alien competitor. Otherwise native labour is gradually replaced by immigrants, and the supply of native workers in occupations free from immigrant competition increases and so tends to lower the rate of remuneration in these occupations also. The native workers who are not successful in finding a job elsewhere or in getting promoted as a complement to immigrant labour, must adapt themselves to the new wage rates or become unemployed.

The impact of cheap immigrant labour on the relatively high

native wage standard may also take a more indirect form. If the supply of unskilled labour is abundant, it may be assumed that less capitalistic methods of production will become more profitable, that the demand for labour-saving capital equipment and correspondingly the rate of remuneration for the qualified labour producing such capital equipment will fall.[1]   Moreover, the demarcation between immigrant and native labour is never very rigid; a constant transfer takes place from the former to the latter. The work of immigrants can be looked upon as a kind of apprenticeship of indefinite duration. As soon as the immigrant has made some progress in assimilation, he is able to compete with native labour in its own field. The segregation of immigrants in national units, which, as we have seen, has been characteristic of mass immigration, is in the interest of native labour, at least from this point of view, because it prevents or retards assimilation and hence the transfer of immigrants into the higher wage groups.

All these cases of immigrant labour replacing native labour and lowering the wage level are so conspicuous that the hostile attitude of native workers to mass immigration of cheap unskilled labour seems at first sight quite consistent and reasonable. But such an attitude does not take into account the less obvious effect of immigration as a factor complementary to native labour. The experience of past periods of large-scale immigration, mainly into the U.S.A., indicates that the immigration of unskilled labour provides the more progressive elements among the native workers with new opportunities for promotion to higher-paid jobs. If industries expand as a result of the lower costs of production resulting from the employment of cheaper labour, a relatively large number of foremen is required to supervise and instruct the newcomers. In spite of the tendency to replace semi-skilled and skilled labour by the now relatively cheaper immigrant labour, new openings for the former will be created, as in practically all industries unskilled and skilled labour are to a large extent co-operative. "It is only because the new immigrants have furnished the class of unskilled labour that the native workman and older immigrants have been raised to the plane of an aristocracy of labour."[2] But the increase in output requires under normal conditions of demand a reduction of the prices for the product. If the demand for the products produced by immigrants

---

[1] The possibility of co-operation will be discussed below.
[2] E. Hourwich, *Immigration and Labour*, p. 12.

is inelastic, the reward per unit to native labour as a complementary factor may not increase. On the other hand, if the cheap immigrant labour is mainly absorbed by industries producing directly or indirectly "wage goods", the fall in prices will increase the purchasing power of money wages and therefore raise the *real wage rate*.

The net effect of immigration on the wage rate is thus compounded of various tendencies: substitution tends to reduce it, co-operation and a lower price level for goods to raise it. It depends on the changes in the aggregate demand for goods and services and in the demand for and supply of the other factors of production, which of the tendencies affecting the wage level will become dominant. The effect of migration on some of the forces which determine the nature of these changes will be discussed later, but it is obvious that even a comprehensive study of the possible implications could not cover all the combinations which are likely to occur in real life. Since it is practically impossible to eliminate the effect on the wage level of all the other interacting and permanently changing forces, such as the state of technique, the propensity to invest and to consume, the balance of trade, etc., it is a matter of conjecture whether in particular cases immigration has *in the long run* an unfavourable effect on the wage level. In the case of the U.S.A. during the period of large-scale immigration of unskilled labour, competent opinion is divided. A marked characteristic of the American labour situation during the period of new immigration before the First World War was the comparatively low rate of pay for unskilled workers. The "pick and shovel man" received only slightly more in the U.S.A. than in Europe, relatively to the wide wage differential between the American and European skilled worker. "The cause is not far to seek. The enormous influx of immigrants maintained a great supply of unskilled labour and kept down its pay."[1]

The adverse effect of immigration on the wage level is presumably less marked for the trend of average real wages in the U.S.A. during this period than for the lowest categories. But in spite of the rapid economic development average real wages did not increase during the period of large-scale immigration from 1899 to 1914. Taking average real wages in 1899 as 100, they never rose during this period above 109 (in 1905), and fell to 93, 102, 103 and 96 from 1911 to 1914. M. D. Anderson has shown

[1] Taussig, *International Trade*, p. 59.

that in 16 out of the 28 years from 1899 to 1927, and in 7 out of 15 years from 1899 to 1914, real wages and immigration varied inversely.[1] It is obvious that after the 1914 war, when the volume of immigration was only small relative to the total labour supply, immigration is unlikely to have had any appreciable effect on the general wage level, so that we are concerned only with the period 1899–1914. If we assume that it takes some time for the wage level to adjust itself to changes in the supply of labour, so that changes in wages may lag one year behind changes in immigration, we find with this lag the inverse relation in the year to year variation much stronger, since volume of immigration and average real wages then move in the same direction only in three years out of fourteen, while in eleven years an increase in immigration can be associated with a fall in real wages during the following year, or a decrease in immigration with a rise in real wages.[2]

The suggestion that the "new" immigration has increased real income per head of the total population and in the long run has at least not markedly reduced the level of real wages in the U.S. is supported by statistical evidence. But this evidence lends support to the view that during certain periods the number of admissions exceeded the absorptive capacity of the country, so that the necessary adjustments lagged behind and temporary economic dislocations with an adverse effect on the wage level could not be avoided. It seems doubtful whether a less rigid policy of discrimination against the new immigration than that pursued by the U.S. during the inter-war period would have depressed the wage level for white native labour. When large-scale immigration from Southern and Eastern Europe was discontinued, vacancies in former immigrant jobs, in spite of the heavy unemployment, were not taken up by white natives, but were given to a large extent at sub-standard wages to negroes from the Southern States or to Mexican labour which is not subject to the immigration restrictions.

If minimum wages can be enforced over the whole of the trade, or if the closed shop policy is generally introduced, as happened before the 1939 war in various countries of immigration, native workers are fairly well protected against the undercutting of their

[1] M. D. Anderson, *Dynamic Theory of Wealth Distribution*, p. 129.
[2] Anderson examines the correlation when changes in immigration are lagged one year behind the changes in wages. The result for 1899–1914 is a *positive* relation in 11 of the 14 years. This indicates that immigrants tended to flow in more rapidly when real wages had increased in the preceding year.

wages by immigrant labour. An efficient enforcement of these regulations is likely to cause a reduction in the inflow of unqualified labour, but its extent depends partly on conditions in the countries of emigration and on opportunities for immigrants elsewhere. These immigrants who are able to find employment at the legal wage rates can affect the existing wage level only when wage rates lie above the legal minimum, but they may be able to compete with native workers by harder work and greater efficiency and therefore increase unemployment among the natives and weaken their bargaining power. The closed shop principle enables trade unions to prevent such a development by excluding immigrants from membership. Immigrants are then pushed into those occupations where they have to meet with less resistance and where they are often less useful from an economic and social point of view. Friction between immigrants and natives is then almost unavoidable, unless the economy is fast expanding.

Of all categories of immigrants the unskilled labour group from countries with a low standard of living is most likely to depress the existing wage level. Immigration of other groups which do not compete with native labour is from the labour viewpoint more desirable. As the entrepreneur class and capitalists are generally in favour of free immigration, because an increase in the supply of labour is likely to increase their profits and their share in the total national income, so the wage-earner is interested in any immigration which is likely to increase the supply of other factors of production and the demand for labour. As we shall see later, in periods of political stability migration of capitalists does not necessarily imply a transfer of their funds from the country of emigration to that of immigration; movements of capital occur independently of those of its owners, and therefore the immigration of capitalists can only under certain circumstances be associated with an increase in capital investment. But the capitalist immigrant as consumer and taxpayer will have a favourable influence on the wage level. Entrepreneurs who are prepared to invest their own funds in the new country after their immigration are most likely to raise the wage level. The supply of labour remaining unchanged, an increase in capital investment and entrepreneur activity tends to raise marginal productivity and remuneration of labour, as we can assume that labour, capital and entrepreneur activity are in the main complementary factors of production, especially in new countries with an abundant supply of unused natural resources, and that therefore the effect of substitution will remain relatively small.

A similar effect may be expected from the immigration of technical and skilled labour which usually occurs in connection with foreign capital investment in countries with a low wage level and little developed capitalistic production. The immigration of a relatively small number of technical experts and qualified workmen may then raise the wage rates and real income of the natives. Whether this result will be actually achieved depends largely on the circumstances which have led to the movement.

A few examples may be given in order to illustrate various types of this co-migration of capital and technical labour. The Russian Industrial Revolution which began about the turn of this century would have been impossible without foreign loans and without the immigration of foremen, skilled workers and technical experts, mainly from Germany. Moreover, a high protective tariff for manufactured goods was a condition of this industrialization. During the inter-war period many U.S.A. companies established branch factories in Canada which were usually financed with U.S. capital and used to a large extent immigrants from the U.S.A. for their managing staff and their technical workers. This movement was partly due to the lower wage level in Canada, which made the import of manufactured goods from Canada to the U.S.A. profitable, partly to the high protective tariff on these goods in Canada which led on the Canadian market to the replacement of imported by Canadian-made goods. Similar considerations account for the establishment of U.S.A. branch factories in Europe. The Ford Motor Works for instance profited from the relatively low wage rates in Eire. Not only were Ford tractors built there by American engineers and Irish workmen for the Irish home market and that of large parts of Europe, but they were even exported to the U.S.A. British industry found it necessary in order to compete with certain lines in the Far East to transfer capital and technical labour to India and to produce there, using cheap Indian labour. The oil industry in Mexico and South America was developed by capital and technicians from the U.S.A., that in Iraq mainly by British experts and capital. In these cases the incentive to the movements was provided by the existence of unused natural resources which promised high profits and which could only be exploited by co-migration of capital and technical labour. All these migratory movements brought about an increase in the demand for unskilled labour in the country of immigration and therefore—under the given circumstances—had presumably a favourable effect on the wage level in the country of immigration. It is, however, a matter of controversy whether the policy of high protection, without which some of these movements would not have occurred, had not an opposite effect by outweighing the advantages of the immigration through raising the costs of living and depressing real wages in the country of immigration. This issue will be discussed in the next chapter.

Only a few conclusions of general validity can be drawn from our inquiry into the effect of migration on the wage level. We have to remember that any migration releases a multitude of other forces which, working interdependently, affect the trend of the wage rate and determine what wage reduction is necessary in order to absorb a given amount of immigrant labour. When a certain easily absorbable volume of migration has been reached, the absorption of a relatively small number of additional immigrants would require a relatively large fall of the wage rate. A fall in the supply price for immigrant labour, however, is likely to bring about changes in the prices of the other factors of production and of the product, and the net result is generally an increased demand at a lower price level which has a counteracting effect on the declining trend of the wage rate. But time is required before these adjustments can become effective. Therefore, as already suggested, a constant flow of immigrants at a rate which is always so regulated as to allow for the necessary adjustments, can be absorbed more easily and with less pressure on the general wage level than the same amount if added at one time.

c. Development of Sweated Industries

Demand curves for labour indicate what wage reduction is necessary in order to absorb a given number of additional workers; if the demand for immigrant labour is highly elastic, a small fall in the wage rate will suffice to absorb a relatively large number of immigrants. Obviously a certain time is required for any change in the number of employed to take place. The demand curve for a particular type of labour will therefore vary in shape according to the period of time in which the changes are supposed to occur. Generally speaking the demand for labour is less elastic over a short period than over longer periods which allow for adjustments to become effective in the supply of and the demand for other factors of production and in the demand for the product, though on the other hand adjustments in the supply of factors of production rival to immigrant labour which need time, may reduce the demand for immigrants over the longer periods. With capitalistic production, provided the existing capital equipment is not used much below optimum capacity, the proportion between capital equipment and labour is rather rigid, so that over the short period only a limited new supply of labour can be absorbed, and any appreciable rise in the number of employed implies a relatively heavy fall in the physical marginal productivity of labour, and therefore, under normal conditions, a heavy fall in the rate of remuneration. The elasticity of demand over longer periods largely depends therefore upon the extent to which the necessary adjustments of capital equipment take place.

The response of highly capitalized industries to the incentive to employing more labour afforded by a fall in the wage rates for immigrant labour, when its supply increases, will be slower and less marked than that of those industries whose production is labour-intensive, that is to say, which are using a relatively large amount of labour. It will be less marked, because a given fall in the wage rate has in a capital-intensive production only a comparatively small direct effect on the costs of production and therefore on the price of the product; it will be slower, because an expansion of production by using more labour relatively to capital equipment requires a rearrangement and replacement of the existing equipment. It can therefore be assumed that the fall in prices of goods whose production is labour-intensive is likely to be heavier than that of goods whose production is capital-intensive, and that—provided differentials in relative elasticities of demand have not an opposite effect—the demand for the former will rise more than that for the latter.

These reasons account for the fact that, if demand and supply on the labour market are in equilibrium, new immigrants can relatively easily be absorbed by those trades, occupations and industries which work in a combination with only little capital. No capital investment at all is needed for certain kinds of personal services. Experience shows that, of all types of unqualified immigrant labour, domestic servants can be absorbed most easily.

As their production consists in the services they render to the consumer, any fall in the rate of their remuneration is fully reflected in the price of their product. Domestic service in countries with high standards of living is widely considered as socially inferior, and the native population often prefers unemployment to this occupation. During periods of general unemployment the demand for domestic servants remained relatively unaffected, and during the depression they were practically the only type of unqualified labour which was admitted by the immigration countries. Various other types of consumable personal services have become immigrant jobs during periods of heavy immigration. The immigrants find openings as waiters, etc.; the boot-blacking business in various American and Canadian towns was almost monopolized by Greek immigrants. In the distributive trades immigrants are found mainly in those lines whose expansion requires only little or no capital, even if the demand for these services is inelastic. News vendors, pedlars and various types of middleman, working as entrepreneurs or on a commission basis, are occupations open to immigrants, especially if they have to meet elsewhere the resistance of organized native labour. In industry those branches which are labour-intensive and need but little fixed capital equipment for their production, can absorb over the shorter periods a relatively large number of immigrants. A typical example is the development of the clothing trades during the period of free immigration.

Wages for unskilled or semi-skilled labour represented a very important cost item in the manufacture of cheap clothing. The effect of wage reduction on the cost price was therefore relatively high. As free competition prevailed both in the production and the distribution of these goods, the gains accrued automatically to the benefit of the consuming public in the form of lower prices; the reduction of prices made for an increase in sales and output. A large part of the demand for cheap clothing in England and the United States until the latter part of the last century was met by imports from low-wage countries. By reducing costs of production, native producers in both countries were enabled to undersell the importers and to replace imported goods by native goods on the home market, so that the conditions existed for a large expansion of production and a relatively large number of additional workers could be absorbed by the clothing industry. This, however, could be achieved only by making production as labour-intensive as possible and by paying to immigrants wages much below the native level. The result in both England and America was a revival of the home industries in the form of sweated industries. These sweated industries which did not require capital investment in equipment and but little working capital for their expansion, became one of the outlets for the pressure on the labour market, caused by the increase of immigration from low standard of living countries about the turn of the century. The new industries tended to concentrate at the points of cheap immigrant labour. In England it was at London, in Whitechapel, where Jewish refugees mainly from Tsarist Russia had congregated; in the United States it was the East Coast—New York—which supplied the sweated trades with unskilled or semi-skilled labour, mainly of Jewish and Italian origin; on the West coast San Francisco became a new centre of the clothing industry, using, as long as it was available, almost exclusively Chinese immigrant labour.

The appalling social conditions associated with the sweated industries were partly due to unscrupulous exploitation of the new immigrants by the entrepreneurs, usually themselves immigrants of not much longer standing; partly the necessary result of the rapid expansion of a new industry which depended largely upon a constant reduction of labour costs.

On balance, it would seem that the immigrants absorbed by these industries brought a net gain to the receiving countries, from a purely economic point of view. Generally speaking, they did not replace native labour, but rather raised the real wages of the natives through the price-fall of the wage goods they manufactured. They created additional employment in other industries, mainly the textile industry. Cotton and wool manufacture were appreciably influenced by the development of the ready-made clothing industry. Both in England and in the United States medium and cheaper grades of textiles were now exported in the form of ready-made garments, whereas it would have been impossible to sell the fabrics from which the garments were made.[1]

The immigrants themselves were, in spite of their subsistence earnings, in most cases better off than they would have been at home, and they might expect that in due course their conditions would improve. These expectations proved correct; the wage

---

[1] Cf. Clark, *History of Manufacture in the United States*, Vol. II; *Reports on the Volume and Effects of Recent Immigration from Eastern Europe*, Cmd. 7406, 1894; *Reports to the Board of Trade on Alien Immigration*, Cmd. 7113.

differentials became narrower,. the sweated industries were gradually replaced by more capitalistic methods of production, but the clothing industries continued to expand and remained competitive on the world market.[1]

It is, however, easy to see that economic expansion by the development of sweated immigrant industries is a method which belongs to the past, and would be bound to fail if it were attempted under present social and technological conditions in any country of immigration.

For other industries in the U.S.A. it is less evident that the inflow of immigrants can be associated with a similar expansion of production. Immigrants were to a large extent absorbed by mining and the iron and steel industry, in cotton mills and textile factories; they performed indispensable work in building canals, railroads and highways. The demand for labour in all these occupations was, apart from cyclical fluctuations, continually growing, and would not have been met without immigration. But expansion in these industries, after the two-shift system had where possible been adopted, could only occur *pari passu* with new capital investment, and, when the latter lagged behind, wage-cutting immigrants tended to replace that part of native labour which did not succeed in being promoted to supervisory posts. "The opportunities for the new hands depend upon the expansion of industry and the resources of the country. Provided this expansion occurs there is no overcrowding of the labour market. The new resources and new investments demand new labour, and, if this expansion is strong enough, the new labour as well as the existing labour may secure advances in wages."[2] When this overcrowding of the labour market occurred at various periods of large-scale immigration into the United States, it was certainly not the case that no new resources were available or that the U.S. economy was unable to provide the capital necessary for industrial development.[3] It is rather the formation of bottlenecks which accounts largely for the overcrowded labour market.

[1] The clothing industries have remained the industries with the lowest capital investment per wage earner. In 1928 in Pennsylvania, the amount was in the manufacturing of:

Shirts	$563		Cigars	$851
Women's clothing	800		Men's clothing	900

as compared with:

Pig iron	$19.658		Cement	$13.926
Coke	15.627		Iron and steel bars	10.026

(Bliss, *Structure of Manufacturing Production*, Nat. Bureau of Economic Research, 1939).

[2] Prof. J. R. Commons, in *Report of the Industrial Commission*, Vol. XV.

[3] But cf. Chapter VII, 2.

They were due to a rate of immigration, temporarily above absorptive capacity, which did not allow the time necessary for capital adjustments to become effective.

D. INTERDEPENDENCE BETWEEN THE DEMAND AND THE SUPPLY OF IMMIGRANT LABOUR, THE DEMAND AND SUPPLY OF CAPITAL AND OF GOODS

The statement that the usefulness of an increased labour supply depends under otherwise stationary conditions on a proportionate increase in capital investment, does not exclude the possiblity that the new labour supply may be the cause of increased investment activities. It may be assumed that population increase in general tends to increase the propensity to consume and to increase investment opportunities. At a given state of technique, a growth in private real investment is with·a stationary or declining population largely limited to the form of a deepening of capital. The deepening process means that more capital is used per unit of output, and implies on our assumption a continuous fall in the rate of interest. "The rate of interest at any moment would be such that every form of capital equipment yielding more than that rate had already been installed. The actual rate of interest would thus represent the yield of the most remunerative forms of capital not yet installed."[1] Under these conditions a growth in investments depends—apart from possible State intervention—upon a fall in the rate of interest or on a narrowing of the margin between the current rate of interest and the prospective yield of the investment. It is, however, unlikely that without Government intervention the rate of interest will decline sufficiently—in the absence of population growth or other stimuli to investment—to equate savings and investments at a level consistent with full employment; the marginal efficiency of capital will tend to fall below the current rate of interest.

If the active working population is growing, real investment can take the form of widening the capital equipment; as a proportional growth of capital is then required to preserve the same structure of production, new investment can take place without a fall in the rate of interest or in the marginal efficiency of capital. The conclusion consistent with this line of argument is that population growth will tend to stimulate investment activities, and as it is the growth of the active working population which

[1] Hawtrey, *Capital and Unemployment*, p. 35.

has to be taken into account, the same conclusion applies to the effect of immigration on investment activity. If natural increase keeps the net growth of the labour force in harmony with the amount of saving intended for investment which is available for the widening of capital, any further increase in population through immigration would tend to lower the amount of capital equipment per head and therefore normally of real income per head also. But this would not be the case if without immigration the economy were not expanding sufficiently to provide the adequate investment outlets necessary to avoid a rise in unemployment and a fall in real income. But little new investment is required if a declining population is kept stationary through immigration.

Our general conclusions, that the usefulness of an increased labour supply depends, under otherwise stationary conditions, on a proportionate increase in capital investment and that immigration tends to stimulate investment activities, need further discussion.

In the case of large-scale immigration the new supply of labour is, as we have seen, likely to press on the wage level before investment activity can adopt itself to the new conditions, and we must therefore take into account in such a case the effect of falling wage rates on capital investment.

As labour and capital are partly co-operant and partly rival, an increase in the quantity of labour not only requires new investment to co-operate with the new labour, but will to a certain extent replace capital equipment and so release capital equipment for co-operation with the new labour supply. But obviously this process can only be a slow one owing to the specific nature of most industrial equipment. If the fall in wage rates makes the application of less capitalistic methods more profitable than before, some of the existing equipment may become obsolescent, but its use will be continued over a short period so long as the prime costs of the more capitalistic process are not higher than the costs resulting from a shift to less capitalistic production. Generally speaking, the relation between labour and capital is predominantly one of co-operation,[1] and the volume of immigrants likely to be absorbed by the replacement of capital and the transition to less capitalistic production is both for industry and agriculture comparatively unimportant.

The effect of falling wage rates on investment activity is determined by various counteracting factors, so that any general-

[1] Cf. Pigou, *Economics of Welfare*, p. 662.

ization seems impossible. For instance, it has been shown that investment reacted quite differently on the wage-reduction which took place in the United States in 1920 and on that of 1929.[1] In 1920–21, when general opinion held that prices and wages had been kept too high, the wage reductions were followed by a general revival of investment activities which accounts for the boom period 1922–29; under the different circumstances of 1929–30 larger wage reductions could not produce a similar effect.[2]

The main reason why investors do generally not react—under conditions of free competition on the labour market—to wage reductions so readily as the wider range of investment opportunities would justify is that usually with a falling price and wage level is associated the expectation that wages will continue to fall and that it will therefore be more profitable to postpone investment. On the other hand too optimistic expectations concerning the rate of future immigration may lead to over-investment in housing and similar lines of production which are likely to profit most directly from immigration. The element of uncertainty as to the future trend of immigration is in the case of regulated immigration largely reduced; investors are provided with a sounder basis for their expectations if they know that the volume of immigration will be kept in harmony with the country's absorptive capacity.

Wage reductions, even if accompanied by a fall in the price of wage goods, are likely to bring about a shift in the distribution of incomes which is more favourable to entrepreneurs and rentiers. As their marginal propensity to save is relatively high, a larger share of the national income may become available for investment.

Moreover, the assumption which underlay our argument that immigration does not alter the state of technique, has to be qualified. This necessity is obvious in the case of immigration of technical labour and of all other types of immigrants who are able to improve the stock of technical knowledge in the receiving country.[3] Their immigration is likely to increase real income

---

[1] Cf. Sweezey, "Population Growth and Investment Opportunity," in *Quarterly Journal*, 1941, p. 65.

[2] The fact that the volume of U.S. immigration was relatively high in 1921–24, and had become severely restricted by 1929, has hardly any connection with this phenomenon.

[3] This contribution to technical knowledge in the U.S. is not confined to highly qualified immigrants. The dried fruit industry, for example, grew up in recent decades in Southern California when a number of South Europeans had settled there (cf. Ohlin, p. 363).

per head in more than due proportion. The state of technique may also be affected to a certain extent by the immigration of unskilled labour. When the price of unskilled labour falls relatively to that of other factors of production, it is likely that new inventions will be made and new processes developed with a view to substituting unskilled labour for these factors. The arrival of the "new immigration" in the United States had this effect. The new inventions, however, were generally not capital-saving but rather skilled-labour-saving. The large-scale employment in mining and manufacture of these immigrants who had no previous industrial experience of any kind, was made possible only by the invention of new machines and the application of new processes, which largely reduced the amount of skill and experience formerly required. In bituminous coal mining the invention of the mining machine replaced the skilled pick or hand miner. Other inventions in textile and in iron and steel factories had a similar effect.[1]

During the period of large-scale immigration, rapid population growth in general, the opening-up of the new continents, and technical progress provided ample opportunity for capital-widening investment. For this period the assumption that the demand for goods in general is fixed by the supply of goods in general seems to be borne out by the facts. The demand for labour is then not determined by the demand for goods, but mainly by the supply of capital and by the technical coefficients of production. Unemployment is on these assumptions either frictional or voluntary, and it is taken for granted that any expansion of production in accordance with the law of the market will produce a corresponding increase in demand; the economic significance of immigration lies therefore in its possible contribution to the volume of production. Its stimulating effect on consumption is under such circumstances rather irrelevant. The indisputable fact that "every migrant has a mouth and two arms and his children have a mouth and no arms" has always been stressed in order to show that the immigrant is not only a competitor but also a customer of the natives. But so long as a general deficiency of demand was practically unknown and savings found adequate investment outlets, it did not much matter what part of his income an immigrant preferred to consume; his two hands were of more importance than the mouths he had to feed.

[1] Davie, *Immigration*, p. 238.

E. MIGRATION UNDER CONDITIONS OF GENERAL UNEMPLOYMENT

In recent years this attitude has become almost reversed. The theory that supply creates its own demand seemed to be contradicted by the fact of chronic depressions, and it was held that an effective demand at a point of equilibrium short of full or optimum employment accounted for a contraction of economic activities which could not be explained as merely of cyclical character. When in all immigration and emigration countries a large percentage of the population of working age was unemployed and the existing capital equipment was used far below capacity, the main criterion of the usefulness of any type of immigration became its ability to stimulate the demand for goods. In Britain this situation led to the somewhat paradoxical result that during the period of general unemployment, apart from special cases, only immigrants in the non-working age-groups—below 18 or above 60—were admitted. Many other countries, for instance France, Switzerland, and several Central American Republics, pursued an immigration policy on similar lines, preventing their immigrants from exercising any productive activity, whether paid or unpaid. It is easy to see that with these restrictions immigration was confined to certain categories of refugees. Generally speaking, immigrants who merely consume without adding directly to production were considered as the most welcome type, provided that the means for their livelihood could be provided without public assistance. The line of argument supporting this policy runs as follows: As the contraction of real income is due to a deficiency in demand for consumers' goods, any additional demand for these goods will tend to reactivate idle equipment and idle man-power. When consumption has been adjusted to the capacity of the existing capital equipment, any further increase in consumption necessitates additional investment. In accordance with the acceleration principle, the increase in investment will be on a larger scale than the expansion of consumption, and this new investment is likely to lead to a more than proportionate increase in employment through the effect of the multiplier.

This argument is conclusive, if the funds now spent on the purchase of consumers' goods for immigrants would not have been used for similar purposes if immigration has not occurred. If the immigrants so admitted are of independent means, they will normally transfer their funds from the emigration to the immigration country. This unilateral transfer of purchasing power may be achieved merely by a reduction of the idle credit balance of the country of emigration in the currency of the country of immigration. In this case the immigrant's consumption represents a clear increase in the demand for goods of first order in the immigration country and is therefore likely to have the desired effect. The transfer may, however, imply the purchase of currency of the immigration country by the country of emigration, and this transaction may lead to an increase of imports from the country of emigration or to a decrease of exports from the country of immigration, and thus partly cancel out the gain.

In recent years refugees without means have been admitted in various countries as immigrants without permission to work, if other people provided for their cost of living. This does not, of course, alter the issue, if the necessary funds are transferred from abroad and are not to be repaid. If the funds are collected in the country of immigration, no international transfer of purchasing power takes place, but it may be presumed that funds which had been idle or invested (in the form of loans or shares) are switched over to consumption. It is less probable that those who gave these funds will curtail their own expenditure on consumers' goods. If they did so, this would probably mean an increase in the demand for wage goods at the expense of the demand for luxury goods, and therefore not necessarily a net gain for production; in England, for instance, a considerable percentage of wage goods have to be imported, whereas many luxury products such as motor cars are almost entirely produced by the national industry. These few possible exceptions, however, are unlikely to invalidate in real life the general principle that the increase in the general demand for consumption goods brought about by the admission of immigrants has in a period of depression a favourable effect on the real income of the receiving country and is likely to hasten recovery and a fuller employment of the idle factors of production. As soon as full employment has been reached—as for instance in Britain under war conditions—the situation is again reversed. An increase in the demand for consumption goods can then be met only at the expense of the production of non-consumers' goods (instruments of production, armaments and export goods) and is likely to lead to a rise in prices for consumption goods which at that stage is as undesirable as the wartime alternative of smaller rations per head. When in 1940 Germany had reached full employment before Italy entered the war and imported Italian miners to work in German mines, the arrangements made were designed to curtail as much as possible the consumption of these "immigrants" in Germany. Their food was imported from Italy, prepared by Italian cooks, and cash payments were made in Italian currency, to be sent to Italy.[1]

Even if in the receiving country unemployment is fairly widespread, it seems very doubtful whether a policy of excluding immigrants from any work is based on sound economic reasoning. The recognition that under certain conditions a country may experience involuntary unemployment[2] does not imply that the demand for labour is everywhere and with respect to all groups of labour met at the prevailing wage level, and that any vacancy can be adequately filled from the pool of unemployed. Even in a period of industrial stagnation, some industries will grow, owing to a shift in demand, while others contract; workpeople should then move from the declining to the expanding industries. But this necessary adjustment often does not take place. A large number of the unemployed are elderly people, somewhat unadaptable to an unfamiliar employment, and a surplus of unemployed labour may remain attached to the industries and areas where employment has declined in spite of unsatisfied demand for labour in other areas and industries. It is the greater adaptability and mobility of the immigrants which would prevent the formation of bottlenecks due to an insufficient supply of labour to growing industries and which are likely to delay recovery.[3]

The theory which sees in a deficiency of effective demand the main reason for general unemployment may be used to explain why the U.S.A. has been unable since the Great Depression to reach an adequate employment level in peacetime. It has been argued that the chronic unemployment in the U.S. during the decade before the 1939 war was due largely to a lack of investment outlets caused by a decline in the rate of population growth. The population of the industrialized section of the United States increased by 10 per cent from 1916 to 1922, and

---

[1] Further aspects of the relation between business cycle and migration will be discussed below.

[2] It is, of course, more difficult in real life than in theory to determine whether a depression is chronic or temporary and whether unemployment is involuntary, voluntary or frictional.

[3] Cf. *The Population Problem*, H. O. Henderson, p. 87; A. Plant, p. 129.

again by 10 per cent from 1922 to 1928, but the increase from 1930 to 1936 amounted only to 3 per cent; similarly the population of the entire country increased from 1922 to 1928 by 9.1 per cent, and from 1930 to 1936 by only 4.3 per cent.

"During the Great Depression, accordingly, there did not accumulate any such backlog of housing shortage as had developed in the period 1916–22, and there was not the pressure from a continued rapid growth in population such as occurred in the period 1922–28. The 'extensive' or expansionist outlets for investment in housing, incident to population growth, are thus in large part gone."[1] This decline in population growth has, as Professor Hansen suggests, a profound significance for investment outlets; it differentiates our age from the nineteenth century when "a perfectly enormous amount of capital" was absorbed for no other reason than the tremendous rate of population growth.[2]

But this argument does not lead Professor Hansen to the conclusion one might expect, namely that a resumption of large-scale immigration would be desirable for the United States, as it creates investment outlets for capital-widening which are, according to him, essential for reaching full employment. He admits that the United States can absorb a considerable increase in population, and can doubtless *absorb in the long run a larger volume of immigration than any other part of the world.* "But there are good reasons why this country could not, without endangering her own security, loosen her immigration restrictions."[3] One reason is the assimilation problem discussed in a previous chapter; the other reason he gives is that the U.S. will be compelled to undertake in the next decade a difficult structural reorganization of her economic life.

Population growth (through immigration or through natural increase) is undoubtedly a major factor in keeping an economy in full employment by providing opportunities for capital-widening. It is, however, more questionable whether the mere addition of new people is likely to have the same effect *after dislocations have actually occurred.* The normal type of immigrant, the unskilled worker without funds, will not substantially increase the aggregate effective demand for consumers' goods until he has found employment, and it is not easy to see why his mere

---

[1] A. H. Hansen, *Full Recovery or Stagnation?* p. 300.
[2] *Ibid.*, p. 313.
[3] *Ibid.*, p. 253.

existence should lead entrepreneurs to take a more optimistic view of the profitability of new capital investment, and so induce a resumption of investment activity and increased employment.

It is true that, if the immigrants are assisted by public funds, they will create an additional demand for consumers' goods, including durable consumers' goods such as houses. Their immigration is therefore likely to have a favourable effect on employment and investment activities. But the immigrants constitute not only additional demand for but also additional supply of labour. They would reduce unemployment only if the number of new openings were larger than the number of new immigrants seeking employment. Other forms of public spending, for instance schemes for the clearance of slums or an increase in the expenditure on assisting the unemployed, may have the same stimulating effect on employment; these measures would then be a more efficient means of reducing unemployment, since they do not imply an increase in the labour supply.

F. Migration and Structural Readjustment

Similar arguments apply to the usefulness of immigration in bringing about structural readjustments. We have shown in Chapter IV, 2, why such structural readjustments can be achieved much more easily and less painfully with an increasing population, but it depends on the particular case whether the advantages of a population increase brought about by immigration compensate for its possible disadvantages. In the case of the U.S.A. the need for structural readjustment, on which Hansen's argument is based, is most urgent in the agricultural sector of production. The dislocations in American agricultural production are neither mainly the effect of the declining rate of American population growth nor are they likely to be mitigated by immigration. They are due rather to the decline of the population growth of America's overseas customers, to a fall in the *international* demand for her agricultural production, to increasing production both in America and in countries competing with her in these lines, and to a fall in the national demand for these goods as a consequence of the higher standard of living and of changed dietary habits.[1]

---

[1] The *per capita* consumption of cereals has declined by one-third since the beginning of the century. Totalling all foods on the basis of either farm or retail prices or calories, there has also been a significant decline (cf. O. E. Baker in *Am. Economic Journal*, Suppl. 1939, p. 387). According to the estimates of the International Institute

It has been estimated that in 1940 one-half of the pre-war farm population (30.2 millions) could with the aid of current technology supply the agricultural products needed by the U.S.A. for domestic consumption and export.[1] But in American agriculture the technical coefficient of production in respect to labour is continually decreasing. At the same time the supply of farm labour is increasing owing to the high rate of natural increase in rural districts. From 1922 to 1929 the average (internal) emigration from the farms amounted to 1,300,000, but the slump brought a reversal of the trend, and in 1932 the farms had a net immigration of 260,000 persons. Emigration was resumed after 1932, but was only about half that in the pre-depression period. Unable to obtain employment in the cities, the surplus farm population has been backing up on farms at a rate of 400,000 a year, and represented with the urban unemployed a huge unabsorbed supply of labour. Professor Spengler estimates that 10–16 millions of persons of productive age will transfer from the rural farm population to the non-farm population between 1930 and 1960.[2] This would imply that 5.6 to 9 millions of jobs will have to be developed outside agriculture for the employables flowing out of the farm population, in addition to 3.1 million jobs for the increase in the rural non-farming population and about 1 million jobs for the increase in the urban population of productive age.

Such a redistribution of population would imply an increase of 25–30 per cent of the number of employed outside agriculture; it would still mean a decline in the rate of growth, since the corresponding figure for 1910–1930 is 45 per cent, or 12.6 millions. It appears, however, that surplus agricultural labour and immigrant labour are largely competitive, that the resumption of large-scale immigration would be prejudicial to the absorption

of Agriculture the world production of wheat reached in 1938 a new record figure. The wheat production of North America rose from 235 million quintals in 1937 to 291 millions. Other foodstuffs capable of replacing wheat in the diet, such as rye, potatoes, rice, have also reached new high figures of production. Cotton production in U.S. had fallen in 1938–39 by about 35 per cent owing to the reduction by more than one-third of the area cultivated, but cotton stocks amounted in 1939 to 55 per cent of the production=14 million bales, of which 11 million bales were financed by the Treasury (cf. League of Nations, *World Economic Survey*, 1938–39, I.L.O. *Yearbook*, 1938–39).

[1] J. J. Spengler, "Population Trends and Economic Equilibrium," *Journal of Political Economy*, 1940, p. 156 ff. According to the U.S. Bureau of Agricultural Economics average farm employment in 1940, amounted to 10.6 million persons. This figure includes proprietors and self-employed, unpaid family workers, and wage and salary workers.

[2] O. E. Baker estimated that there was merely through natural increase a yearly surplus of 200,000 farm boys who cannot be absorbed by agriculture.

of this surplus population without proportionately stimulating the demand for agricultural products. The labour coming from the farms is mostly not trained for any skilled city job, and must seek employment at unskilled or semi-skilled work. The same characteristic applies, as we have seen, to immigrant labour. Moreover, our previous argument that immigrant is more mobile than native labour was scarcely valid in the United States during the depression. It has even been held that the high mobility of the U.S.A. unemployed was a dislocating factor which rather tended to delay recovery.[1]

With the entry of the U.S. into the war the problems of structural adjustment and population redistribution found a temporary solution. Between four and seven million people left the farms to join the armed forces or take up city jobs. The labour force actually employed in agriculture declined from 9.4 millions in 1939 to about 8.1 millions in 1944. This outflow, combined with the war-time increase in the demand for agricultural products, produced a marked labour shortage in the agricultural sector. But it has been estimated that in spite of insufficient supply of labour and machinery, farm production could be increased by about one-third of the pre-war average. Further progress in mechanization and technology is likely to lead to a substantial reduction in the amount of man-power per unit of farm production.[2] With a labour force of 7.5 millions, implying a decrease of 8 per cent from the 1944 low, the physical volume of agricultural production per head of the total U.S. population would probably lie 10 to 20 per cent above the 1939 level.[3] In any case the pressure from the farm population on employment opportunities in the non-agricultural sectors is likely to persist in the post-war years.

Industrial reconversion and the provision of jobs for about 9 million demobilized members of the armed forces are even greater and more urgent post-war problems. Undoubtedly this

---

[1] Not less than 12 per cent of the total population 5 years old and over lived in 1940 in a county or large city different from that where they had lived in 1935.

[2] *National Budgets for Full Employment*, National Planning Association, p. 66 (Planning Pamphlets Nos. 43, 44).

[3] *I.L.O. Yearbook*, 1938–39, points out that 195,000 workers had been displaced by the introduction of 65,000 mechanical maize pickers and that similar developments are expected to take place in the cotton industry. After the war, the complete mechanization of the sugar-beet industry will displace some tens of thousands of migrant labourers. The trend towards one-man operation (one-man hay baler, one-man all crop combine) means that one man with machines can farm alone a larger acreage than he used to do with several hired hands plus seasonal help (*Fortune*, June, 1945, Farm Column).

setting is not conducive to a re-orientation of U.S. immigration policy. There may, however, be a case for a substantial rise of the immigration quota after the U.S. economy has become adjusted to peace-time conditions. It should be realized that full employment of labour and capital equipment means for the post-war U.S. a national product of 170–190 billion \$—a real increase of about 50 per cent over the 1940 peace-time record. Unemployment is bound to occur to the extent to which expenditure on consumption and investment would fall below the value of the national product consistent with full employment. And it has been argued that such a gap is unavoidable, if the pattern of total expenditures (private investment, private consumption, and public expenditure) were in the post-war period to follow past relationships. Then post-war expenditure on the 1940 level would generate unemployment to the tune of some 20 millions, i.e. an unemployment rate of about 33 per cent.

A substantial part of the additional expenditure required to ensure full employment is likely to be allocated to the development and conservation of America's natural resources. A number of projects for the development of irrigation, power, navigation, and flood control as well as for soil conservation have been already authorized or are under consideration by Congress. Their object is primarily to provide opportunities for settlement and better jobs for the native population.[1] But if they materialize the discrepancy between the enormous absorptive capacity of the U.S., resulting from abundant natural resources and capital equipment, on the one hand, and her low population density and slow population growth on the other, will become even more marked than before the war, while the economic reasons against a positive immigration policy will have been largely removed.

When the structure of American economy has been adjusted to the requirements of a peace-time production consistent with a high level of employment, immigration might again become an important means of maintaining a steady rate of economic progress and of preventing a relapse into general unemployment.

It seems that the immigration policy of the Dominions during the period of transition to peace-time conditions will be governed by similar considerations. Though it would be much easier to recruit suitable immigrants from Britain and liberated Europe

---

[1] The Columbia Basin Project of the U.S. Bureau of Reclamation alone will provide livelihood for at least 350,000 on new farms or in new industries.

before the potential applicants have been re-housed and re-settled
in their old countries, the Dominions have to give priority to the
more urgent claims of their native populations.[1]

G. MIGRATION AND THE BUSINESS CYCLE

In the preceding discussion of the bearing of migration on
wages, unemployment, chronic depression, and structural adjustment we have covered ground which is essential for the under-
standing of the mechanism of the trade cycle. We need not go
into the many controversial issues connected with the explanation
of this mechanism in order to see that major changes in the
volume of migration may be both the cause and the effect of
cyclical fluctuations. It may be argued that immigration tends
to delay the downturn of the cycle by supplying new labour for
industrial expansion without a corresponding rise of the wage
level, but this may lead to an excessive expansion in the capital
industries and increase the severity of the subsequent depression.
On the other hand it is likely, as we have shown, that certain
types of immigrants will hasten recovery during a period of
depression. The sudden cessation of a constant flow of immigrants
is bound to have an adverse effect on income and employment
in those industries which had previously satisfied the demand of
the immigrants during the period of transition until their economic
absorption. Our argument presumed that the typical immigrant
depends on finding employment soon after his arrival, as he has
usually only a small amount of savings on which he can live during
the transition period.[2] But it is easy to see that the aggregate of
this demand must have been considerable in the case of large-
scale immigration for those immediately concerned. Since widespread unemployment is likely to prevail during periods of
depression it seems that these favourable effects of immigration
are more than compensated by the adverse effect of unqualified
immigrant labour on the prospect of bringing the native labour-
market into equilibrium.

Under conditions of free migration fluctuations of the business
cycle coincide in practically all immigration countries with
fluctuations in the volume of immigration. In Argentina net
immigration fell during the nineties, when slump conditions pre-

---

[1] Cf. *Migration within the British Commonwealth*, British Government White Paper,
June, 1945 (Cmd. 6658). Australia's post-war policy was discussed above, p. 113.
[2] The size of the capital brought in by immigrants will be discussed in the next
chapter.

vailed, to 397,000, from 855,000 in the preceding decade, and rose again during the more prosperous following decade to 1,177,000. Brazil during the boom period of 1887–1898 had an annual immigration of 83,000 as compared with 24,000 in the six preceding years and 55,000 during the period of deflation from 1895 to 1905.[1] Jerome, investigating the correlation between business fluctuations and fluctuations in the volume of migration, found that migration is predominantly determined by business conditions in the immigration country.[2] When the business cycles of the two countries run parallel, migration appears greater during the upswing of the cycle and during the boom and contracts with a declining market and less employment opportunities in both countries. Generally the pull incentive is much stronger than the push incentive, so that if the business cycles in both countries show different fluctuations, the volume of immigration is not markedly affected by the cycle of the emigration country except in the case of absolute destitution, which may increase assistance from abroad, or political persecution. This correlation is, however, subject to a time lag of several months, and also during a heavy slump leaves a volume of immigration which cannot be readily absorbed.

The result of Jerome's investigation coincides with what common sense would have expected. As business fluctuations are generally more violent in immigration countries, the disparity between the income levels in the two countries becomes wider during the boom than it is during a depression. As the migration of prospective emigrants is largely financed by their friends or relatives in the receiving country, it is obvious that the prosperity of the latter will tend to increase the volume of migration. A certain time-lag is unavoidable, since it is not always easy for the general public to recognize the downturn of the business cycle in its earlier stages, and since time must be allowed for the period between the decision to emigrate and the actual immigration. That "the number of incoming immigrants is sufficiently large, even in depression periods, to suggest that, even though there may be extensive emigration, the adjustment of the recent immigrant to industry is an ever present and serious problem,"[3] is simply the result of the free system of migration within a free economic system. The incentive to migrate remains, in spite of

[1] Cf. Ohlin, op. cit., p. 331.
[2] H. Jerome, Migration and Business Cycle.
[3] H. Jerome, op. cit., p. 241.

slump conditions in the country of immigration, so long as the disparities between the standards of living in different countries are such that an immigrant can become better off by wage-cutting and replacing native labour than he was before his emigration.

H. CAPITAL VALUE OF MIGRANTS

Before summing up this chapter we must consider the validity of the argument, often put forward, that migration normally involves a gain for the receiving country and a loss for the sending country in that the typical migrant represents a considerable capital asset.

A country from which emigration takes place bears the cost of maintaining the emigrants during the unproductive period of their lives, while it is the country to which they migrate which derives the direct benefit of their productive energies. It is thus a costly business for a country to bring up children who later migrate abroad, and under modern conditions this cost is tending to increase. The upbringing of children now entails a considerable charge not only upon the resources of their parents, but, as the result of the development of public education, maternity and child welfare services, etc., during the last two generations, upon the public funds as well. It may be computed roughly that for every child who attains school-leaving age there has been spent £100 from public funds on education alone, while the total cost of upbringing to the State and to the parents may be put at upwards of £300. If the individual upon whom this expenditure has been incurred migrates at an early age to another country, it is obvious that the community secures little or no direct economic return.[1]

Consequently the receiving country is likely to gain from "the acquisition of a number of individuals, at the beginning or in the early part of the productive period of their lives, on whom it has spent nothing during their non-productive childhood and adolescence."[2]

A study of family budgets conveys a rough idea of the amount of private expenditure required to bring up a child until he reaches adolescence and begins to become self-supporting. For the U.S.A. the cost involved has been investigated by Lotka and Dublin. They calculated the average cost of raising a child in a typical American family of moderate income (annual income of the head of the household: $2,500). They found that on the basis of 1935–1936 prices $6,790 is spent on a child up to his 16th birthday and $7,762 up to his 18th birthday. If allowance is made for losses by death and for interest on expenditure ($2\frac{1}{2}$ per cent), total private investment in bringing up a child of

[1] Report of the Committee on Empire Migration, Cmd. 4075.
[2] Inter-Departmental Committee on Migration Policy, 1934, Cmd. 4689.

16 amounts to $8,414 and for a child of 18 $9,862. These figures, however, do not include the value of the personal services of the mother or the cost of public education and other services furnished by the community for which there is no direct charge, e.g. medical care.[1] The capital value of these public services is difficult to assess. But a rising tendency has been obvious during the last decades and is likely to become more marked in the future, mainly for two reasons: In order to check the decline in fertility the State in many countries has undertaken to relieve the burden of parenthood by paying children allowances in cash or in kind and by providing services which aim at reducing the drudgery of the mother in large families. This policy tends to raise the total cost of bringing up a child, because higher public expenditure is offset only partly by lower private expenditure. Moreover in the "social service" State high priority is given to the needs of children and adolescents. Expenditure on their health and education is regarded as a sound social investment likely to bring high dividends when they have reached working age.

The losses for the sending country and the gains for the receiving country arising from the migration of young adults, however, seldom balance.

It is a fact that countries of immigration show a marked preference for immigrants in the pre-productive period, unless they have to meet with an immediate shortage of labour. The reason for this preference is that the education the adult immigrants have received in their native country is often not in line with the requirements of the country of immigration. This has been observed in the case of Empire migration. Though education in the United Kingdom and in the various Dominions is based on the same language and the same cultural background, it is widely held in the Dominions that adults who have completed their education outside the Dominion are less adaptable and less welcome as immigrants than youths whose education becomes a charge on the public funds of the receiving country.[2]

The same argument applies *a fortiori* to immigrants who have been brought up in a different language and in a cultural environment widely different from that of the receiving country. In this

---

[1] Cf. A. J. Lotka and L. I. Dublin, *The Money Value of a Man*. The figures quoted above are taken from more recent publications which bring the data of this book up to date (Metropolitan Life Insurance Co., Statistical Bulletin, Vol. 24, Nos. 9–11, Vol. 25, No. 1).

[2] In 1944 the Australian Cabinet approved a Governmental Scheme under which Australia will take 17,000 child migrants a year from British and European sources, in age groups of 6 to 12 years for alien children, and 6 to 14 years for British children.

case the problem of assimilation with all its economic implications, which we have outlined in Chapter V, alters the issue to a certain extent. Expenses for adult education become necessary, and measured by possible results, the yield of this expenditure is probably lower than that spent on the education of immigrants of pre-working age.

1. CONCLUDING REMARKS ON THE ECONOMIC EFFECT OF MIGRATION

Our inquiry into the various factors which govern the demand for immigrants led us to examine the effect of immigration on the wage rates, on the standard of living of the native working population, on investment activity, on the demand for goods, on unemployment, and on structural adjustment through internal migration. Two other factors, closely interconnected with those discussed: international capital movements and international trade, had also to be mentioned, but it seems best to leave their further examination to a separate chapter in view of their importance as possible alternatives to migration.

We had to focus our attention on the demand for unqualified immigrant labour, since it is mainly with immigration of this type that the receiving country has to reckon in the case of large-scale immigration, though a relative increase in the number of semi-skilled and skilled would-be emigrants can be presumed. The admission of immigrants with special qualifications is less problematic; immigration of these types may—as we have seen— affect the vested interests of small sections of the native population, but is unlikely to depress real income per head or the standard of living in the receiving country. It has been suggested that the specificity of factors of production has undergone a continuous secular increase. Technical progress and an increasing degree of fixity of the technical coefficients of production tend to depress the demand curves for unskilled labour.[1] Such a trend would adversely affect the capacity of industrialized countries to absorb unskilled immigrant labour. But other factors, the increasing demand for personal services and better facilities for acquiring semi-skill, for instance, may have a counteracting effect.

Spengler in *Chicago Economic Journal*, 1940, p. 156.

CHAPTER VII

MIGRATION, INTERNATIONAL TRADE AND INTERNATIONAL CAPITAL MOVEMENTS

"The development of international intercourse must necessarily be hampered unless it takes place simultaneously in every sphere—that is to say not merely in the international trade of goods but also in the circulation of capital and the movement of men." By adopting this resolution the Assembly of the League of Nations[1] emphasized the close relationship between the men, money and market aspects of international economics. An examination of this relationship is the object of this chapter.

It is easy to see that movements of capital and goods *may* occur without corresponding migratory movements; indeed, the classical theory of international trade is based on the assumption that international mobility of capital and labour is practically non-existent, whereas within a single country both are supposed to be freely mobile. In the preceding chapter we have seen that in the past migratory movements occurred which were not dependent upon corresponding movements of capital, and which to a certain extent tended to reduce the volume of international trade by enabling the receiving country to produce commodities which had previously been imported.

On the other hand we have seen various instances of migratory movements whose close interdependence with capital movements or international trade was evident. The new continents were able to absorb the huge masses of immigrants from Europe up to the turn of the last century only; (1) because there was a continuous flow of capital exports from Europe to these countries which provided the necessary capital equipment for the immigrants; and (2) because free trade had made possible the export of agricultural consumers' goods such as wheat and other raw materials, cotton and wool for instance, from the new countries to Europe. We also dealt with various cases of co-migration, where either capital investment requires the co-migration of unskilled labour, technical labour or entrepreneurs, or the

[1] Meeting of October, 10, 1936.

231

migration of entrepreneurs in industry or farming, or of rentiers, depends largely on the possibility of having funds transferred to the new country.

All this suggests that there is no one-way causal relationship between migration and the movements of capital and goods. In some cases migration can be considered as the cause of the other movements and in others as the effect, but often their interdependence is such that it is not possible to distinguish between them.

Though it is scarcely possible to overrate the importance of a co-operation between the movements of men, money and goods in bringing about economic readjustments of international dislocations and in increasing the level of income in general, it cannot be overlooked that to a certain extent these movements may be considered as substitutes for one another. Obstacles to migration may lead to an increase in the volume of capital movements or international trade and conversely. The significance of this substitutional effect will be discussed in the last part of this chapter.

It goes without saying that throughout the history of migration the immigrant with some means of his own has had, other things being equal, a much better chance of success than the immigrant who had to earn his living immediately after his arrival, notwithstanding the fact that at all times a relatively large number of capitalist immigrants have soon joined the ranks of the destitutes, while others, after starting without any means, became highly successful within a relatively short time. But such exceptional cases do not invalidate the general rule.

The amount of capital which an immigrant needs in order to ensure him a fair chance of success naturally differs widely in each individual case. Generally speaking, we have to distinguish between immigrants into urbanized and industrialized regions and immigrant-settlers on the land. The financial problems which the settler on the land has to face were discussed under the heading "Methods of Settlement" (page 150 ff.). In the present context it is important to realize that settlement is no longer possible without substantial capital investment for each undertaking; there is little scope for that type of pioneer settlement which for half a century after the Napoleonic wars absorbed a large part of the immigration into the new continents. Moreover the modern immigrant cannot expect to save as a wage-earner in the new country the capital necessary for settlement. Since the number of would-be immigrant settlers with sufficient capital is likely to remain small, and for other reasons to be mentioned later, the future of immigration for settlement depends largely on the possibility of providing the bulk of the necessary capital from outside sources.

Immigrants into urbanized and industrialized regions are generally less dependent on capital. As outlined in Chapter VI (p. 200 ff.), their capital requirements are usually confined to the amount necessary to help them over the transitional period of adjustment. In the case of mass immigration, success is largely determined by the rate of economic progress and capital investment in the receiving country, which again in most sparsely populated new countries depends upon capital imports from outside sources.

In examining the effects of migration on capital movements we have therefore to consider:

(i) the funds transferred by the immigrants themselves; and
(ii) capital imports by third persons or agencies in the form of investment which is either the cause or effect of migration.

1. CAPITAL TRANSACTIONS OF IMMIGRANTS

Two items in the balance of payments of a country are directly associated with immigration:

On the credit side: funds brought in by immigrants.

On the debit side: immigrants' remittances and funds taken out by returning migrants.

Both are essentially different from normal financial transactions. They represent a definite transfer of purchasing power from one country to another, whereas the normal transfer of purchasing power as the result of foreign investment or foreign lending is followed by a transfer in the opposite direction in the form of payments on interest or profit or on amortisation.

A. FUNDS BROUGHT IN BY IMMIGRANTS

Broadly speaking the available statistical evidence indicates that the funds brought in by immigrants have always been small relatively to the values brought into countries of immigration through foreign lending and international trade. As already

9*

pointed out, during the period of large-scale immigration the vast majority of immigrants, though not absolutely destitute, arrived in the new countries with means allowing of only a very short period of transition for the search for a job. That this was the case in the United States may be concluded from statistics published by the U.S. Department of Labour (Annual Report of the Immigration Commission). According to these reports the following average amount per head was exhibited to the inspectors by the landing immigrants:

Year:	1895	1896	1897	1898	1899	1900	1901
$	16.3	11	15	17	17	15	15

Year:	1902	1904	1905–09	1910–14	1915–19	1920–24
$	16	26	22.5	33	73	62

Year:	1925–29	1930–34	1935	1936	1937	1938	1939
$	73	108	140	169	178	217	302

The corresponding yearly total amount of money exhibited by immigrants on their arrival in the United States was:

1895	. . $ 4.13 million		1920–24 .	$34.3 million
1900	. . 21 ,,		1925–29 .	22.3 ,,
1909	. . 17.3 ,,		1930–34 .	9.2 ,,
1910–14	. 34.3 ,,		1935–39 .	11.88 ,,
1915–19	. 17 ,,			

These figures are not so significant as they may at first sight appear. They reflect the tendency, already mentioned for the U.S. immigration to become more capitalistic when its volume contracted as a consequence of the restrictions which discriminated mainly against the countries of new immigration whose immigrants had the smallest amounts of money to show.[1] Undoubtedly the stricter application of the public charge clause and the growing difficulty of finding a job immediately after arrival had the same effect, and may have discouraged many prospective immigrants with modest means. For three main reasons, however, no definite conclusions can be drawn from these statistics as to the capital amounts actually brought in by immigrants; these are obviously higher than the amounts indicated by the statistics.

(1) Many of the immigrants did not make accurate returns,

---

[1] For instance, in 1900 the average amount of $15 compares with an amount per head of immigrants of the following nationalities: Scots: $41.51; Japanese: 39.59; English: 38.9; Greek: 28.8; German: 28.6; North Italian: 22; Irish: 14.5; Slovak: 11.7; Portuguese: 10.5; Polish: 9.5; South Italian: 8.8; Hebrew: 8.7; Lithuanian: 8.

they were suspicious of the reasons for requesting such information and thought it wiser to admit to much less than they really possessed. At certain periods the immigration officers were satisfied when the immigrant could show $25 in cash plus the amount necessary to cover the costs of the journey to his inland destination, so there was no reason for showing more.

(2) The more prosperous immigrants do not carry their whole capital with them, but have the greater part of it transferred in advance through banking institutions.[1]

(3) The immigrants who entered the U.S.A. as tourists and only later decided to stay on, and those who entered the country illegally, are not covered. Their inclusion would increase the total amounts, but possibly not the amounts per head. During the inter-war period rigid currency restrictions in various countries of emigration resulted in large-scale illegal money transfers. The immigrants concerned will probably have been reluctant to disclose these amounts to the immigration authorities.

The estimates for the period 1898–1908 made by Sir George Paish of the amounts actually brought in by the immigrants at their arrival (hence not covering transfers by banking institutions, etc.) are much higher than the official figures. He puts the yearly total amount at roughly $50 millions or $50 per immigrant.[2]

For the inter-war period a certain revision of the figures of the U.S. Department of Labour shown above is contained in the returns for immigrant funds in the balance of payments figures published by the U.S. Department of Commerce. The following figures for 1923–35 are not always strictly comparable, as the methods of calculation were altered in various years. For instance the 1928–31 figures include $7 millions each year for goods brought in by immigrants (personal effects). In 1929 the original amount of $23 millions was raised to $28 millions to allow for 62,500 illegal immigrants, each of them supposed to have brought in $80. In 1926 the official amount was raised from $21 millions to $35 millions to allow for under-statements of the immigrants and for illegal immigration. It is not clear from the attached explanatory notes whether these factors have been taken into account in later years.

---

[1] "It is becoming more and more common for immigrants to send money ahead through banking institutions, but no one has attempted to state the amount thus sent" (Immigration Commission Report, 1901, quoted by Hall, *Immigration*).

[2] Sir George Paish .The Trade Balance of the United States, 1910, p. 182.

Funds of U.S. Immigrants brought in from 1923-1935 (in $ millions)

1923	.	. 60		1930	.	. 33 ⎫
1924	.	. 46		1931	.	. 10 ⎬
1925	.	. 40 ⎫		1932	.	. 6 ⎬ average 11.4
1926	.	. 35 ⎬		1933	.	. 3 ⎬
1927	.	. 35 ⎬ average 32.6		1934	.	. 5 ⎭
1928	.	. 25 ⎬		1935	.	. 4
1929	.	. 28 ⎭				

From 1936 the returns include estimates of the remittances received by immigrants from abroad, which in the preceding years apparently were considered as negligible. As only a small part of these remittances is sent to immigrants who arrived during the same year, the following figures for 1936–1938 have no relation to the number of arrivals during these years.

Amounts brought in by U.S. Immigrants plus Remittances received by Immigrants (in $ millions)

1936	1937	1938
24	25	35

The statistical information available is not sufficient to justify an estimate of the amounts brought in by immigrants through banking institutions or similar channels. The difference between the total amount and the amount brought in "for immediate use" is probably only slight for the period of new immigration before the First World War, since the evidence indicates that the vast majority of the arrivals were practically without means of their own and could afford the cost of the voyage only through the financial help of relatives or friends in the new country, so that immigrants with considerably more means than they disclosed to the authorities must have been rather exceptional. Strictly speaking, a large part of the sums exhibited does not represent an inflow of new capital; they are merely remittances from the new country sent to the old country in order to finance the migration of the receiver; they are not always genuine assets of the immigrant, but often mere loans which in due course have to be repaid. This argument does not apply equally to the period of agricultural immigration, when the immigrants included a considerable number of farmers who were prepared to invest the proceeds of the sale of their old farms in a new one,[1] or in

---

[1] An official enquiry made by the Immigration Commissioner in 1856 showed an average of $68.08 *per capita*. It was then discontinued because it became apparent that many immigrants had put the amount too low, suspecting that the question was asked for fiscal motives. F. Kapp, one of the commissioners, estimated that the amount brought in by each immigrant was at least $100. Cf. R. Mayo-Smith, *Emigration and Immigration.*

the purchase of land, nor to the immigration during the period
of restriction, especially after the great depression. But even if
we allow generously for these unaccounted-for amounts brought
in by immigrants, it is safe to say that the capital brought in
directly by immigrants did not at any period of American
immigration fully meet the demand for widening production,
caused by the population increase through immigration, and left
ample scope for widening investments to non-immigrants abroad
or in the new country. Savings of immigrants of longer standing
of course contributed to meet this demand for investments, but,
as we shall see presently, a considerable proportion of their savings
was sent abroad for relief or investment or taken back in the case
of re-migration.

An examination of the figures given for the inflow of capital
into other countries of immigration gives rise to qualifications
similar to those made in the case of the U.S. immigration. For
the pre-1914 immigration into *Canada* we owe to Jacob Viner a
comprehensive estimate of the capital brought in by immigrants.[1]
He arrives at a total for the period 1900–1913 of $411,809,000
or $138 per head. This is a figure almost 200 per cent higher
than Paish's above-mentioned estimate for U.S. immigration
during a similar period. The explanation of this difference is
the large share of immigrant farmers and farm labourers from the
U.S.A. in the Canadian balance of migration. This type of
immigrant accounts for 17 per cent of the total immigration during
the period under consideration, but for 64 per cent of the amounts
brought in. Viner allocates $500 per head to the farmers and
farm labourers coming from the U.S., $100 to other immigrants
from the U.S.,[2] $500 to immigrants arriving as saloon passengers,
$50 to steerage passengers from Great Britain and $25 to steerage
passengers from other countries.[3] It should be mentioned that
only a part of the $412 millions can be considered as a unilateral
transfer of purchasing power; a part represents foreign loans, for
instance sums borrowed by U.S. farmer sons from their fathers

---

[1] J. Viner, *The Balance of Canada's International Indebtedness*, 1900-1913.

[2] Figures published by the Superintendent of Immigration for the *per capita* value
of cash and effects of immigrants from the U.S. to Canada vary between $809 in
1906 and $1,539 in 1911. F. W. Fields estimates the average value of effects and
capital brought in by U.S. settler immigrants at $850 (350+500). Both are con-
sidered by Prof. Viner as over-estimates. Cf. *op. cit.*, p. 41.

[3] Any adult immigrant not going to assured work had to show $25, any child
under 18 half that sum; if the landing took place during the four winter months both
categories had to show twice as much (*Dominions Royal Commission Rep.*, Part I, 1912,
p. 85, Cmd. 6516.

for the purchase of a homestead in Canada, and to be repaid
after a few successful harvests.[1]

For the inter-war period the following figures are taken from
Balance of Payments published by the League of Nations since 1923.

Amounts brought in by Alien Immigrants into Canada
(total amounts in $ millions)

Year	Total	$ per head	Year	Total	$ per head
1920	7.5	54	1929	14.1	88
1921	5.8	63	1930	11.1	105
1922	8.1	123	1931	5.2	180
1923	12.4	92	1932	4.4	210
1924	13.8	111	1933	4	280
1925	15.2	179	1934	4	325
1926	15.6	112	1935	1.8	160
1927	14.5	92	1936	1.7	146
1928	14.8	88	1937	1.6	106

The amounts brought into *Australia* are estimated in the
Report of the Dominion Royal Commission at £12 per head up
to 1914. Roland Wilson in his estimate arrives at £15 for the
period 1914–20, and £20 for 1920–30. In the following figures,
for which R. Wilson is presumably also responsible, it is assumed
that immigrants from British and North American countries
brought in from 1928 to 1931 £30 per head, in 1931 and 1932
£25 per head, those from other countries £25 and £15 respectively per head.[2]

Amounts brought in by Immigrants into Australia[3]
(in £ 000's)

1928	1929	1930	1931	1932	1933	1934	1935
1072	705	360	207	238	239	336	357

The changing share of immigrant capital in the capital
import of Australia and New Zealand during 1871–1903 is
indicated in Coghlan's estimates.[4] If we accept his figures, the
percentage of immigrant capital in the total capital imports for
private and State investments was:

1871–75	1876–80	1881–85	1886–90
19%	9.7%	7%	4.5%
1891–95	1896–1900	1901–02	1903
14%	5.8%	10%	4.8%

---

[1] Viner, *op. cit.*, p. 43.

[2] Authority for admission as immigrants was confined during the period of
depression to close dependent relatives of persons already settled in Australia and
persons who could produce their own capital to the amount of £500 (Australian
currency) in each case. Other cases having special features are considered on their
merits (*Yearbook of Australia*, 1935, p. 562).

[3] League of Nations, *Balances of Payments*, 1923–39.

[4] Roland Wilson, *Australian Capital Imports*, 1871–1930.

The published figures for *New Zealand* show considerably higher amounts per head than those for the countries previously discussed; they have been supplied by the New Zealand Immigration Department and cover personal cash and effects, but exclude all immigrants who have received "assisted passages". The latter circumstance provides an explanation for the differentials relatively to the other countries up to 1932, when assisted immigration was practically discontinued.

Amounts brought in by non-assisted Immigrants into New Zealand per head
of non-assisted Immigrants (totals in £ 000's)

Year	Total	Per head	Year	Total	Per head
1928 . .	320	78	1933 . .	72	41
1929 . .	317	70	1934 . .	81	53
1930 . .	346	64	1935 . .	103	56
1931 . .	160	57	1936 . .	151	58
1932 . .	80	54	1937 . .	251	58

The statistical evidence for the remaining countries of immigration is still more vague than that for the countries discussed; even a comprehensive investigation, therefore, would have to reckon with a wide margin of error. The figures given above and their interpretation will suffice to convey a general idea of the magnitude of the capital movements which may be directly associated with normal migratory movements, though it has not been possible to assess fully the amounts brought in by capitalist immigrants. They do not, however, quite adequately reflect the abnormal character of the migratory movements during the years preceding the war of 1939. The rigid application of the immigration restrictions and slump conditions in the traditional immigration countries brought practically to a standstill all movements of migrants with modest means which had been typical for the preceding periods. At the same time the flight from Nazi-occupied Central Europe caused the emigration of a considerable number of capitalists, mainly refugees from Germany. Data are available for the capitalist immigration into Palestine. According to official figures 17,653 persons possessing a capital of at least £1,000 entered Palestine during the four years 1933–36. They represent 11 per cent of the total Jewish immigration during this period. About a third of them came from Germany. The possession of at least £1,000 was the condition for admission outside the labour schedule (cf. Chapter V, 2) but a great many of them brought in much higher amounts ranging up to £10,000 and £20,000.[1]

Though Palestinian immigration has differed in various respects from the refugee immigration into other countries, there is some reason to believe that the percentage of capitalists has not been much lower during this period among the immigrants to most other countries overseas than to Palestine. The main flow of the capitalist emigration from Europe obviously went to the U.S.A. According to the U.S. Department of Commerce many of the refugees who came from Europe in recent years had previously built up balances in the U.S. totalling many millions of dollars. On the arrival of the owners these accounts were changed from foreign to domestic addresses, thus tending to reduce the foreign balances item of the balance of payments without any actual repatriation having occurred. It was estimated in the balance of payments study of this Department covering 1939 that such transfers amounted to between $200 million and $300 million, that is, from twice to three times as much as immigrants had exhibited during the whole decade 1930–1939. As pointed out, this estimate covers only those accounts which were registered under foreign addresses and on arrival of the owners transferred to domestic addresses. It therefore does not take into account various forms of invisible transfer, for instance, the exporting of goods below their real value and leaving the profits from such transactions in trust of the American importer. On the other hand, contrary to the assumption of the U.S. Department of Commerce, not all the accounts which were transferred in 1939 from foreign to domestic addresses may be associated with immigration. In order to avoid the blocking and possible confiscation of their accounts, foreign owners may have been induced to transfer them to the addresses of friends or trustees residing in the U.S.A.

B. TRANSFER MECHANISM

Clearly the outflow of capital from the emigration countries must approximately[2] correspond to the amount brought by the immigrants into the receiving country. For immigrants from the United Kingdom the transfer of these amounts represented no

---

[1] *Palestine Royal Commission Report*, p. 284.

[2] The amounts need not necessarily balance. A part of the outgoing money will be spent during the voyage, and some emigrants may remain tourists for some time before they become settled.

difficulty, since the U.K. has been a capital-exporting country during the whole period of large-scale emigration from the British Isles and since the amounts needed by the emigrants were relatively small compared with the capital exports for investment. But the countries of new emigration which suffered from chronic lack of capital likewise did not encounter serious transfer difficulties as a consequence of their large-scale emigration. They had reason to expect that in the long run their emigrants would supply a much larger amount of foreign currency than they had taken out. They might be considered as prospective re-migrants and as senders of remittances during their absence. As we shall see presently, the sums so transferred from immigration to emigration countries were substantially larger than those required for emigration. The transfer mechanism was not at all affected by the many emigrants who obtained their funds by direct remittances from abroad. These were earmarked for the emigration, and would not have been sent had currency restrictions prevented their re-transfer.

The transfer problem became acute only for countries with no surplus of capital funds for export and without unilateral remittances from abroad, and with a volume of emigration involving the transfer of relatively large capital funds. Such was Germany's situation before the war of 1939. In Germany there had already been a tendency towards the emigration of capitalists during the years of tension preceding Hitler's advent to power in 1933. As early as 1931, in order to discourage emigration of this type, a tax of 25 per cent *ad valorem* was imposed on the property of capitalist-emigrants having fortunes of RM. 200,000 (£16,000) or more. Under the "New Order" exemption from the flight tax was restricted to property of RM. 20,000 or less. The capital funds of prospective emigrants became "Blocked Marks" which could be transferred only at a high and continually increasing discount. They could be sold against foreign currency only to the German Golddiskontbank, and an ingenious method was found of using these funds for subsidizing the German export trade or attracting foreign funds to long-term investments in Germany. To simplify a procedure in reality very complicated, we might say that the transfer mechanism of emigrant funds was governed by the following principle: Foreign buyers of certain goods were allowed to acquire blocked marks at a discount against foreign currency and to use them for the settlement of a certain percentage of the amounts they owed to the German exporter, while the remainder had to be paid in foreign currency. This system was extended to the purchase of real estate and mortgages in Germany by re-migrants of "pure German race" and by foreign investors who would never have thought of making these investments without this opportunity of acquiring blocked marks at a discount. So at the expense of the emigrants, German exports were subsidized and the transfer of emigrant capital had, broadly speaking, no adverse effect on Germany's balance of payments, but on the contrary added to her stock of foreign currency. So long as the rate of exchange for these blocked marks stood as high as 60–80 per cent of the normal Reichsmark value, as was the case during the first years of the Nazi régime, this method of transfer was under the circumstances not too unfavourable to the emigrants, as the official rate of exchange for the German Reichsmark was undoubtedly fixed at too high a level relatively to the purchasing power of many other currencies at that time. The emigrant could therefore transfer to many countries in spite of the discount as much purchasing power as his funds had had in Germany. Gradually, however, the uses to which blocked marks could be put were more and more limited, and the rate of discount rose to 82 per cent, until eventually the whole transfer system broke down.

Special arrangements had been made for the capitalist immigrants to Palestine. They were given an opportunity of buying shares or debentures of institutions working in Palestine, as for instance the Jewish National Fund, against German currency. These institutions bought from the proceeds of the sales various kinds of capital equipment in Germany, for instance building materials for houses, drain-pipes, and agricultural machinery. Other imports from Germany were paid for in Pal. £, subject to the condition that these payments were earmarked for the capital transfer of emigrants to Palestine; a small discount accruing to the buyer of the goods was deducted. All these purchases by Palestinian Jews in Nazi Germany were, of course, made solely with a view to facilitating Jewish migration from Germany to Palestine.

No reliable figures have been published showing the amount of the funds transferred by emigrants from Germany during this period. The German balance of payments for 1934 and 1935 only contains debit items of 120, and 100 million Reichsmark respectively, covering emigrant funds, but no details as to the composition of these amounts are given.

c. FUNDS SENT OUT OF THE COUNTRY OF IMMIGRATION BY
     IMMIGRANTS

Three main outflows of money from immigration to emigration countries, caused directly by immigrants, account for the compensatory effect of migration on the balance of payments of the emigration countries. These are:

    (1) Tourist expenditure;
    (2) Immigrant remittances;
    (3) Funds taken out by returning immigrants.

i. *Tourist Expenditure by Immigrants*

(1) It is obvious that only a small percentage of the total amount spent by tourists abroad is due to immigrants visiting their old country. The total payments on account of tourists' expenditure abroad for the world as a whole (including commercial travellers, students, etc.) may in 1929, a year of relatively heavy international tourist traffic, have exceeded $1,700 million and may have fallen by 50 per cent in subsequent years.[1] About 25 per cent of this amount is due to travellers from the U.S.A. (in 1929: $436.6 millions). About 15 per cent of the U.S. expenditure is due to alien residents (in 1929: $63 million).[2] The following figures apply to the expenditure of alien American tourists (immigrants visiting fatherland)[3] in $000,000, 1931–1934 (total U.S. tourist expenditure in brackets):

1931	1932	1933	1934
52 (590)	15 (447)	10 (292)	10 (314)

Considering on the one hand that alien residents represent only the non-naturalized part of the immigrant population and that the expenditure of immigrant visitors from countries other than the U.S. is by no means negligible, and on the other that only a part of the expenditure is spent in the country of emigration, a rough estimate would lead to an annual transfer of $15–30 millions, or about 2 per cent of the total expenditure, accruing to countries of emigration through visiting emigrants. It may be assumed that it was mainly visiting emigrants who spent in 1929 $1.3 million in Poland, 0.9 million in Rumania, 0.3 million in Estonia and 0.3 million in Lithuania, these figures representing the expenditure of U.S. tourists during that year. It is, of course, more difficult to estimate the share of emigrants in the amounts brought by tourists into such countries of emigration as have in

[1] League of Nations, *Balance of Payments*, Vol. 1935, p. 43.
[2] *Ibid.*, Vol. 1939, p. 142.
[3] *Ibid.*, Vol. 1935, p. 190.

general a considerable international tourist traffic, for instance Italy, Great Britain, Greece and Czechoslovakia.

ii. *Immigrant Remittances*

During the period 1924–1929 remittances from emigrants involved the international transfer of about $600 millions per annum, corresponding to about 2 per cent of the payments on account of international goods in 1929. After 1929 the total volume markedly contracted, though less than the volume of international trade. The gold value of emigrant remittances fell in 1932 to 60 per cent, in 1933 to 40 per cent, in 1934 and 1935 to 30 per cent of what it had been in 1929; in later pre-war years the value fluctuated between 35 and 40 per cent of the 1929 figure.[1] It should, however, be noted that these estimates, which are based on information from the countries concerned, are subject to a wide margin of error. For instance the returns from the U.S., which account for about one-third to one-half of the total, had to be revised in 1937, when a new enquiry by the U.S. Department of Commerce found that the value of the remittances had been under-estimated in previous years, so that the corrected figure for 1936 became 50 per cent higher than the original estimate for the same year. The figures given for various countries of emigration seem, however, to be more accurate.

During the period of free migration the share of the U.S. in the total was probably well over 50 per cent. It was estimated by the U.S. Immigration Commission in 1907 at $275 millions. Charles F. Speare calculated in 1908 that out of the savings of the foreign-born $250 millions a year are going abroad, and that the annual increase is about 10 per cent.[2]

Generally speaking, the value of emigrant remittances tends to increase with increasing prosperity in the immigration countries and with an increasing volume of migration, but there are various counteracting forces which affect the fluctuations of the value. This becomes apparent if we remember that the remittances are made for a number of entirely different reasons.

(a) The estimate includes the transfers made by temporary and seasonal workers, which are considerable in certain years, especially in the cases of Poland, Italy and Canada.

(b) Remittances made to relatives in the old country. These probably represent the main item in the balance of migrants'

---

[1] L.o.N., *Balance of Payments*, 1923–1939.
[2] In *North American Review*, 1908, cited by Paish, p. 183.

transfers. As the breadwinners of a family often leave dependants behind with a view to bringing them to the new country as soon as they can afford it, they will during this period of transition, if possible, support their families by remittances. But when they have become settled and are able to pay the passages and to send the landing money for the rest of their families, these remittances will be discontinued, and part of their earnings will be spent by their families in the new instead of in the old country. Clearly, this process will require less time in periods of prosperity in the new country than in periods of depression, so that in many cases immigrants will reduce or entirely stop their remittances during a period of prosperity. On the other hand more rigid immigration restrictions which prevent the immigration of friends or relatives will tend to increase the volume of remittances during a depression in the country of emigration.

(c) Remittances for investment. A considerable number of immigrants, especially prospective re-migrants, tend to invest their savings in the old country. Investments in Italy have always been very popular with Italian immigrants. This tendency, however, is adversely affected by a falling trend in the rate of exchange and by currency restrictions in the country of emigration, which may prevent the transfer of the interest or the re-transfer of the funds, by a relatively low rate of interest, or in general by unstable political and economic conditions in the emigration country.

(d) Remittances made for various other reasons. These include cash legacies by immigrants to friends or relatives abroad —their volume is determined by factors similar to those discussed under (b)—contributions to political parties, notably in the case of Eire, contributions for charities in the old country, etc.

We can presume from this variety of motives for sending remittances to the countries of emigration that the amounts sent to the various countries are proportionate neither to the number nor to the wealth of their emigrants. Charles F. Speare distributes $230 millions of the 250 million of his estimate as follows:

Receiving country in 1907	Total amount from the U.S.A. in million $	Amount per foreign born capita (in $)
Italy	70	30
Austria-Hungary	65	28.10
Great Britain (incl. Ireland)	25	7.14
Scandinavia	25	15
Russia	25	14.50
Germany	15	4.05
Greece	5	50

A similar calculation for 1929 gives the following result:—

	(million $)	$ per head
Italy	46.2 (45%)	25.6
Greece	25.3 (67%)	144
China	22.5 (19%)	490
Poland	18.1 (59%)	14.3
Eire	11.7 (—)	15.7
Russia and Lithuania	11 (56%)	8.2
Czechoslovakia	10.5 (59%)	21
Hungary	6.6 (92%)	24
Norway	4.6 (—)	13
Rumania	4.5 (94%)	32
Yugoslavia	4.5 (27%)	21.5
Finland	1.5 (32%)	10.6

The number of foreign-born persons for the calculation of the second part of this table is taken from the 1930 U.S. Census. The percentage in column 2 indicates the share of the U.S.A. as country of origin in the total amounts received. Italy used to receive large amounts from Italian emigrants in Argentina and from seasonal workers in France. The estimate of remittances sent to China in 1930 from the Straits Settlements amounts to $15 millions, from Siam to $7 millions and from the Philippines to $4.5 millions. In the total amount for Poland the receipts from seasonal workers in Germany are included.

iii. *Funds Taken Out by Returning Immigrants*

As already mentioned, the distinction between countries of immigration and of emigration has become somewhat artificial with respect to the actual balance of migration since 1931. But there has always been in all immigration countries a certain outward movement both of natives and re-migrants, accompanied by corresponding movements of capital. Natives, that is to say in the case of the new continents descendants of earlier immigrants, migrate and have migrated, for instance, to a large extent in both directions between the U.S.A. and Canada and between Australia and New Zealand; the same applies to the re-emigration of immigrants from one new country to another. It may, however, be assumed that in the long run the resulting capital movements roughly balance. It occurs not seldom that wealthy citizens of the new countries after their retirement take up residence in Europe. In that case they usually leave a great part of their investments in the new country, so that to a large extent only the transfer of their incomes, or of the amounts they actually spend, is involved in these movements. A similar tendency can be found with wealthy re-migrants. Especially when investment conditions are less stable or lucrative in the country of re-migration, they tend to distribute their risk by transferring only part of their funds. Nevertheless the outward movements of funds caused by re-migration have been considerable. In the later inter-war years these movements markedly contracted owing to the precarious political conditions in Europe.[1]

In the U.S. returns the amounts taken out by returning immigrants have been contained since 1927 in the remittances made by immigrants. In 1927 they were estimated at 9 per cent of the total remittances or at 57 per cent of the amounts brought in by immigrants during the same year, whereas the number of re-migrants was only 23 per cent of the number of immigrants. Australia during the eight years 1928-1935 had £5,127 millions taken out and only £3,514 millions brought in by migrants. Of the old countries, Italy and Poland seem to have profited most from the return movement.

2. CAPITAL IMPORTS IN GENERAL INTO COUNTRIES OF IMMIGRATION

Before discussing the economic significance of the capital movements in both directions which originate with the migrants themselves, we have to examine the second source of capital supply which can be associated with immigration: foreign lending and foreign investment. Immigration is of only secondary importance for determining the volume of foreign lending and investment. The most important stimulus to the export of capital for long-term investment is the margin between the marginal efficiency of capital abroad and at home, taking into account differentials in the risk premium; that is to say, the flow of capital is governed by conditions in the countries both of export and of import. Migration, therefore, is likely to stimulate the export of capital to immigration countries only if the yield of capital in the export country becomes smaller as a consequence of emigration, or if immigration brings about a higher rate of interest for the lender and expectations of a higher marginal efficiency for the investor.

In the preceding chapter (p. 210 ff.) we discussed how far the

---

[1] The propaganda of the totalitarian governments in Italy and Germany among their emigrants abroad had some success in initiating a return movement, but in the long run economic considerations proved stronger than nationalistic arguments.

number of openings for immigrants and their remuneration is determined by the amount of capital equipment available to co-operate with the new supply of labour. It is evident that the marginal efficiency of immigrating capital must similarly be affected by the amount of labour available to co-operate with the new supply of capital imported from abroad.

New countries are generally characterized by an abundant supply of natural resources and a relative scarcity of capital and labour; the marginal productivity of both labour and capital is relatively high owing to their abundance of natural resources. As their rate of saving is only small, new investment depends largely on foreign capital exports. When foreign capital has been attracted by the high marginal productivity of capital, investment activity will grow and labour tend to become the only scarce factor of production. This means that labour will claim a greater share in the total product at the expense of capital and the inducement to invest will become smaller, unless immigration occurs to prevent the supply of labour becoming scarce relatively to that of capital. If the new demand for labour caused by the growing investment activities is not met by an elastic supply, wage rates may soon become so high that the prospective yield of capital investment becomes unattractive.

Natural increase is in sparsely populated countries an inadequate source of labour supply—even if the rate of natural increase is high, as was the case in most new countries during their period of large capital imports—especially as with rapidly growing populations the number of new entrants into the labour market represents only a relatively small percentage of the natural increase owing to the time-lag of some fifteen years before an increase in the number of births can affect the labour supply, Moreover, as already pointed out, during the whole period of colonization it was relatively easy for the wage-earner to become an independent farmer. These opportunities and the constantly growing number of farms created so many new openings that the net increase in the supply of labour, due to natural increase, could have been easily absorbed at a constant or rising wage level with little or no capital import. A substantial import of capital therefore required a corresponding importation of foreign labour in order to prevent a rapid rise in the wage level. Practically all investment opportunities implied a considerable expenditure on wages, so that the yield of any new investment depended largely on the wage rates which had to be paid during the period of construction. This applies to the building of new railways, which represented by far the largest field for foreign investment, to road building, and to all other kinds of public services, such as water works, gas works, power plants and sanitation.

The statement that foreign investment is largely dependent upon an elastic labour supply in the import country during the period of construction still holds good under present conditions, though perhaps to a somewhat smaller extent. It is possible to-day to open up inaccessible regions by establishing new air lines which require only a relatively small expenditure for wages in the country of investment, but prime costs in air transport are still so high that only in exceptional cases can it be regarded as an adequate substitute for all other means of transport which require large amounts of labour for their construction.

This qualification with respect to air transport applies also to a second reason why the volume of foreign investment is largely determined by immigration: the railroads and other public services with large overheads, which were the main object of foreign investment, could become profitable only with a much more fast-growing population, with more colonization and expansion of production than could be achieved through natural increase. The expectation of high profits which induced British capitalists to invest their savings in North American railway ventures was mainly based on the anticipation of a growth in the volume of immigration. It was presumed that the lands brought into easy reach by the new transport facilities would attract enough immigrants to bring the traffic quickly to full capacity and to produce a high yield by the sale of land to immigrants' In South America the development was different; there foreign investment tended to follow immigration, and the inflow of cheap immigrant labour provided the incentive to increased investment of British and North American capital.

The causal relationship between immigration and capital imports is in many cases doubtful. The two movements often coincided, because, when general conditions were favourable to immigration, they were usually also favourable to capital investment in the new country. But it is evident that the peopling of the new continents would have taken place much more slowly than it actually did, if the absorptive capacity of all new countries had not been increased by a flow of foreign loans and investments during their immaturity.

A. FLOW OF CAPITAL AND GOODS

i. Into the U.S.A.

In the U.S.A. capital imports first attained large proportions after the Civil War up to the slump of 1873—a period of large-scale immigration relatively to the preceding and following decades. From 1864 to 1873 the U.S.A. had a net capital import of 507 million gold dollars after deduction for interest payments, whereas the following and preceding periods are characterized by a considerable outflow of capital.[1] The total foreign capital in 1873 is estimated at $1,500 millions, mainly railroad and Government bonds. This amount was reduced by capital losses and withdrawals during the following period of depression, but by 1890 it had risen again to $3,000 and to 5,000–7,000 million in 1914. Much of the later increase in foreign investment, however, is due not to new capital imports, but to the reinvestment of payments on interest, dividends and amortisation. During the years before the First World War, when the U.S. experienced her record immigration, net capital imports markedly contracted. The amount of new loans per annum during this period is estimated at about $100–150 millions as compared with an average of $200 millions during various preceding periods. The amount of interest payable on previous loans had risen to $200 millions per annum. Moreover, the growing export of capital from the U.S.A. for investment abroad must be taken into account. The first appreciable outflow of capital into foreign countries, mainly Canada and Latin America, occurred about 1900, and is estimated at over $600 millions. It had risen to over $2,000 millions by 1914.[2] The amount of interest from abroad for this period has been estimated at about $50 millions per year. A further strain on the U.S. balance of payments was exerted by the remittances of earlier immigrants. As we saw earlier in this chapter, the value of these remittances may have exceeded $250 millions per annum before 1914.[3] Four main factors, the contraction of new borrowing, the increase in American investments abroad, the large amounts of interest due to foreign

---

[1] Cf. Graham, *International Trade under Depreciated Paper in the U.S.*, 1862–1879, quoted by Ohlin, *op. cit* p. 452.

[2] Cf. Wright, *Economic History of the U.S.*, p. 865.

[3] That part of the remittances which can be considered as foreign investment may be contained in the above-mentioned estimate of U.S. capital exports for investment abroad. As Taussig suggested, the available statistical evidence is too vague to give much confidence in the precise accuracy of many of these figures. None the less the trend of the capital movements and its bearing on the volume of immigration can be made out with sufficient clearness.

creditors, and the rise in the value of immigrants' remittances, account for the negative balance of payments from capital transactions of several hundred million dollars and for the positive balance of trade of about $400 millions which can be assumed for the U.S. during the period when she had to cope with the task of absorbing more than one million immigrants per year. It is true that she had become less dependent on capital imports in so far as the rate of her own capital accumulation had risen. But it seems that the reversal in the flow of capital movements contributed to the dislocations caused by the U.S. mass immigration, and that larger imports of capital equipment would have reduced the difficulties which the U.S. then experienced in absorbing her immigrants (cf. Chapter VI, p. 202 ff.).

ii. *Into Canada*

In this respect conditions in Canada were significantly different. The same period 1900-1913 is there characterized by heavy borrowing and by a rapidly increasing volume of immigration. Both capital imports and immigration were greater than ever before or after this period. Average *net* immigration per year amounted to 166,200 from 1900 to 1910 and to 214,300 from 1911 to 1913 as compared with 37,500 from 1891 to 1900 and 88,700 from 1881 to 1890. The population of Canada increased by 30 per cent from 1900 to 1910 and by 45.8 per cent from 1900 to 1913; roughly 54 per cent of this increase was due to immigration. A comparison of these figures with the corresponding figures for the U.S. suggests that the problem of absorbing her immigrants was much more difficult for Canada than for the U.S. Population in the U.S. increased from 1900 to 1910 by only 14.9 per cent, and of this smaller increase only 41.8 was due to immigration. It is mainly Canada's large capital imports which account for the fact that her relatively much larger immigration caused less friction than in the case of the U.S.[1] The amount of outside capital in Canada increased from $1,200 millions in 1900 to $2,448 millions in 1910, an increase of 104 per cent, and to $3,700 millions in 1913, an increase of 208 per cent. During the previous decades interest payments on older loans had exceeded new borrowing in amount. These data clearly show that the increase in the supply of capital was relatively much greater than the increase in population and in

[1] Other reasons are, for instance: cheaper land prices, lesser population density, and the large percentage of immigrants from the U.S. and U.K.

the supply of labour. This is indicated by the fact that the index of wages rose to 148.9 (1900 = 100), and that practically no unemployment existed during this period.[1] Labour had become scarcer relative to capital in spite of the heavy immigration. A large inflow of capital without corresponding immigration would have driven wages to so high a level that the marginal productivity of capital would soon have fallen below the current rate of interest and no further foreign borrowing or foreign investment would have taken place. On the other hand the same volume of immigration without a corresponding import of capital would probably have led to a conspicuous fall in the level of wages and to serious dislocations. As it was, the period of large-scale immigration and capital import was for Canada a period of general prosperity. Viner is doubtful, however, whether this prosperity was sound or was based on over-optimistic speculative anticipation of future economic development.

iii. *Into Australia*

A close interdependence between the volume of immigration and the volume of capital imports is less evident in the case of *Australia*. The period 1871–1885 is characterized both by a substantial rise in capital imports and by heavy immigration. But after 1885 net immigration fell while capital imports continued. In the nineties Australia experienced net emigration, but capital imports, which had fallen markedly at the beginning of the decade, were later resumed at an average of £8 millions a year. From 1904 to 1911 there was a net export of capital, consisting mainly in interest and repayments of earlier borrowings, but after 1906 immigration rapidly increased. As already suggested, Australian immigration was over various periods preceded by capital investments which created openings for future immigration.[2]

B. FINANCING OF IMMIGRATION THROUGH CAPITAL IMPORTS

Whether a period of prosperity brought about by foreign borrowing can be considered as sound depends largely upon "whether the borrowings were used wisely or were squandered

---

[1] Most of these data are taken from Viner's *Canada's Balance of International Indebtedness*, 1900–1913.
[2] Cf. R. Wilson, *Australian Capital Imports*. In *Peopling of Australia* Copeland has calculated the correlation between capital imports and immigration. He found that *r*, the coefficient of correlation, is only +0.49, but he shows that the smooth curves for both values "suggest that movements in the series are in fact related".

in unwise investments or extravagant living."[1] Often this becomes clear only when the later stages of the credit cycle have been reached. In the case of loans capital exports become necessary for the debt service. This loss of purchasing power will lead to a reduction of real income in the paying country. The net result in the long run can be beneficial, under conditions of adequate employment, only if the imported purchasing power has been spent for producing assets which yield more than the annual debt-charge. Experience shows that a relatively large volume of immigration can be absorbed without much friction if a large amount of foreign lending is forthcoming. But the net result may be only an additional burden to the country if the expenditure, made with a view to attracting and settling immigrants, proves to be unreproductive; that is to say if in the long run the contributions to the national income made either directly or indirectly by the immigrants are not large enough to cover the necessary payments on interest and amortisation for the foreign loans raised on their behalf. For instance, it would appear to be unsound policy to borrow money for a settlement scheme for immigrants which is based on subsistence farming and leaves no profit margin for the debt service or any other advantage to the community. For this reason the rate of interest may be regarded as one of the factors which may determine the volume of immigration. If it is possible to borrow money on favourable terms, many projects for the settlement of immigrants may be considered from the economic standpoint as reproductive government investment which would have been extra-marginal at a higher rate of interest.

The question therefore arises: What are the factors which enable immigration countries to obtain on favourable terms loans for the settlement of immigrants? The most important stimulus to the export of capital is a wide margin between the current rate of interest in the capital-exporting and the capital-importing countries. The prospects of borrowing on easy terms, therefore, will be best—other things being equal—when the rate of interest in the capital-exporting countries is relatively low. Another important factor is the difference in the risk premium for home and foreign lending. Normally lending to the Government at home is associated with the least risk. But things may be different if the currency or the political situation in the home country is unstable, as was the case in Europe before the 1939 war. The

---

[1] Viner, *op. cit.*, p. 302.

tendency will then be to export capital to countries with a stable currency and a settled political situation even if the current rate of interest there is much lower than at home. The borrowing countries, however, did not gain much from this opportunity. The capital lent from such motives went mainly to countries which did not want it. It was almost exclusively short-term money which could not be used for investment purposes and was therefore rather a burden than an asset for the importing country.

Apart from this exceptional case foreign lending is generally considered more risky than home lending. If the borrowing country has once repudiated its foreign debts, it will be able to borrow abroad—at least for some time—only on very unfavourable terms. Default on their foreign liabilities seemed to various countries of immigration an easy way of getting rid of their debts when their investments proved to be a failure. But such repudiation made further borrowing very difficult, it prevented economic expansion and it reduced the capacity for absorbing immigrants still more than in the alternative case where countries of immigration, for instance Australia, had to cope with a heavy debt burden caused by unsuccessful immigration schemes.

Yet other considerations determining the direction of the flow of capital exports must be taken into account. So long as Great Britain was the main capital-exporting country, membership of the British Empire constituted a valuable advantage in this respect. Apart from the fact that the British capitalist could obtain better information about conditions in the British Empire than in other borrowing countries, and apart from the smaller political risk involved in such lendings, the Colonial Stock Acts, by making certain national debts of Dominions and colonies trustee investments in the United Kingdom, provided an effective incentive to prefer lending within the Empire. Loans to other immigration countries were encouraged when they served to finance the export of manufactured goods from the capital-exporting country. For instance, the greater part of the British loans made to Argentina was used for the purchase of material for railway construction and other British export goods needed for the development of that country; the borrowing country could therefore obtain the loan on relatively favourable terms.

The extent to which foreign *investment*[1] contributes to increase

---

[1] That is to say the creation or purchase of actual capital assets abroad in contrast to foreign lending.

the absorptive capacity of countries of immigration is governed by factors similar to those which determine foreign lending. The risk involved in foreign investment is normally much greater than in foreign lending; the investor therefore expects a higher yield than the lender, and this may consist either in high dividends or in a rise in value of the investments. Often investors greatly over-estimated the prospective yield or under-estimated the cost of their projects. Huge amounts were lost, especially by investors in American railway shares and bonds. The consequences for the country of immigration were: conditions of depression, a contraction in investment activities and in the volume of immigration. New investors could be attracted only by Government guarantees or other privileges tending to reduce risk. But to a certain extent the losses incurred by the investors were gains to the receiving country; the assets of these malinvestments could be acquired at a price which made the operation of the project profitable.

On the other hand extremely successful foreign investments, especially when the privileges granted to the entrepreneur gave them the character of monopolies, were not always helpful to the development of countries of immigration. If, for instance, the exploitation of natural resources by foreign capitalists leads to profits out of proportion to the efforts contributed by the investors, the profit transfers, like payments of tribute, are likely to drain the country of its potential wealth and to slow down further development.

It depends largely on the particular case whether it is better to finance the opening-up of a new country by foreign lending or by foreign investment. Normally both will be required, but it seems that the economic key positions on which the country's further progress depends should be developed, if possible, through foreign lending rather than through foreign investment.

It should be noted that the profit expectations underlying the investment activities in the new countries up to 1914 were based largely on the anticipation of a growing rate of immigration and that failures were often due merely to over-optimistic estimates of the volume of immigration which the new investments would attract. Broadly speaking, the rate of immigration for settlement on the land was never seriously impaired by a deficiency of public investment.

In this respect conditions for new immigration have remained favourable in most immigration countries. In the United States the present railway and highway systems and other public services could in most parts of the country cope with the demands of a much larger population with only insignificant increases in overhead costs. Australia's expenditure on development has far exceeded the needs of the existing population. A large part of the capital spent on railway construction was expended with a view to attracting more immigrant settlers and in the full knowledge that these railways could pay only when the country had a larger population, and it is still true that the profitability of the Australian railway system depends on a denser population (though the development of road transport is another important factor in the losses). Victoria has spent more than £10,000,000 on irrigation works, but as there are too few farmers to make full use of the water supply provided, this enterprise has not become profitable.[1] Conditions in Canada are similar. The 55,000 miles of Canadian railways remained up to 1939 a heavy burden; their financial success requires a much larger population. R. H. Coats estimated in 1926 that an early increase of three million people would meet the immediate requirements of Canada and that an annual immigration of 200–250,000 people would work in this direction.[2] The free land in easy reach in Canada has receded, but there are still large unoccupied sections contiguous to the railways, under private ownership, so that further expansion does not depend upon additional railway or highway construction.

The preceding argument leads to the conclusion that, in general, capital imports tend to increase the volume of immigration, and that in the case of undeveloped countries with a small rate of capital accumulation large-scale immigration is likely to be beneficial only if capital imports are forthcoming. Correspondingly, capital exports can generally be considered as detrimental to immigration. From this point of view the immigration of immigrants with their own capital may be considered as the best way of providing the capital required for the widening

---

[1] J. W. Gregory, "Some Effects of Current Migration Restrictions", p. 206, in. *Problems of Population.*

[2] *Population Problems, in the U.S. and Canada,* p. 180. The Federal Government is faced with an annual deficit below operating charges amounting to millions of dollars on the railroads for which it is financially responsible. . . . The immediate future presents a prospect of heavy taxation to meet the obligations incurred in constructing public works, pavements and roads, sufficient for a population much greater than they are likely to have for many years" (Viner, *Canada's Balance of Payments,* p. 305). The financial position of the railways has improved during the war, but this does not alter the point at issue.

of production which is a consequence of the immigration, as in new countries there is normally no surplus of funds intended for investment, which could be used for financing immigration.[1]

3. EFFECT OF CAPITAL EXPORTS FROM IMMIGRANTS

A. ON THE COUNTRIES OF IMMIGRATION

During the first stages of the borrowing cycle the effect of foreign loans is similar to that of the transfer of immigrant funds. But borrowing implies a transfer of funds in the opposite direction for the debt service, whereas no such capital movement can be associated with the transfer of immigrant funds.[2] If it is true, as our argument led us to assume, that the capital exports from countries of immigration, which are typical for the later stages of the borrowing cycle, tend to reduce the opportunities for economic expansion and the capacity to absorb immigrants, we may conclude that immigrant remittances must have the same adverse effect.

But here it becomes necessary to distinguish between the different purposes for which these remittances are made. As we have seen, they are made in part to finance other immigrants, and a substantial part of them is retransferred to the country of immigration, so that the whole transaction may be considered as the financing of immigration from savings made in the receiving country. Similar qualifications apply to the remittances of the breadwinner to his family left behind in the country of emigration. They are sent to support the family until the breadwinner can afford to bring them to the new country. A part of his income is consumed abroad during this transition period, which later will be consumed in the country of immigration. For instance, in the case of remittances from the U.S.A. to Poland, the recipients will exchange their dollar claims against Polish currency and use the proceeds for buying necessaries produced in Poland. The acquisition of U.S. currency will enable Poland to import from the U.S. more agricultural machinery and other manufactured goods which she does not produce at all or not so efficiently as the U.S.; or she will be able to maintain the volume of her imports and reduce the volume of her exports of primary com-

---

[1] The case of production under conditions of deficient effective demand will be discussed later.

[2] Apart from the exceptions discussed on p. 236 of this Chapter.

modities, retaining more for inland consumption. The final effect of these remittances for the U.S.A. is that part of the immigrant's income is spent on the purchase of manufactured export goods instead of on that of domestic wage goods. The discontinuance of the remittances after the family has joined the breadwinner may therefore result only in a shift in demand in the U.S.A. from export goods to wage goods.

With these qualifications it appears that immigrant remittances, in the same way as other unilateral capital transfers like tribute payments, tend to affect adversely the standard of living in the paying country. Their tendency is to bring about an excess of merchandise exports, a "favourable" balance of trade, lowered money incomes and lower domestic prices in the remitting country, and higher incomes and prices in the receiving country. The barter terms of trade are likely to become less favourable for the remitting country. For not only has it to export gratis the tangible goods which serve to meet the remittances, it *may* lose also through the circumstance that it gets less imported goods in exchange "for the exports which are the commercial items in the accounts." "Whether we look at the gross terms or net terms, the tribute causes it to give more of its own goods unit for unit, in the exchange for the goods of the other country." [1]

B. ON THE COUNTRIES OF EMIGRATION

For some emigration countries the higher incomes and prices for domestic goods, and lower prices for imported goods, resulting from immigrant remittances and from the capital transfers of returning immigrants seem to have been the main advantage received from emigration. [2] There is little doubt that generally speaking such remittances from abroad greatly contributed to bring to the emigration countries some relief from population pressure. But the general experience that tribute payments, if not spent wisely, may do more harm than good to the receiver applies also in this case. The undesirable effects of such an inflow of money became evident, for instance, in Greece during the first decade of this century.

---

[1] Taussig, *International Trade*, pp. 118, 121. Taussig points out that the case of remittances representing gifts or charitable contributions "is like that of a tribute and also unlike". There is no *quid pro quo*, but they are made voluntarily, not under compulsion. The donors "have the satisfaction approved by the moralist of doing a merciful deed. . . . On principles of a higher or sublimated utilitarianism, they suffer no loss, nay, reap the highest gains, through the whole gamut of the performance".
[2] Cf. Chapter V.

Professor Fairchild's study of the conditions of Greek immigration almost gives the impression, clearly unintentional, that the remittances had such unfavourable consequences for Greece that she would have been better off if her emigrants had sent none and had returned without means. The remarkable fall in foreign exchange is considered as the foremost of these undesirable effects. So long as the amount of the remittances remained small, 100 gold francs or gold drachmas would secure 160 paper drachmas; during the period of heavy remittances from abroad, the rate fell below 108. The principal home market commodities grew dearer in spite of the spectacular rise in the value of the Greek internal currency, and prices of imported goods did not fall proportionately. This had the undesirable effect of increasing the cost of living for the average Greek who did not receive payments from abroad. But, as Fairchild admits, the payments served a very useful purpose by putting the currency of the country on a sound basis. Another beneficial result was the paying off of a large number of real estate mortgages and the marked fall in the rate of interest. But this low rate of interest, according to Fairchild, did not stimulate business activity in Greece. On the contrary the abundant supply of money which was coming into the country without labour encouraged the tendency to prefer leisure, to give up work, "to spend the days in the coffee houses talking politics". The money was not used to develop productive industries but rather in luxuries and "in putting up new churches, bell towers, etc."[1] Fairchild's pessimistic views, which are based mainly on personal impressions, are to some extent supported by the statistical evidence he provides, though it is, of course, difficult to eliminate the possible effect of other factors on the development of the Greek economy during this period.[2]

Apart from undesirable psychological effects which may result in the receiving country from the unilateral transfer of purchasing power, certain economic consequences of the transfer may in some circumstances tend to reverse the position, and to make it more desirable for a country to pay tributes than to receive them; to have immigrants sending out remittances, than immigrants transferring capital from abroad. This became apparent mainly during the inter-war period.

[1] Fairchild, *Greek Immigration*, p. 222 ff.
[2] Observations similar to those made by Fairchild in Greece have been recently reported from the coastal region in South-East China, from which migrants have gone to the South Seas (Ta Chen, *Emigrant Communities in South China*).

4.   SIGNIFICANCE OF THE CAPITAL MOVEMENTS
ASSOCIATED WITH MIGRATION UNDER CONDITIONS
OF DEFICIENT DEMAND

Our examination of mass immigration into the new continents up to 1914 led to the conclusion that capital imports to the new countries tended to create opportunities for immigration, and that capital exports from the new countries which were due to payments for the debt service or to immigrants' remittances tended to contract the absorptive capacity of those countries. We arrived at this conclusion on the assumption that in the immigration countries natural resources were abundant but capital and labour relatively scarce and fully employed. We ignored the problem of deficient effective demand, that is to say, periods of depression in the immigration countries with unemployment and production below capacity were considered as disturbances of merely temporary nature, due to structural changes and friction. These assumptions may be considered as fairly realistic for an analysis of the economic development up to 1914. As pointed out in the last chapter, during the inter-war period the problem of general unemployment had become so conspicuous that an analysis which treated full employment of the factors of production only as a limiting case, had to be regarded as more realistic. In discussing the effect of migration on general unemployment, we had to show that in certain circumstances immigration is likely to increase aggregate consumption and to provide an incentive to new investment, so that it would bring about fuller employment of labour and of capital equipment.

Conditions of general unemployment as a consequence of a deficiency in effective demand on the home market were characteristic during the inter-war period for various former countries both of emigration and of immigration, viz., for those which had reached higher stages of capitalistic production and a relatively high standard of living. When the immigration countries had to cope with the problem of finding adequate investment outlets or of stimulating the consumption of the primary goods they produced, immigration and capital imports rapidly contracted, but at least in theory the close correlation between migration and capital movements observed up to 1914 became less evident and less necessary. The "double absurdity" of the inter-war years "when every country seemed anxious to sell but not to buy, while the great creditor countries were willing and indeed eager to lend but reluctant to receive interest payments in the shape of increased imports, is the outcome of this struggle for bringing idle factors of production into employment."[1] For reasons already given, immigration may then be desirable in order to stimulate consumption and to create new investment outlets, and we saw that for this purpose immigrants with independent means may be more desirable than those without any means; but capital imports in general are considered undesirable, since they may be associated with an increase in the import of goods, and less opportunity for export. Under conditions of surplus capacity no foreign borrowing is required in order to settle new immigrants, and even immigrants' remittances may help to bring about fuller employment of existing capital equipment and to overcome slump conditions. Since incomes earned by producing export goods add to the demand for home-produced consumption goods without adding to their supply, such incomes are likely to create secondary employment and may facilitate the absorption of immigrants.

The immigration countries, except the U.S.A., may be considered to have been the victims rather than the cause of this development which led to the breakdown of international intercourse in the form of migration, capital movements and trade during the inter-war period. Their capacity to absorb further immigration was curtailed mainly by their inability to sell their products to their former customers in industrialized Europe. This was due partly to the declining rate of population growth in Europe, partly to the restrictions on international trade. It induced the countries of immigration, whose economy depended on the production of primary goods for export, to pursue a policy of structural readjustment by promoting industrialization and secondary production; a development which was hastened by the outbreak of the war, and is bound to go on after it. This tendency is relevant to our present argument in two respects:

(1) The transition from primary to secondary production requires the immigration of qualified labour—unskilled labour will be largely supplied from the surplus population in primary production[2]—and new capital equipment which cannot be provided on the internal market of the immigration countries; it is therefore likely to lead to a certain revival of immigration and to imports of capital equipment. On the other hand, in spite of

[1] Condliffe, *Reconstruction of World Trade*, p. 105.
[2] Cf. p. 221.

all objections to trade restrictions, it must be admitted that the transition from primary to secondary production is easier when the new industry is protected against foreign competition during this transition period. A regulation of the movements of goods, men and capital is therefore the expedient indicated for these countries. The tariff policy of Australia, for instance, has created a new demand for industrial labour and thereby increased Australia's absorptive capacity for immigrants.

(2) The present problem of new countries is to create an internal market for their primary production, which is favoured by abundance of natural resources, and to provide the producers of primary goods with manufactured domestic goods; in other words to become more independent of international trade. The efficiency of secondary production, however, depends much more on economies of scale than that of primary production. The industrialization of the new countries which is based on the substitution of domestic for imported goods can be successful only if the internal market is large enough to ensure a certain minimum output. The conclusion from this argument is that, in line with the tendency towards industrialization in the new countries, new capital imports and new immigration will be required; both are necessary in order to establish secondary production in relatively sparsely populated countries.

These joint movements of capital and men to the new countries are in one important respect different from the migratory and capital movements of the nineteenth century.[1] Then they brought about a greater international division of labour and a rise in the volume of international trade through the exchange of the primary goods produced by the new against the manufactured goods of the old countries. The same effect cannot be expected from movements which aim at the industrialization of the new countries. It is true that the industrialization of an agricultural country does not necessarily mean that its demand

---

[1] The same "apparently pre-ordained" harmony of interests which governed migratory movements during the nineteenth century can be found with the international movements of capital, and accounts largely for the close correlation between both movements during that period. "It seems to have been something like a law of nature that the countries whose investors were rich enough to want to lend abroad were also the countries whose industrialists were ingenious enough to need, and enterprising enough to find, an expanding market for the products of large-scale industry; while the countries which were poor enough to borrow were also the countries which were sufficiently simple in economic structure to have a high demand for the specialised products of factory industry." Borrowing countries were growing in power to produce wealth, and kinds of wealth which the lending countries wanted, so that it was not too difficult for them to pay interest on their borrowing (D. H. Robertson, *Economic Essays and Addresses*, p. 178).

for manufactured foreign goods will contract after the new capital equipment has been installed. The new countries will then be able to produce many goods at home which were formerly imported, but on the other hand a new demand will be created in them for many goods which require specialization and an international market. But it is likely, if present tendencies continue to prevail, that the range of manufactured goods to be imported to new countries will become smaller with growing industrialization and immigration. As soon as the new countries have created an adequate internal market for their production, they are less dependent on the export of their primary products and the import of secondary goods. A reversal of this tendency may occur if the terms of trade should become more favourable to them as a consequence of their growing economic independence.

5. MIGRATION, INTERNATIONAL TRADE, INTERNATIONAL CAPITAL MOVEMENTS, AS ALTERNATIVES

We have found a close positive correlation between migration, international capital movements, and international trade. Though it was not always possible to determine the causal relationship between them, we showed that in the past migratory movements tended to call forth movements of capital in the same direction and an increase in the international exchange of goods, that international capital movements provided new incentives to migration and international trade, and that an increase in the volume of international trade created opportunities for migration and capital investments abroad.

We have now to discuss the significance of migration and international movements of capital and goods as mutual substitutes in bringing about readjustment in the case of international discrepancies in real income per head. This process of readjustment is entirely different in a predominantly free system from that under national planning as developed by economic nationalism mainly during the inter-war period, or under international planning.

A. UNDER CONDITIONS OF FREE MIGRATION

Within a predominantly free system existing differentials in standards of living and real income per head of the working population, due to an uneven geographical distribution of productive factors, will *tend* to become equalized by the combined effect of an unrestricted flow of mobile factors of production and of free trade. But, broadly speaking, each of these movements tends to smooth out existing income differentials.[1] If for instance trade reacts immediately when for some reason international price margins have become wider, equilibrium may be reestablished mainly through an increase in the volume of trade, and less scope may be left for movements of the more slowly reacting factors. Conversely, if capital or labour responds more readily to the new incentive, prices of goods will tend to become readjusted without the intervention of trade. This may happen if high transport costs for the goods in whose production each country has comparative advantages, prevent the development of trade relations between them.

Readjustment through factor movements between two countries one of which has an abundant supply of capital and the other of labour can be achieved by a transfer of capital from the former to the latter, or by migration from the latter to the former, or by simultaneous movements in both directions. Which of these will prevail depends to a large extent, though of course not exclusively, on the propensity of labour to emigrate and the propensity of the owners of capital to invest abroad, in both the countries concerned.

In real life conditions in France and Poland from the end of the First World War until the great depression approached this situation, and may serve as an illustration. In France the supply of capital became abundant, mainly owing to the inflow of reparation payments, and the supply of labour scarce owing to the declining trend of her population increase and to her losses in man-power during the war. Poland's economy during the whole inter-war period was characterized by a chronic scarcity of capital, aggravated by her attempts to shift from agricultural to industrial production, and by an abundant supply of labour, due to her rapid population increase. Unfavourable transport relations for commodities between France and Poland impeded the development of mutual trade. Polish labour immigrated to France and French loans went to Poland, the French propensity to lend to Poland being enhanced for political reasons. These loans enabled Poland to pursue her programme of industrialization and to absorb part of her redundant labour supply at home.

---

[1] The growing importance of exceptions to this rule has already been remarked.

Capital and labour moved in opposite directions and both movements tended to reduce population pressure in Poland.[1]

If transfer relations for commodities are favourable and factors of production relatively immobile it is conceivable that readjustment and relief from population pressure can be reached merely by an expansion of international trade without corresponding movements of labour or capital for investment. To describe the mechanism of this process, we may consider two countries with a factor combination similar to that of Australia and Japan and assume conditions of *laissez-faire*, no differential in the rate of interest of both countries and little external mobility of "Japanese" labour. "Australia," with abundant land and a scanty supply of labour, whose reward is therefore high compared with the reward to the owners of land, will import goods requiring much labour and export goods requiring much land which she can produce at a comparative advantage. "Japan", with a surplus of labour and scarcity of natural resources, will import goods requiring a large amount of natural resources relative to labour, and export goods for whose production much labour is needed.

This exchange of goods tends to equalize the prices of commodities and factors in both countries; the exporting industries will expand and the production of goods which have to compete with the imported goods is likely to contract; that is to say, the aggregate demand for labour will rise in "Japan" and fall in "Australia". The share of labour in the national dividend will become greater in "Japan" and smaller in "Australia", but the national income will rise in both countries provided that fairly full employment of the factors of production can be maintained. These changes in income are likely to lead to a narrowing of the margin between the income levels of the working population in both countries and therefore to reduce the incentive to immigrate into the country with the higher level. Whether this would have happened in this particular case depends to a large extent upon the relative elasticities of demand for "Japanese" export goods in "Australia" and for "Australian" export goods in "Japan", since the terms of trade are largely determined by the relative demand for export goods in both countries. It is quite possible

---

[1] During this period factor movements between France and Poland were, in fact, not entirely free, but subject to various restrictions. It may, however, be assumed that similar movements in opposite directions would have occurred in the absence of these restrictions. During the period of free migration capital exports from countries of immigration to countries of emigration were mainly confined to immigrants' remittances.

that real income per head would have risen more in "Australia" than in "Japan", so that trade expansion would have widened the gap. But even then the propensity to emigrate from "Japan" might have become smaller; as we have seen in earlier chapters, the economic motive for emigration is not only the prospect of earning a higher income abroad, but also the absolute level and the trend of real income at home. Though the pull from the prospects of high incomes in "Australia" might have become stronger, "Japanese" potential emigrants might have preferred the slow rise of their standards of living at home to the less certain prospect of a rapid rise brought about by emigration.[1]

It is likely, however, that, in spite of the specialization, a more efficient factor combination and higher real income per head in both countries might be reached by improving the external mobility of "Japanese" labour, for instance by advancing the costs of transport to would-be emigrants or by other offences against the *laissez-faire* principle.

A similar reasoning applies to the trade relations between the U.S.A. and Japan. On our assumption of free trade and fairly full employment, the U.S.A. could have absorbed a much larger volume of Japanese export goods than Australia and have brought a marked relief to Japan's population pressure, with real income and probably also real income per head of the working population rising in both countries. Under the economic conditions which prevailed in the U.S. before the war, taking into account unemployment and price rigidities, this could have been achieved probably only at the expense of the standard of living at least for a substantial part of American wage earners.[2]

B. UNDER CONDITIONS OF NATIONAL PLANNING

It is mainly due to the tendency to mutual substitution between the movements of men, goods and capital that in the systems of national planning which economic nationalism had developed during the inter-war period each of these movements

---

[1] This argument does not imply that the gain of Japan from a re-establishment of free trade or free migration would have prevented her entering the war. According to Colin Clark average real incomes rose in Japan more rapidly than in any other country of the world during the inter-war period, namely, from 198 International Units in 1909–13 to 380 I.U.'s in 1935–38.

[2] Ohlin, discussing what the effect would be if the U.S. turned to free trade or to a very low tariff, holds that it is not certain that the national income of the U.S. would be increased, still less that the standard of living of the manufacturing workers would rise, but he expects that the farming population would benefit, *op. cit.* p. 317. A good deal of the following argument is due to the same source.

had become subject to strict regulation. "National planning involves not merely the suspension of *laissez-faire* as regards movements of trade and investment. It involves also the suspension of *laissez passer* as regards the movements of men." [1]

During the inter-war period, movements of factors and commodities became more or less rigorously restricted in practically all countries. The natural consequence was that the forces aiming at a readjustment of the international disequilibrium had to rely on the gaps left in the network of restrictionism. When one of the outlets for adjustment was barred, the pressure on the remaining two became correspondingly greater.

The restriction of migration gave rise to capital movements which otherwise would have occurred not at all or only on a smaller scale. For instance, it may be assumed that less capital would have been exported from the U.S.A. to Europe during the inter-war period if the restriction on American immigration had not reduced the scope of widening investment in the U.S. [2] Similarly the complete exclusion of Japanese and Chinese immigrants from the main countries of immigration may partly explain the fact that high protective tariffs proved not to be prohibitive against Japan's export goods. The embargo on the import of cheap Japanese labour led to an increased pressure of cheap Japanese export goods not only on the markets of the immigration countries, where this pressure could be met by discrimination against Japanese imports, but also on neutral markets, where the export goods of the countries of immigration had to compete on equal terms with those from Japan. It can, however, be argued that in the case of Japan and other low standard of living countries with a rapidly increasing population, the volume of unrestricted immigration from such countries would not have been large enough to affect their export prices substantially, since the volume of unrestricted migration remains always limited by the imperfect international mobility of man.

[1] This applies to "planning" in a wide sense, from its mildest form, the suppression of private production and exchange by government intervention, to complete control of the whole economic mechanism from a centre. L. Robbins, *Economic Planning and International Order*, p. 37. Prof. Robbins argues in this context: "If national planning raises the standard of life, it is important that the increase should not be absorbed by immigrants." It seems that this argument serves more to show the shortcomings of planning on *national* lines than the advantages of a free system. It is also in a free system important for the inhabitants of an autonomous area to prevent their relatively high standard of living being absorbed by immigration. Autonomous countries of immigration, therefore, tend to abandon the system of free migration as soon as they suspect that immigration makes for a fall in the standard of living of the native population.

[2] Robbins, *op. cit.*, p. 90.

The foreign trade of the European countries which were mainly affected by the restrictions on migration—as outlined in the first part of this chapter—was largely stimulated by free migration. Their economic structure offered little opportunity of substituting export of goods for export of labour; the contraction of emigration could not be associated with an expansion of their export trade, the complementary aspect prevailed in the relationship between the two movements.

We have now to consider under what conditions migration is likely to be affected by restrictions on international trade. In this context we are less concerned with the ultimate effect of trade restrictions on the standard of living in the country which has imposed them; we have rather to examine how far various types of protective measures are likely to attract immigrants, or to stimulate emigration.

It has been argued that duties on agricultural goods in manufacturing countries tend to stimulate emigration by raising the rent of land and lowering the level of real wages. Labour becomes less scarce relatively to land, and the prices which rise as a consequence of the tariff are predominantly wage-goods prices. "If labour could move freely between European countries the food duties in certain of them would drive a part of their population to others which carry on a policy of comparatively free trade, e.g. England, Holland and Scandinavia. . . . In the absence of immigration restrictions the inflow for instance of Germans into Scandinavia would no doubt be considerable."[1]

The question whether duties on manufactured goods have an attracting or repelling effect is more complex. Such duties tend to raise the relative scarcity of manufacturing labour and therefore the price of this factor relatively to other factors of production. Since in the normal case the goods subject to protection are not wage goods, the real income of the industrial worker is likely to rise, provided that the supply of capital is sufficient to meet the increase in the demand for capital caused by a shift of production to the protected industries; and provided that the possible decrease in the national dividend is but slight. It depends entirely on the particular case whether a country becomes more attractive to foreign manufacturing labour through the imposition of duties on manufactured goods, and whether a contraction of the agricultural labour market will exert a compensating effect on changes in the volume of immigration.

[1] Ohlin, *op. cit.*, p. 362.

An examination of the probable effects of duties on manufactured goods in new countries under the economic conditions prevailing before the war allows of a more positive statement. The most urgent economic problem for these countries is the structural readjustment of their production. The elasticity of demand for the goods in which they specialize was so low on the world market during the pre-war period that adjustment without planning would have led to a rapid fall in the level of wages and to a large-scale contraction in the volume of production. As these countries did not offer sufficient opportunities for a switchover to the production of export goods with more favourable conditions of demand, the consequences would have been a rapid fall in the standard of living, unemployment, and emigration. The alternative was government intervention to subsidize the existing export industries, to protect the money wage rates of labour and to encourage the production of manufactured goods for the home market. Protectionist duties on the import of manufactured goods served the last purpose. Industrialization, made possible through protection, created new openings for redundant labour and served as a substitute for emigration. It can hardly be doubted that the transition of agricultural countries toward industrialization is generally possible only if the industry of the "infant country" is adequately protected against competition from well-established foreign industry. In the given conditions, taking for granted that the fall in world demand for the export goods of the new countries represents a secular trend, the possible disadvantages of a protectionist tariff are by far outweighed by its obvious advantages. The alternative, including re-migration from the sparsely populated new countries to the densely populated countries of emigration on a much larger scale than it actually occurred, would certainly have been a less satisfactory solution.

Industrialization of agricultural countries implies the immigration of technical labour. The effect of protection is therefore not only to prevent emigration, but also to attract certain types of immigrants. Moreover the development of home industries is likely to have a cumulative effect. It creates on the home market a new demand for the export goods of the agricultural countries. This tends to hasten the recovery of the production of primary goods and so to lead to a general increase in the capacity to absorb immigrants, and through this new immigration to a further strengthening of the internal market of the new country.

Similar reasoning applies to the effect of protection on agricultural countries of emigration. In this case also, industrial protection may be regarded as a substitute for emigration. Restrictions on immigration directed against emigration from these countries have become prohibitive. The choice left to them was (apart from institutional internal reforms), a *possible* fall in their standard of living, as the primary effect of protection, mitigated by an increase in employment, or a *certain* further fall in their low standard of living through a further reduction in the prices of their export goods or a contraction in the volume of their production.

c. Future of International Factor Movements

Is it wishful thinking to assume that the period of economic nationalism, with the decline of international migration, trade, and capital movements, has come to an end with the end of the Second World War?

It is true that decisions as to the regulation of international factor movements are likely to remain dominated by national policies, although the consternation caused by the use of atomic weapons may compel nations to adopt a less selfish attitude. Even before the advent of the atomic bomb it was widely recognized that a "beggar my neighbour" policy applied to international relations must ultimately defeat its own end, and that the need for lasting peace should overrule all other considerations. On this basis, there is a wide field for international co-operation in the control of factor movements.

Most official and unofficial discussions of post-war reconstruction deal comprehensively with the importance of re-establishing international trade and capital movements and with methods designed to encourage and regulate such movements. The problem of migration is often entirely neglected,[1] or it is suggested that revival of large-scale migration is undesirable for social and political reasons and that there are no empty spaces left for the settlement of emigrants from over-populated countries. Such reasoning leads to the conclusion that readjustment through international trade and capital exports is preferable to the promotion of international migration. But it is easy to see that some of the arguments which can be put forward to show the political and social dangers of migration as an instrument of international adjustment apply also to trade and capital move-

[1] As to the future agenda of U.N.O. see page 169 Footnote.

ments. Without the creation of conditions of international political security and the spirit of co-operation any kind of international intercourse may be prejudicial to security. From the strategic point of view trade which leads to a more advanced international division of labour is objectionable; so is the export of capital which may enable the potential enemy to become more self-sufficient.

Adam Smith's famous remark that man is of all sorts of luggage the most difficult to transport, has lost little of its validity to-day. The technical difficulties have become negligible. As experience shows, whole populations can easily and with little cost be transported from one country or continent to another. But the problems of absorption and assimilation in the receiving countries and to a certain extent the problems connected with the loss of population due to emigration have become more serious. Such difficulties suggest as a general principle that the machine should come to the men rather than the men to the machines. As Walter Lippmann has put it: "A civilized life is impossible for nomads who settle nowhere and do not put down deep roots in a particular place. Capital has to be more mobile than labour, sufficiently more mobile to compensate for the inevitable and desirable human resistance to a migratory existence. This is not to say that all the generations must remain for ever rooted in the place where they happen to be. But it does mean that the tide of population must move slowly if old communities are not to be devitalized by emigration and new communities overwhelmed by unassimilable immigration."[1]

We have tried in previous chapters to analyse the forces which tend to impede the absorption and assimilation of a relatively small volume of immigration, and we reached the conclusion that they are to a large extent man-made and that there is a wide scope for reducing the obstacles to large-scale migration. Even so, if we can regard international movements of goods, capital and men as alternative means of economic readjustment producing the same results, the former two methods would be preferable to the last. But are they likely to produce the same economic effects? Is it in the long run possible and desirable to avoid a more equal population distribution through migration, by planning export of capital from the "have" countries to the "have not" countries, by the expansion of inter-

[1] Walter Lippmann, *The Good Society*, p. 213.

national trade and by encouraging over-populated countries to adjust their social and demographic structure?

. Notwithstanding the mutual interdependence of the movements of capital, goods, and men which has been discussed in the first part of this chapter, broadly speaking, each of these movements tends to bring international commodity and factor prices nearer to equality and to raise the total volume of production. Readjustment of disequilibrium predominantly through trade leaves the geographical factor distribution unaltered. The effect is mainly reached by a more efficient division of labour and is therefore subject to the same limitations as the benefit to be derived from greater international specialization in a *laissez-faire* economy (cf. pp. 265–266). Migration does not necessarily imply a more advanced international division of labour, but it leads normally to a more efficient factor combination. Readjustment mainly through capital movements leaves the geographical distribution of the population unaltered, but it is likely to bring about a more efficient combination with respect to the capital equipment co-operating with a fixed amount of labour and national resources. The factor combination and presumably the aggregate volume of production will therefore be entirely different according to the extent to which movements of goods, capital or men are used in order to obtain a new position of equilibrium.

In a free system the new combination is largely determined by the relative mobility of the factors, and it is easy to see that results must fall short of the theoretical optimum so long as one of the three factors is kept immobile. With a planned economy it is possible to bring about that factor combination which under given circumstances appears to be most desirable, taking into account economic, social, and political considerations. This can be done by encouraging those movements which subserve this end and by discouraging movements likely to lead to a less favourable geographical distribution of factors and real income. This applies to the planning of migration, international trade and capital transactions as well as to the co-ordination of the three factor movements. It would be the purpose of an international planning authority to find a workable compromise between many divergent interests in order to make the plan acceptable to the national units concerned. It would have to reconcile the efforts of national vested interests in wealthy countries to maintain the *status quo*; the tendency of highly industrialized countries to protect their agricultural production with a view to preserving a harmonious balance between urban and rural occupations; the reluctance of countries of immigration to admit immigrants of different cultural and ethnic background, on the one hand; the pressure from poor countries to have differentials in international standards of living equalized, and the desirability of having world production maximized on the other. The nature of this compromise depends largely upon the weight given to each of these considerations and upon the concept of human welfare which is accepted as the ultimate end of the plan. The principle seems to be established that international action in the economic and social sphere will depend largely on the consent of the nations concerned, that co-operation within the United Nations has to be secured by persuasion and incentives and not by compulsion.

In this setting, as we have tried to show, there is scope for a much greater volume of migration than that which could develop during the inter-war period. But we also cannot fail to recognize that there is no basis for a resumption of international migration on a scale similar to that which occurred before World War I. The open spaces available for colonization have been greatly reduced since the heyday of pioneer settlement in the second half of the last century, and the type of white immigrant suitable for pioneer work has become scarce. New methods of settlement requiring relatively large amounts of capital investment will have to be developed if the remaining empty spaces are to be filled. It seems unlikely that the restrictive immigration policy of the U.S. will be fundamentally changed. Though she could probably absorb in the long run a larger volume of immigration than any other part of the world (see above, page 221), her contribution to the problem of mitigating population pressure will consist rather in the promotion of international trade and in the granting of development loans to over-populated countries and to sparsely populated countries desirous of admitting immigrants than in the opening of her frontiers to large-scale immigration.

There is no reason to discard as fantastic the suggestion that Canada, Australia, New Zealand and most South American countries could attain a considerably higher level of living if they would embark upon a policy of planned immigration with a view to doubling or trebling their population size within a generation or so, and indeed several of the governments concerned have reconstruction plans under consideration which envisage the resumption of large-scale immigration. Difficulties in recruiting the necessary number of immigrants may arise in connection with the declining population trend in Europe, and it is difficult to see how such ambitious schemes could be implemented without removing the present discrimination against would-be immigrants from countries which have still a fairly high population increase. Such a policy, as we have seen, is not necessarily incompatible with the desire of the new continents to maintain their character as "white man's land". Population pressure due to rapid increase will, it is true, be most marked in Oriental countries, while a number of European countries are greatly concerned with the prospect of population decline and therefore reluctant to lose as emigrants the most active elements of their population. But Eastern, South-eastern and Southern Europe had before the war a considerable surplus population, and most countries in these regions are likely to experience a fairly high rate of increase in numbers for the next generation even if vital losses during the war are taken into account. Shortage of would-be immigrants is at present and will probably be for the next few decades the least obstacle to the peopling of the sparsely-populated new continents.

If the preceding argument is valid, it still remains to be seen to what extent the *change in outlook* as to the desirability of immigration into sparsely populated under-developed countries or into fully developed countries faced with the prospect of population decline will be followed by a *change in migration policy*. "In immigration, as in foreign trade, the restrictive attitude is apt to possess the greater popular appeal. The benefits of increased population are general and slow in making themselves felt. The dislocations, the injuries to the interests of special groups and classes which may be the immediate consequence of an influx of newcomers are quickly felt, are resented and often exaggerated." [1] We have examined the nature of these dislocations and injuries and have tried to outline the means by which they could be minimized.

Though mass migration is essentially a child of the nineteenth century, migration of free individuals from one country to another has throughout Europe's history contributed greatly to the advancement of human welfare. It took on different forms and had different significance in each period. The *laissez-faire* system of the nineteenth century is associated with the peopling of the new continents by emigration from Europe; it is likely that the

[1] W. H. Chamberlin, *Canada To-day and To-morrow*, 1942.

effect and volume of international migration will be less spectacular in the twentieth century, that the rapid rise of standards of living which was the result of nineteenth-century migration cannot be repeated under the entirely different economic and demographic situation which we have to face to-day. But if we are right in assuming that we are approaching the "age of planning" and that the breakdown of international co-operation has been overcome, planned migration in the post-war world will play an important part in the promotion of economic and social progress.

BIBLIOGRAPHY

ABBOTT, EDITH, *Historical Aspects of the Immigration Problem* (Chicago, 1926).
——, *Immigration: Select Documents and Case Records* (Chicago, 1924).
ANDERSON, M. D., *Dynamic Theory of Wealth Distribution*, 1940.
Anglo-American Committee of Enquiry regarding the Problems of European Jewry and Palestine, Report (April, 1946). Cmd. 6808
Australia Yearbook, 1935.

BAKER, O. E., "Present Day Population Trends and American Agriculture," *American Economic Review Supplement* (March, 1940).
BARKER, SIR ERNEST, *National Character and the Factors in its Formation.*
BEVERIDGE, SIR WILLIAM H., *Full Employment in a Free Society* (London, 1944).
BLISS, *Structure of Manufacturing Production* (National Bureau of Economic Research, 1939).
BOAS, F., "Changes in the Bodily Form of Descendents of Immigrants" in *Am. Anthropologist*, vol. xiv.
BOWLEY, A. L., "The Laws Governing Population", discussion in *Journal of the Royal Statical Society* (January, 1925).
BOWMAN, ISAIAH, Ed., *Limits of Land Settlement*, Council of Foreign Relations (New York, 1937).
BRIGHAM, C. C., *A Study of American Intelligence* (Princeton, 1923).
British Policy in Palestine: Statement of Policy by Winston Churchill, Secretary of State for the Colonies (June, 1922). Cmd. 1700
BROWN, JOHN W., *World Migration and Labour*, Supplemented by Report of World Migration Congress (London, June, 1926), (Amsterdam, 1926).
BRUNS, J. R., "Wartime Fertility and the Future Population of Australia," in *Economic Record* (December, 1943).

CAMPBELL, A., *It's Your Empire* (London, 1945).
CARLTON, F. T., *The History and Problems of Organised Labour*, 1911.
CARPENTER, N., *Immigrants and Their Children.*
CARR, E. H., *Nationalism and After* (London, 1944).
CARR-SAUNDERS, A. M., *The Population Problem*, 1922 (Oxford).
——, "Service in Life and Work," *Magaz. of the Rotary Movement*, vol. 7, No. 28.
——, *World Population* (Oxford, 1936).
CHAMBERLIN, W. H., *Canada To-day and—To-morrow*, 1942.
CHARLES, ENID, "Population Problems in the British Overseas Dominions" *Annals* (January, 1945).
CHEN, TA, *Emigrant Communities in South China*, Oxford University Press (London, 1939).
CLARK, COLIN, *The Conditions of Economic Progress* (London, 1940).
CLARK, V. S., *History of Manufactures in the United States*, Vol. II.
COATS, R. H., The Immigration Programme of Canada, in *Population Problems in the United States and Canada* (Boston, 1926).
Committee on Empire Migration (Cmd. 4075).
COMMONS, J. R., *Report of the Industrial Commission*, Vol XV (U.S.A.).
CONDLIFFE, J. B., *Reconstruction of World Trade*, 1941.
CUNNINGHAM, W., *The Growth of English Industry and Commerce in Modern Times* (Cambridge, 1917), Part II.

DAVIE, MAURICE R., *World Immigration* (New York, 1936).
DENNISON, S. R., *The Location of Industry and the Depressed Areas* (Oxford, 1939).
Dominions Royal Commission, 1912, Report, Minutes of Evidence, Part I, 1914 (Cmd. 6516).

DOUGLAS, PAUL H., *The Theory of Wages* (New York, 1934).
DUNCAN, E. W. G., and JONES, C. V., *The Future of Immigration into Australia and New Zealand* (Sydney, 1937).
DUNCAN, HANNIBAL G., *Immigration and Assimilation* (Boston, 1933).

EGERTON, H. E., *A Short History of British Colonial Policy*, 1897.
EGGLESTON, F. W., *Population Problems*.
EGGLESTON, F. W., and PACKER, G., *The Growth of Australian Population* (Melbourne, 1937).

FAIRCHILD, HENRY PRATT, *Greek Immigration to the United States*, New Haven (Yale University Press, 1911).
——, *Immigration* (New York, 1933).
——, *Outlines of Applied Sociology*.
FAUCHILLE, P., "The Rights of Emigration and Immigration", in *I.L.O. Review*, Vol. IX, p. 320.
FERENCZY, I., "Modern Migrations", in *Encyclopaedia of the Social Sciences*.
——, *The Synthetic Optimum of Population, An Outline in International Demographic Policy*, *I.I.I.C.* (Paris, 1938).
FINER, H., "The T.V.A., Lessons for International Application," I.L.O. (Montreal, 1944).
FISHER, ALLAN G. B., "Education and Relative Wage Rates", *International Labour Review*, Vol. 25, 1932.
FOERSTER, R. F., *The Italian Emigration of Our Times*.
FORSYTH, W. D., *The Myth of Open Spaces* (Melbourne, 1942).
FRANK, TENNEY, *An Economic History of Rome* (Jonathan Cape, London, 1927).

GARTH, T. R., *Race Psychology*.
GINI, C., *The Cyclical Rise and Fall of Population in Population* (Lectures on the Harris Foundation, 1929) (Chicago, 1930).
GLASS, D. V., "Estimates of Future Populations in Various Countries", *Eugenic Review* (January, 1944).
——, *Population Policies and Movements* (Oxford, 1940).
GRAHAM, F. D., "International Trade Under Depreciated Paper in the U.S., 1862-1879, *Quarterly Journal of Economics* (February, 1922).
GREGORY, J. W., "Some Effects of Current Migration Restrictions", *Problems of Population*, ed. J. H. W. Pitt-Rivers (London, 1932).
GUILLET, EDWIN C., *The Great Migration: The Atlantic Crossing by Sailing Ship since 1770* (New York, 1937).
GUNN, G. T., and DOUGLAS, PAUL H., "The Production Function for American Manufacturing in 1919", *American Economic Review*, 1941, p. 70ff.

HALL, PRESCOTT F., *Immigration* (New York, 1906).
HANSEN, ALVIN H., *Fiscal Policy and Business Cycles* (New York, 1941).
——, *Full Recovery or Stagnation* (New York, 1940).
HANSEN, M. L., *The Immigrant in American History* (Harvard, 1940).
HARKNESS, D. A. E., "Irish Emigration", *International Migrations*, Vol. II.
HAWTREY, R. G., *Capital and Employment*, 1937.
HECKSCHER, ELI F., *Mercantilism*, 2 vols. (London, 1935).
HENDERSON, H. D., "Economic Consequences", *The Population Problem*, ed. T. H. Marshal (London, 1938).
HICKS, J. R., *The Social Framework* (Oxford, 1942).
HITCHINS, FORD H., *The Colonial Land and Emigration Commission* (Philadelphia, 1931).
HOURWICH, I., *Immigration and Labour*, 1912.
HUXLEY, J. S., HADDON, A. C., CARR-SAUNDERS, A. M., *We Europeans* (London, 1935).

Inter-Departmental Committee on Migration Policy (Cmd. 4689), 1934.
"International Institute for Intellectual Co-operation (I.I.I.C.), *Peaceful Change* (Paris, 1939).
"International Institute for Intellectual Co-operation" (I.I.I.C.), *The State and Economic Life* (Paris, 1932).
International Labour Office Year Book of Labour Statistics (Montreal, 1943).
International Labour Office Yearbook (1938-1943).
International Labour Office (I.L.O.), *The Migration of Workers* (Geneva, 1938). "Studies and Reports Series O (Migration No. 5)".
International Labour Office, *Technical and Financial International Co-operation with regard to Migration for Settlement.* "Studies and Reports Series O (Migration), No. 7". (Geneva, 1938).
International Labour Office, *An International Enquiry into Costs of Living.* "Studies and Reports Series N, No. 17". 1931.
International Labour Office, Series O: No. 1 *Migration Movements,* 1920-1923 (Geneva, 1925); No. 2 *Migration Movements,* 1920-1924 (Geneva, 1926); No. 4 *Migration Movements,* 1925-1927 (Geneva, 1927).
International Labour Office, *Migration Laws and Treaties* (Geneva, 1928), "Studies and Reports, Series O (Migration), No. 3".
International Labour Review, "The Organisation of Migration for Settlement (May, 1938).

JENNINGS, H. S., *The Biological Basis of Human Nature,* 1930.
JEROME, HARRY, *Migration and Business Cycles* (Nat. Bureau of Economic Research I., New York, 1926).
JOHNSON, ST. C., *Emigration from the United Kingdom to North America* (London, 1913).

KEYNES, J. M., "Some Economic Consequences of a Declining Population", Galton Lecture, 1937, *Eugenics Review* (April, 1937).
KIRKPATRICK, CLIFFORD, *Intelligence and Immigration,* Mental Measurement Series No. 2 (Baltimore, 1926).
KISER, CLYDE V., "Recent Trends in Birth Rates among Foreign and Native-White Married Women in Up-State New York", *Milbank Memorial Fund Quarterly XIV,* 173-179, 1936.
KLEENE, J. A., *Profits and Wages* (New York 1916).
KUCZYNSKI, R. R., *The Balance of Births and Deaths,* 2 vols, New York (The Brookings Institute, 1928, 1931).
KULISCHER, E. M., *The Displacement of Populations in Europe,* I.L.O. (Montreal, 1943), Series O, No. 8.

LAING, SAMUEL, *National Distress: Its Causes and Remedies,* 1844.
LASKER, B., *Asia on the Move: Population Pressure, Migration and Resettlement in Eastern Asia under the Influence of Want and War* (New York, 1945).
League of Nations, *Balances of Payment,* 1923-1939, vol. 1935, *Balances of Payment,* vol. 1939.
League of Nations, *World Economic Survey,* 1938-1939 (Geneva).
LIPPMANN, WALTER, *The Good Society* (London, 1937).
LOTKA, A. J., and DUBLIN, L. I., *The Money Value of a Man* (Ronald Press, New York).
LORIMER, FRANK, and OSBORN, FREDERICK *Dynamics of Population* (New York, 1934).

MALLER, J. B., Vital Indices and Their Relation to Psychological Factors, in *Human Biology,* 5, 94–121.
MALTHUS, THOMAS ROBERT, *An Essay on the Principle of Population,* Revised Edition (London, 1807) (Everyman Edition).

MANNHEIM, K., *Diagnosis of Our Time* (London, 1943).

MANTOUX, P., *The Industrial Revolution in the Eighteenth Century* (London, 1934).

MAURETTE, F., and SIEWERS, E., "Immigration and Settlement in Brazil, Argentina and Uruguay, *International Labour Review* (February, March, 1937).

MEADE, J. E., *An Introduction to Economic Analysis and Policy* (Oxford, 1937).

Migration within the British Commonwealth, White Paper issued by the U.K. Government (June, 1945), (Cmd. 6658).

MUKERJEE, R., *Population Problems in South-East Asia* (Allahabad, 1945).

MYRDAL, ALVA, *Nation and Family* (New York, 1941).

MYRDAL, GUNNAR, *Population, A Problem for Democracy* (Cambridge (Mass.), 1940).

National Commission on Law Observance and Enforcement, publ. No. 10 (Washington).

National Planning Association, *National Budgets for Full Employment*, Planning Pamphlets, Nos. 43, 44 (Washington, 1945).

National Resources Committee, *The Problems of a Changing Population* (Washington, 1938).

NOTESTEIN, F. W., "Problems of Policy in Relation to Areas of Heavy Pressure", *Demographic Studies of Selected Rapid Growth, Milbank Memorial Fund*, 1944.

——, and others, *The Future Population of Europe and the Soviet Union*, 1944.

OHLIN, BERTIL, "Interregional and International Trade", *Harvard Economic Studies*, 39 (Cambridge, Mass, 1935).

OSBORNE, F., *Preface to Eugenics* (New York, 1940).

Oversea Settlement Board Report (May, 1938), (Cmd. 5766).

OVERTON, R. C. M., *The Growth of the American Economy* (ed. Williamson), 1944.

OWEN, A. D. K., "The Social Consequences of Industrial Transference", *Sociological Review* (October, 1937).

Pacific Relations Series, *The Peopling of Australia*, Vol. I, ed. Phillips and Wood (Melbourne, 1930); Vol. II, ed. F. W. Eggleston, (Melbourne, 1933).

PAISH, SIR GEORGE, *The Trade Balance of the United States* (Washington, 1910) (National Monetary Commission).

Palestine Royal Commission Report, 1937 (Cmd. No. 5479).

PARK, R. E., Assimilation, in *Encyclopaedia of the Social Sciences*.

PEARL, RAYMOND, *The Biology of Population Growth* (London, 1926).

——, "On the Rate of Growth of the Population of the U.S. since 1790 and its Mathematical Representation", *Proceedings of Nat. Acad. of Science*, Vol. 6, No. 6.

PELZER, K. J., *Pioneer Settlement in the Asiatic Tropics* (New York, 1945).

PENROSE, E. F., *Population Theories and Their Applications* (Stanford, 1934).

PETTY, SIR WILLIAM, *Natural and Political Observations mentioned in a Following Index, and made upon the Bills of Mortality* (London, 1662) (Reprint).

PIGOU, A. C., *The Economics of Welfare* (London, 1920) (4th ed., 1932).

Pilgrim Trust, *Men without Work*.

PIPPING, H. E., "The Concept of Standard of Life", *Economic Essays in Honour of G. Cassel*.

PIRENNE, HENRY, *Economic and Social History of Medieval Europe* (London, 1936).

P.E.P. (Political and Economic Planning), *People for the Commonwealth*, Broadsheet No. 226 (London, 1944).

PRICE, A. GRENFELL, *White Settlers in the Tropics* (American Geographical Society, 1939).

REDDAWAY, W. B., *The Economics of a Declining Population* (London, 1939)

Report on the Volume and Effects of Recent Immigration from Eastern Europe (Cmd. 7406) (1894).

Report to the Board of Trade on Alien Immigration (Cmd. 7113).

RIEGEL, *Introduction into the Social Sciences*, 1940.

ROBBINS, LIONEL, *Economic Planning and International Order* (London, 1937).

——, "The Optimum Theory of Population, *London Essays in Economics in Honour of Ewin Cannan* (London, 1927).

ROBERTSON, D. H., *Economic Essays and Addresses*, 1931.

ROLL, E., *A History of Economic Thought* (London, 1938).

ROSTOVTZEFF, M., *The Social and Economic History of the Roman Empire* (Oxford, Clarendon Press, 1926).

——, *History of the Ancient World*, Vol I; *Social and Economic History of the Hellenistic World*, Vols. I–III.

Royal Institute of International Affairs, *Unemployment an International Problem*, 1935.

Royal Institute of International Affairs, *Great Britain and Palestine*, 1915–1939.

SABINE, GEORGE H., *A History of Political Theory* (London, 1937).

SHAW, C. R., and McKAY, H. D., "Social Factors in Juvenile Delinquency", *Report on the Causes of Crime*, Vol. II, National Commission on Law Observance and Enforcements.

SIEWERS, E., "The Organisation of Immigration and Land Settlement in Venezuela", *I. L. Review* (July, 1939).

SIMPSON, SIR JOHN HOPE, *The Refugee Problem, Report of a Survey* (Oxford, London, 1939).

SMITH, ADAM, *An Inquiry into the Nature and Causes of the Wealth of Nations*, ed. by J. R. McCulloch (Edinburgh, 1863).

SMITH, RICHMOND MAYO, *Emigration and Immigration* (London, 1890).

SOMBART, WERNER, *Der Moderne Kapitalismus*, Vols. I and II (München, 1928).

SOROKIN, P. A., *Social Mobility*.

SPENGLER, JOSEPH I., "Population and Per Capita Income", *Annals* (January, 1945).

——, "Population Movements and Economic Equilibrium in the United States", *Journal of Political Economy*, Vol. 48 (Chicago, April, 1940).

STAEHLE, H., "A General Method for the Comparison of the Price of Living", *Review of Economic Studies*, 1936–1937.

STALEY, EUGENE, "World Economic Development", *I.L.O.* (Montreal, 1942).

STOFFLET, E. H., "A Study of National and Cultural Differences in Criminal Tendency", *Arch. of Psychology*.

STRONG, E. K., *Japanese in California* (Stanford, 1933).

SWEEZEY, "Population Growth and Investment Opportunity", *Quarterly Journal*, 1941.

TAUSSIG, F. W., *International Trade* (New York, 1928).

TAYLOR, G., *Australia: A Study of Warm Environments and Their Effect on British Settlement* (London, 1940).

——, *Environment, Race and Migration* (Toronto, 1937).

THOMPSON, WARREN S., *Population Problems*, 3rd ed. (New York, 1942).

THOMPSON, W. S., and WHELPTON, P. K., *Population Trends in the United States*, 1933.

——, *Estimates of Future Population in the U.S.*, 1940–2000 (National Resources Planning Board, Washington, 1943).

THRASHER, FREDERIC M., "Are Our Criminals Foreigners?", *Racial and National Minorities*, ed. J. S. Roncek (New York, 1939).

TOYNBEE, A. J., "A Study of History", *Royal Institute of International Affairs*.

TRIMBLE, W. J., "The Influence of the Passing Lands", *Atlantic Monthly* (June, 1914).

TURNER, F. J., *The Frontier in American History*, 1920.

U.S. States Bureau of Census: Report on Prisoners, 1923.

United States Immigration Commission, "Abstract of Report on Emigration in Europe", 1911.

United States, "Statistical Abstract", 1943. Washington, 1944.

VINER, JACOB, *The Balance of Canada's International Indebtedness*, 1900–1913 (Cambridge, Mass, 1924).

WAKEFIELD, E. G., *The Art of Colonization*, 1849.

WALKER, FRANCIS A., *Discussions in Economics and Statistics*, 2 vols. (New York, 1899).

——, "Restriction of Immigration", *Atlantic Monthly*, 77, 1895), 822–829.

——, "Immigration and Degradation", *Forum*, 1891 (634-644).

WALSHAW, R. S., *Migration to and from the British Isles* (London, 1941).

WHITTAKER, EDMUND, *A History of Economic Ideas* (New York, 1940).

WILKINSON, H. W., *The World Population Problems and a White Australia* (London, 1930).

WILLCOX, WALTER F., *Studies in American Demography* (New York, 1940).

WILLCOX-FERENCZY, "International Migrations" (National Bureau of Economic Research), Vol. I, *Statistics*, 1929; Vol. II, *Interpretations*, 1931.

WILSON, ROLAND, *Capital Imports and the Terms of Trade Examined in the light of Sixty Years of Australian Borrowings* (Melbourne, 1931).

WOODBURY, ROBERT MOOSE, *International Comparisons of Food Costs* (I.L.O. Studies and Reports Series N, No. 24, Montreal, 1941).

WOOFTER, T. J., *Races and Erthnie Groups in American Life.*

WOSTENHOLME, S. M., "The Future of the Australian Population", *Economic Record* (December, 1936).

World Population Conference, 1927, ed. Margaret Sanger (London, 1927).

WRIGHT, F. C., *Population and Peace* (I.I.I.C.) (Paris, 1939).

INDEX

For Product Safety Concerns and Information please contact our EU
representative GPSR@taylorandfrancis.com
Taylor & Francis Verlag GmbH, Kaufingerstraße 24, 80331 München, Germany

www.ingramcontent.com/pod-product-compliance
Lightning Source LLC
Chambersburg PA
CBHW050703280326
41926CB00088B/2437

* 9 7 8 0 4 1 5 6 0 5 1 4 4 *